AF580907

FIERCE COUNTRY

THE UNTOLD STORY OF THREE WOMEN WHO IGNITED AMERICA'S LOVE FOR THE WILD

HEATHER HANSMAN

HANOVER
SQUARE
PRESS

ISBN-13: 978-1-335-01343-9

Fierce Country

Hanover Square Press
22 Adelaide St. West, 41st Floor
Toronto, Ontario M5H 4E3, Canada
HanoverSqPress.com

HarperCollins Publishers
Macken House, 39/40 Mayor Street Upper,
Dublin 1, D01 C9W8, Ireland
www.HarperCollins.com

Printed in U.S.A.

26 27 28 29 30 LBC 5 4 3 2 1

For my friends who are also my heroes.

I hesitated a long time before writing a book on women. The subject is irritating, especially for women; and it is not new.

—**SIMONE DE BEAUVOIR**

FIERCE COUNTRY

TABLE OF CONTENTS

TABLE OF CONTENTS

INTRODUCTION: THE WRITING ON THE WALL

Bowknot Bend is the high point above a hairpin curve in the Green River. The channel nearly doubles back on itself, and the land between the two branches buckles up, forming a skinny sandstone fin, the only piece of rock the water hasn't yet eroded.

It was screaming-hot July when we came through, past the point of runoff season, when the water flows thick and chalky. The river was starting to reveal the mosquito-laden bottoms and mudflats. Everything felt suspended, moving slow. We were floating along the Green to its confluence with the Colorado River in the middle of Canyonlands National Park, in Utah. Four friends, two canoes, boats loaded heavy with clean water, a groover, granola. We were moving through the spun-out feeling of long river days: eyes open, nowhere to be but there, no pace but the one the water sets—a feeling I'm always chasing.

We'd been playing leapfrog with a group of rowdy Boy Scouts. Fishing their Starburst wrappers out of eddies, watching them sprawl over all the best beaches, listening to them yelling and wrestling into the night. We'd wanted isolation, and instead we got flashes of middle school, echoing across the canyon. You can't control who else is outside.

The boys pulled up at Bowknot Bend just before us, so we waited, huddled under a rock for shade. Itchy hot, crouching in the shadows until they climbed the ridge. Then we clambered up after them, walking out along the fin, looking for a name.

Rivers mark memories. They chronicle the scrape and the ache of time, the rhythm of change over rock. The monolith has been a marker for river runners for more than a century. It's protected now, ensconced in the national park and on the map, but for a long time, this was harsh, wild canyon country where few people came. Early paddlers would scratch inscriptions into the fin at the top of the ridge, etching proof of their presence into the soft red rock.

We climbed over the sandstone ridges, reading messages from long-ago expeditions. I was looking for one in particular. I made my friends stay until I found it: names carved into a concave dip in the sandstone wall, *Aleson-White 1947*.

White is Georgie White, the first woman to guide the Grand Canyon, downstream of here. Georgie's name is revered in small circles of boaters who tell campfire tales about how she'd power her raft through Crystal Rapid, a Coors in one hand, cackling the whole way. Or how she'd hold court at the Lees Ferry boat ramp in her leopard-print catsuit, wrestling with her favorite river rangers, giving them grief for not protecting the place the way she thought they should.

I've heard some of those campfire stories, but what I know is patchy, partly because of the narrative slant of history, partly because Georgie herself was a tall-tale teller. I've heard that Georgie wasn't her real name, and that she mainly subsisted on canned tomatoes and hard-boiled eggs, along with those Coors.

It's fact that she was the only woman to guide the Grand for nearly two decades and the first to own her own company in the canyon. I believe she first came to the river to escape heartbreak, crushed by the death of her daughter, Sommona Rose. I know that in 1945 she jumped into the gut of the Grand Canyon and swam through the rapids with just a life jacket and a few cans of food. And that the next year she did it again. She was trying to learn every curve of the river at a time when hardly anyone had been through it in a boat. Fearless and feckless and reckless and wild. Or maybe not fearless, exactly, but not caving to her fears, which seems even braver to me.

I'd learned those parts of her story in pieces, a few lines on a river map, a plaque in an obscure river history museum, mentions in other people's books. But other than that, it felt like she'd been left out of the broader stories of outdoor adventures and first descents. Once I learned about her, I wanted to know as much as I could.

And Georgie's isn't the only story I wish I'd known earlier. Across the map of my life, between the southwestern ranges where I now live and the northern mountains of my youth, other names started to surface.

I grew up near Thoreau's Walden Pond, where I was told the truest way to be self-sufficient in nature was his, until I learned about Anne LaBastille, another hermit, and environmental leader, who lived alone on a much more remote lake. When I moved to the southern edge of the San Juan Mountains, I was invited to an autumn equinox remembrance of Dolores LaChapelle, who I'd known as an early groundbreaking backcountry skier. I learned that skiing was a sideline to her work as an environmental philosopher whose ideas helped fuel radical advocacy.

The three women were relative contemporaries, born within a few years of each other, carving out space in nature starting in the 1950s when second-wave feminism was taking hold, when the outdoor world was forming into an industry, and when conservation was coming into its own. Georgie kick-started access to outdoor recreation. Anne protected land from Schenectady to South America. Dolores's philosophy of deep ecology and bioregionalism shaped the environmental movement. It still does. But while they might be known in specific small circles, I had to dig for their stories.

As I dug, I got glimpses of Georgie's bullheaded desire for adventure, the way Anne stuck out her neck to protect the place she loved, and Dolores's quest to explain how she felt flying down a mountain—how that connection between body and place—drove her philosophy and politics and rage. I had been thrashing in their footsteps since I was a teenager, learning to navigate turbulent water, going to the woods alone. But I didn't know that they'd been there before me until after I had wrestled my way through. Instead, I'd grown up on tales of young men going west, stories of Chris McCandless decamping to an Alaskan bus or Ed Abbey flinging beer cans out of his car window into the desert. The gap made me question who gets to have adventures, who *wants* to have adventures, and who is considered capable, self-reliant, and brave.

These women are far from the whole of ignored adventurers, but they're a piece. Writer and activist China Galland, who wrote a book called *Women in the Wilderness* in 1980, says she thinks about certain women as pebbles in her shoes, unignorable. These are my particular shoes, and those women kept rubbing my heels, making me wonder what else I had missed.

For me, they offer a more expansive and accurate narrative of the outdoor world, and their stories, haunted by the specter of overuse and extraction, anticipated the creeping edge of climate change. We're seeing their worries play out now. It's too hot in Georgie's canyons, and seasons seem to bring flooding in the Adirondacks, or unstable snow in the San Juans, where Dolores settled.

The problem with heroes, of course, is that no one is perfect. Mine aren't. They bumbled and lied and burned bridges and screwed up. They were often egotistical and angry, driven by an obsessive kind of love. Georgie quipped that she was married to the river after her second marriage to a man blew up. Maybe she was feeling lonely or unmoored when she slid into her leopard leotard and headed to the river. I know I've had that feeling before.

None of it is uncomplicated, but I'm sick of smooth adventure stories and holding up false idols. So I've been hunting down out-of-print books and faded photos and scrambling in the heat to show myself Georgie's inscription. I want to locate myself in the moving flush of history and find a way forward through the past.

GEORGIE WHITE

A RIVER IS A HEAVY THING

I am rowing in the flat water west of Diamond Creek when an eddy sucks the raft into the upriver current. In a half second, the river wrenches the oar out of my hand and sends me spinning. The power of the Colorado doesn't give me a chance to fight.

I am pushing an 18-foot-long gear boat loaded with the shit necessary to take 24 people through the Grand Canyon for 16 days. Literally the shit. I am rowing the boat with the groovers—the portable bathrooms for the trip—and the boat is getting heavier by the day. By now, near the end of our trip, it is so overloaded and pluggy that it takes me several strokes to start the boat moving in the direction I want. But even in the slow water the current is so forceful that it can grab the elephantine boat and throw it halfway across the river.

Over the course of its 1,450 miles, the Colorado River drops 8 feet per mile, more than almost any major river in the world. It is fast and steep, and here in the compression of the Grand Canyon, there is so much water in the channel that sometimes the eddy lines are bigger than the waves. They boil up around us.

A river is a heavy thing. One cubic foot of water weighs 62.5 pounds. It's muscly and fast-twitch and its force compounds with movement. Here, the shore is a dark, slanted rib of metamorphic rock, shot with lighter mica and quartz. The blood-colored basement rock is the oldest geologic formation in the canyon, diamond-hard remnants of an ancient world, some of it nearly 2 billion years old. Those thick-skinned rock walls are so steep and solid that there are no beaches here, just big swirly boils where the current hits the shore.

In the eddy, I shake out my arms and get ready to fight my way into the current. I watch a branch get sucked down in the boil and come up 20 yards downstream.

As I put my back into every push of the oars, holding my angle against the river, I imagine swimming through the current. Imagine what it would do to my body. That's because this is approximately where Georgie White started swimming the river in 1945.

One day in June, a month after VE Day, Georgie and her buddy Harry Aleson jumped in the river here, planning to swim into the mouth of Lake Mead. "When we reached the river we stared in disbelief," she wrote in her memoir, *Woman of the River.* "The current hurtled at breakneck speed downriver, creating huge waves that crashed headlong into giant rocks."

I'm sure they had some idea that the river was running high. Harry had spent years in the nearby canyons. But, unlike now, when we have data on the flows of almost any river in the country, they only had a few points of reference, including a gauge at Lees Ferry, a few miles below the dam, which was installed in 1921.

Maybe it was better that they didn't know much about the conditions so they couldn't overthink them. Plus, at that point, they were committed. To get there, they'd hiked 19 miles down the Diamond Creek access road in the blistering sun. They were wearing sneakers and shorts and carrying life jackets. They each had a backpack stuffed with a double-lidded malt can that held a camera, a thin jacket, candy, powdered coffee, and soup. In Peach Springs, back on the highway, they'd asked the local sheriff to ship some clothes to Boulder City, Nevada, where they were planning to hike out, so they'd have something besides swimsuits to wear on the other side.

Georgie had spent minimal time on the river. Very few people had been there. The core of the Grand Canyon was one of the last places in the western US to be mapped. The United States Geological Survey didn't map the canyon until 1923. By the time she and Harry decided to swim, only a few dozen people had been down the canyon in boats.

Georgie and Harry had spent the previous fall hiking through nearby canyons with little food and water. They were both comfortable with the exhaustion that comes from long days in the desert, where many of the plants and animals could kill you, and where the weather can switch at any second. Georgie claimed that she'd learned to swim in the frigid waters of Lake Michigan, so she wasn't worried about cold or fatigue, but they were wholly unprepared for the swollen river. They couldn't have known what the waves would do to their bodies, how the river would rip them from shore and hurl them downstream.

From the banks they watched the melee of waves and whirlpools and listened to the roar of the river on the rocks. The air held the heavy smell of rotting plants. There were dead things in the water. Their plan had been to swim until they got tired and then stop for a while on a beach, but they quickly realized that they'd be at the mercy of the current. The river was in control.

That's the first thing you learn about running rivers. The average human weighs about as much as 3 feet of water. You are nothing against its force. Fighting the river is futile, so you have to learn to work with the flow. You're committed.

Eventually, Harry got up his courage and waded in. The current immediately grabbed him and knocked him over. He disappeared downstream, his hat trailing behind him, and there was nothing Georgie could do but follow.

She was sucked into the water and washing-machined in the massive eddy line. She tried to pinch her nose closed, but the river ripped her hand away. She kept trying to get above water to breathe, to look for Harry, or to find a slow piece of water where they could wash themselves to shore and rest, but she was hurled between waves and lashed by floating driftwood. It was all she could do to try to keep her face up.

If you've ever been pummeled by recirculating white water, you might know that feeling. Underwater, getting whitewashed, it seems like you'll never surface. You're trying to find glimmers of light, trying to figure out which way is up. Fighting for air as your lungs come closer and closer to popping. The best thing to do is relax, but nothing feels more impossible.

Eventually, Georgie and Harry washed up on the same small beach, freezing and exhausted. They failed to make a fire, and their supplies were soaked, but they sucked on hard candies to gain a few calories and shivered their way through the night. In the morning they made cold instant coffee with chunky river water and then threw themselves back into the morass. There was no escape out of the steep-walled canyon besides downstream.

The second day they made it 27 miles over 9 grueling hours of floating. On the third day, after getting stuck in a driftwood logjam at the top of Lake Mead, they floated to Harry's camp at Quartermaster Canyon, where they gorged on food he'd stashed, before they hiked another 20 miles and caught a Greyhound in their bathing suits. They'd been near death. They still had water in their lungs. But as they flagged down the bus, Georgie was already thinking about doing it again.

Almost sixty years after Georgie's swim, a decade before I'd ever hear her name, I jumped into a different stretch of white water in a similar way. Just my body, a life jacket, the river. I was 18, a rookie river guide in northern Maine, trying to figure out the rush and flow of water and how to move within it.

That summer, my first on my own, I was objectively bad at guiding. I was awkward and often nervous. But I loved the connection and buzz from being outside. And like Georgie, I wanted to see what the river would do to me.

I'd come to the Kennebec River with no previous knowledge, just looking for a summer job that would let me be outside. I was surprised at how much it grabbed me. I loved the ragtag river society where we dogpiled into tents and tumbledown houses. I loved learning the physics of paddling. I loved the river itself, bank full and restless, white with roil and the new kinetics of spring. I could watch it pool for hours, a moving puzzle of force.

The Kennebec cuts through a gray-veined granite gorge. Its water is a specific northern color: leaden blue where it's deep and fast, tannic in the shallows. In my memory the sky is always slightly gray in the gorge, and the white water is gnashing at sharp rock, rushing past eddies, training up into roller-coaster waves. Bigger, I'm sure, in my recollection.

Later, after I'd learned other, wilder rivers, I'd understand that the dam release and the deep channel made the white water there uncomplicated. But back then, it felt like a whole world compressed. I was the youngest guide on the river that summer, and I desperately wanted to have some kind of power.

So one morning after the river came up, I tightened my life jacket and jumped into the river at the boat ramp below the dam. The second I was sucked away from shore I fought to keep my head above water. Years later the thing I remember most is the feeling of waves lifting me up and then letting me go as my body moved downstream. The more I got that sense of motion the more I wanted it. Sometimes I wonder if it might have been different if I'd put myself on another path at 18, or whether that ache was always in me, waiting.

Georgie had her own ache when she first came to the canyon. She said part of why she went down to the river was because she didn't care about living.

Her daughter, Sommona, had been killed in a bike crash the previous spring, her second marriage was on the rocks, and she was spiraling. She said she couldn't feel anything.

She'd met Harry Aleson at a house party that same summer. He was showing some of his photos of the red rock canyons around the Grand. The scenery sparked something in her, and she asked if she could come with him the next time he went back.

Harry was searching, too. "He didn't think much, he just acted," says river historian Renny Russell, who wrote a book about Harry Aleson. Harry had been gassed in World War I and was living off his disability pensions. He'd set up an isolated camp at Quartermaster Canyon, where the Colorado flows into the eastern edge of Lake Mead, and from there he was trying to make a living exploring canyons and guiding people through. He was a bit of an unlikely explorer—he had serious stomach problems to the point that he only ate baby food—but so was Georgie.

Harry had an agenda. He wanted companions for a harebrained hike across the arid, spiny Colorado Strip. Georgie was foolhardy enough to say yes. The two spent the fall after Sommona's death hiking around Lake Mead. Georgie looked upstream at the gush of the Colorado and wanted to see more of the river. They decided to swim.

That first swim switched something in Georgie. Back home in Los Angeles, she wrote letters to Harry outlining the ways she wanted to understand the river. It was all she could think about, which might have been because nothing else was going well. She was grieving Sommona, coping with her husband James "Whitey" White's alcoholism, and bored with her work as an office temp. She kept imagining the river in her mind, the feeling of river and rock, the texture of water, and obsessing over the parts they hadn't yet seen.

Time is excellent at erasing physical pain. It expunges cold and discomfort. Georgie said that as summer turned into fall, she and Harry talked less about the agony of the swim and more about the good parts. "I was also beginning to wonder what it would be like to cover twice the distance we had swum that first summer. After all, there was a lot more river to explore," she wrote.

By the spring of 1946, she'd sold Harry on the idea of

another swim. The river was lower that year, but Harry wrote that the rapids were just as bad as the year before. They had initially attempted to build a driftwood raft, but they couldn't get it over the massive eddy lines. The tiny rubber boat they'd packed quickly sank. Mostly they swam, using the wrist-lock technique they'd invented the previous spring, where they clutched each other's forearms as they floated. Georgie said that on the second swim she could relax more and try to just let the river take her.

They'd slipped into the water unnoticed on the first swim, but the second time they spotted planes circling them above Lake Mead. Harry finally admitted to Georgie that he'd been scared and told some friends in Las Vegas about their plan, in case anything happened to them. When the pair didn't come out of the canyon on time, the friends alerted the authorities. By the time rescuers hit the lake, Georgie and Harry had already made the papers. TWO DROWNED IN GRAND CANYON, the *Boulder City News* headline read.

It escalated from there. Someone called Georgie's mother in LA and told her that they'd found her daughter's body in the river.

Tamor DeRoss was unfazed or perhaps used to hearing outlandish stories about her daughter's escapades. "My mother had great faith in me, however, so she simply hung up and forgot the whole incident," Georgie said.

Her mother might have not cared about the gossip, but a growing curiosity around recreational river running caused the story to spread, even after they turned up exhausted but unscathed. The Boulder City newspaper ran photos of them on a rescue raft barely afloat, Georgie grinning huge. It was the first of her many brushes with the media.

Harry was exhausted by the swim. He swore he'd never do it again, and he turned his attention to finding other ways to bring tourists into canyon country. But Georgie was exhilarated. "I learned more about water and the Colorado River on those two trips than I could probably have learned in ten years any other way," she said.

Today much of the river's mystery is gone. More than 20,000 people raft through the Grand Canyon each year, the majority of them on commercial trips. You can watch videos of all the rapids. You can page through river maps that outline every curve and sandbar. You can ask internet forums what to cook and how bad the bugs will be.

Back then, the only resource was a 1923 USGS map of the canyon, which filled the gaps left by the 1869 John Wesley Powell expedition. Georgie and Harry might have gotten their hands on a copy of Ellsworth Kolb's 1914 book, *Through the Grand Canyon from Wyoming to Mexico*, but at that point no one had done what they'd attempted to do.

Georgie couldn't have known it then, but they were floating through a landscape at the forefront of the American public land movement. Their second swim—which had appeared to be a publicity stunt from the outside—pissed off the authorities in Grand Canyon National Park, who were starting to reckon with increased river traffic and potential danger. The age of unconstrained exploration was ending.

In the previous decade, between 1928 and 1937, 12 people died boating in the Grand Canyon. River historian Otis "Dock" Marston called that period the tragic era, and it had a big impact on Grand Canyon National Park superintendent Miner Tillotson, who had started the job in

1927 open to the idea of boating in the canyon. He quickly changed his stance when two park employees, Glen Sturdevant and Fred Johnson, drowned in Horn Creek Rapid, in 1929, after the canoe they were using for an exploratory trip swamped and flipped.

Tillotson was nervous about what could happen on the river, and Georgie's float got under his skin. In 1946, he wrote to the director of the National Park Service, asking for more regulation and other ways to make sure that they could control the flow of boaters. He cited permit systems in places like Mount Rainier National Park and Grand Teton National Park—and the park's responsibility if rafters were to hurt themselves or die.

By the end of the year, Acting National Park Service Director Hillory Tolson sent out a memo to all the national parks, outlining how Georgie and Harry had violated "section 2.54 of the General Rules and Regulations, which prohibit the placing of any privately owned boat, canoe, raft, or other floating craft upon the waters of any park or monument without a permit from the superintendent." He gave the parks power to regulate rafting and set a permitting system in motion. It fundamentally changed how we access public lands in the US.

Regulation can kill part of the romance of being outside, but the move toward permitting ultimately helped limit overuse and abuse. In the years following Georgie and Harry's swim, river running exploded from a risky niche experience to a vacation cliché. The place needed some protection, but government oversight also felt like it sucked away some of the exploratory magic.

Those early days of river running, when Georgie was swimming into the unknown, make me jealous because they feel so wild.

You can't just jump in the river anymore. These days, passage through the Grand Canyon is highly regulated, expensive, or hard to get, in part because of those constraints set in place during Tillotson's time and the culture that grew up around river running.

I had neither money nor a permit, so the dirtbag in me—who learned to be scrappy from my time as a guide, and who still tries to sneak around the system whenever I can—started scheming.

I decided I'd try to be a swamper, the equivalent of an unpaid river intern, which is often a first step for guides trying to get into the canyon. In February, when the trip was starting to turn in my head, I'd run into a Grand Canyon guide I knew in a coffee shop in Silverton, Colorado. John Shocklee walked in the door layered up against the cold, his dog waiting patiently outside.

We talked about snowpack and how the ski season was shaping up so far, and then I steered the conversation toward summer. "I'm trying to get down the Grand. Do you know anyone who might need help?" I asked, as he leaned on our table, waiting for his mug to get filled.

Two days later he called me. "Are you free in August?" he asked. And then he disappeared back into the vapor of winter for months. I was hopeful that I'd scored a spot on one of his trips, but I wasn't sure.

But, like Georgie must have done when she first met Harry Aleson, I set my heart on a half-formed idea, trusting that it would happen. "I think I'll be gone in August," I found myself telling people. "I think."

In late July, Shocklee called again. “Can you be in Flagstaff on August 2?” he asked. “We’ll rig that day, then head to the river the next.”

Can you row? he texted a few days later. And what’s your last name?

After I texted back (YES! Hansman), I realized I neglected to ask how long the trip was, but I didn’t want to seem high-maintenance when it felt like my tie was tenuous, so on August 1, I threw my river gear in the back of my car and drove across the Navajo Nation toward Flagstaff in the silvery afternoon light of a summer monsoon, still unsure of what I was getting into. In the morning, I met the 7 other members of the crew: 4 guides, 2 baggage boaters, and another swamper. We loaded 6 rafts with the mountain of gear and food we needed for 16 days on the river. That night I slept on the floor of the boathouse, restless with anticipation.

Shocklee works for OARS Grand Canyon Dories, a company with a long history of human-powered boat trips and conservation, thanks to its founders George Wendt and Martin Litton, who began running commercial trips in 1969 and ’70 respectively. The company’s boathouse walls are spackled with decades of raft guide detritus. It’s a history lesson told through snapshots, Christmas cards, news clippings, and broken boat parts. You can track fashion and facial hair, and you can learn stories. I walked along the wall, trying to identify faces in old photos. Georgie ran a different, competitive rafting company, but she’s part of the legacy, so there are photos of her, including one from her notorious 80th birthday party where hundreds of guides showed up. There’s a portrait of her when she’s old and etched with wrinkles, staring down the cameraperson, fire in her steady blue eyes, a can of Coors in her hand. She looks both ageless and ancient, and at that point she probably was. Georgie was about my age, mid-thirties, when she came to the river, and she guided the river into her eighties, hauling motors and running boats until cancer decimated her strength and shrank her to skin and bones—a change she outwardly blamed on the tightening Park Service regulations, which wouldn't let her drink those Coors all day. The photos on the wall tell pieces of the story, and the next day I'd be loading boats at Lees Ferry, getting ready to be a part of it, too.

INTO THE CANYON

Guiding is often full of fish tales, exaggerations of how big the rapids were or how wild your line was. Georgie was good at that. From the get-go, she was twisting things, especially about herself.

The story she told was that she grew up scrappy and poor in the tenement district of Chicago with a father who wasn't around much and a physically disabled mother. Georgie says her mother, who used a wheelchair, supported them by working in a commercial laundry. She was calm in any emergency, unfailingly positive, and suffered no fools. She taught Georgie and her two siblings, Marie and Paul, to be gutsy and gritty and to take care of each other.

"I had a mother who wanted you to have spirit," Georgie told Lew Steiger, the river community's beloved historian who runs the Colorado River Runners Oral History Project, in an interview for the canyon-based periodical *Boatman's Quarterly Review.* "She'd always say, 'You're on the bottom, but everything has to be up from here.' And so that was her thing, that you're already on the floor, you can't get any lower."

Georgie said she learned to swim and understand boats on the cold rocky shores of Lake Michigan, which prepared her for the vicious swims in the Colorado. Living close to the bone made her comfortable with the uncomfortable. It's a nice narrative arc, but it doesn't actually line up with reality.

Records show that she was born Bessie DeRoss in the tiny Oklahoma Panhandle town of Guymon on November 13, 1910. Her father's name was George, and there are records of her going by Georgie as early as 9, following his lead. And census and city directory files have her pegged as Georgie in Denver, where the family moved to chase work, by 1920. Her Chicago childhood was a fabrication.

I have no reason to doubt her stories of toughness and family closeness, but it's unclear why she lied about facts that couldn't have been that crucial to anyone other than herself. What was the point?

I asked her close friend Roz Jirge, who spent countless campfire nights with her. She said that Georgie might have been embarrassed by Depression-era stereotypes about Oklahoma. She also said that Georgie was a deeply private person even though she ended up in a public role. She tried to control the narrative around herself, in part because it felt like she was on shaky ground. Maybe the deception was a defense mechanism. Maybe she told the false stories enough that she started to believe them.

We know Georgie was a sophomore in high school when she met "a handsome, all-American, six-foot, blond young man by the name of Harold Clark," and from her telling, they couldn't keep their hands off each other, so they got hitched. "My mother had hoped that I would wait to get married until I finished high school. But she understood that I had strong sex needs and couldn't bring myself to fulfill them outside of marriage," she wrote in her memoir. "Outside of our sexual relationship Harold and I had nothing in common. In addition, I couldn't commit myself to Harold, or for that matter, any other man."

Commitment or not, in 1929, when she was 18, she and Harold had a daughter, Sommona Rose. Two years later, Georgie left Sommona with her mother so she and Harold could hit the road to find work. They ended up in New York City. It was the gut of the Great Depression, and jobs were scarce. When she was searching for a job, she lied and said Harold was her brother, because no one wanted to hire a married woman. Harold couldn't find work, but Georgie found a job running a comptometer, an early computer, behind the scenes at Radio City Music Hall. She says she was good at it, but she quickly grew bored by the work.

On her days off she would wander the city, and one Saturday in Central Park, she saw a group of people training for a bike race. She was interested and brave, so she asked about the bikes, and soon the bikers were teaching her to ride.

She didn't stick in the city for long. On August 2, 1936, she pocketed a week's worth of her Radio City salary and biked out of New York, bound for California with Harold begrudgingly in tow. They had flipped a coin between Los Angeles and San Francisco, and when LA won, they shipped their belongings there. "We sent what few clothes we had, just so that we could pick them up in California, sure we were going to get there, and started out," Georgie told Steiger.

That sureness feels stunning. Neither of them had ridden farther than the park before. A friend from the cycling club had given them two racing bikes, which had single gears, skimpy brakes, skinny tires, and even skinnier seats. Georgie said her legs felt okay, especially after the first hundred miles or so, but that the seat was so uncomfortable she mainly rode standing up as they crept along the Great Lakes. She fell and broke her hand outside of Chicago, but they kept going. From there they headed south and west 2,000 miles to Santa Monica, California, over the Rockies and across the deserts she'd later come to know well. She was bowled over by the weather and the light, how the high mountain passes around Flagstaff stayed cold in the summer, and the way the unending ribbon of Route 66 kept spooling out before them.

They had no spare tires or sleeping bags and barely any clothes or food. Georgie often claimed that she didn't drink much water, but it's hard to imagine inching across the Midwest in August and September without anything to drink. They didn't carry tents: They'd pull off on the side of the road and bed down in a field, or exchange farmwork for a meal and a place to sleep. She said that at that point in the Depression they were part of a migration west, moving toward the golden idea of California. There were other travelers on the way, so it felt safe. The only time it was scary was when cars on Sunday drives would swipe close by on the narrow roads, unfamiliar with bicycles.

Georgie took to the migratory lifestyle. She'd bathe in creeks or walk into rooming house bathrooms like she owned the place, clean herself up, and then walk out without paying.

Harold hated the sneakiness. The ride increased the friction between them, and their already tenuous relationship unraveled. When they hit California, they were down to their last few dollars and didn't have a plan to make more. In Fontana, California, Georgie sweet-talked them into jobs picking grapes in an orchard. They were mostly paid in wine, but over the harvest they made four more dollars. It was enough to get them to Los Angeles, where she pawned a diamond Harold's mother had given her to make rent.

Her next 5 years are hard to track, but you can feel the restlessness in the scraps of stories. She was pinging between Chicago and LA, flashing between jobs, seemingly unsettled. Her siblings and Sommona came out to join her in California in 1937, but court notices have her living in Chicago in 1941 when she divorced Harold.

By 1942, she met and married James White. Whitey was kind, and in awe of her. He enabled her future raft company, driving shuttle and rigging boats. But he was also an alcoholic whose disease would eventually rupture their marriage.

In those scattered years two things came into focus for Georgie: Sommona and the mountains. She lived away from her daughter for nearly a decade, but once they were in the same place she became fiercely connected to her. Georgie joined the Sierra Club in LA and started hiking and climbing in the San Gabriels and Sierras. She started a biking club, and she took Sommona with her on the hikes and rides. Both of them loved to speed downhill.

During World War II, she was working security at Douglas Aircraft, and on her night shifts she hooked on to the idea that she wanted to fly. If you were a woman, your best option for flying was to be a ferry pilot, the branches of the Army and Air Force that shuttled planes from the factory to air bases and other places they were needed. The age cutoff was 35, and 34-year-old Georgie filled out the application, citing that she was a divorcée with a teenager, pretty sure that she wouldn't be picked.

"I thought, 'Oh boy, I'll probably never get in,'" she wrote in her memoir. "But I did! Much to my surprise, too. And so I was thrilled to death then."

She trained in Quartzsite, Arizona, north of Yuma, close to the Colorado River that she'd come to love. She brought teenage Sommona with her on training trips to Quartzsite. They camped in the fields by the airstrip as Georgie chipped away at her 500 hours of training time, and precocious teen Sommona became so popular with the other pilots that they let her fly, too.

Georgie said that Sommona was a better pilot than she was: The kid was a quick study and a light touch on the stick. When Georgie flew her check-off solo flight, she snuck Sommona into the cockpit, and her daughter flew the second and third rounds of takeoffs and landings.

When Georgie wasn't training, they'd gotten into the habit of biking between LA and Santa Barbara over the course of a weekend, curving up the coast on the 101. They'd head north on Saturday and come home on Sunday.

On June 23, 1944, a Saturday, they were pedaling north, and Sommona was singing, sailing up the shoulder. Georgie was behind her, close enough that she could listen to her daughter's voice, when she heard the screeching of tires and felt herself slammed from behind by a car. Georgie was unhurt, but the side-view mirror slammed Sommona in the back of the head. She hit the pavement, immediately silent.

Georgie went running after the car, which had slowed down but then kept going. It stopped enough that she could see that the driver was in uniform, and she committed the license plate to memory. She dumped the number on the next driver that came up and ran back to Sommona.

Sommona was unresponsive but still warm, and Georgie stayed beside her until the police pulled her away.

The cops tracked down the driver, who had been drinking, and charged him with Sommona's death, but Georgie declined to press charges. She said she couldn't change the past, and it wouldn't bring her daughter back. She sank into mourning. She wouldn't leave the house. She couldn't stop replaying the scene in her mind, hearing Sommona's head hit the ground.

To get her out of her grief, the next month some friends dragged her to the house party where she met Harry Aleson. His slideshow covered his time in the canyons of Utah and Arizona. Georgie, who had to be physically brought to the party, perked up once the slides started playing. By the end of the night, she and Harry had a plan to hike around Lake Mead.

Harry had put together the slideshow because he was trying to recruit people to come with him on an expedition across the Shivwits Plateau, some of the most desolate terrain in the country, north of the Grand Canyon. He was an amateur historian, fascinated by the stories of early explorers, and he wanted to find his own trails through the canyons around the recently built Lake Mead.

After Georgie committed to the trip, Harry put an ad in the Sierra Club newspaper, which pulled in one more person: Gerhard Bakker, a biologist who was interested in the canyon's animals. They had a party.

In August Georgie left LA and headed for Arizona, and together the three hiked out of Harry's camp at Quartermaster Canyon.

It was immediately exhausting. Bakker and Harry both developed debilitating blisters, and the terrain was ruthless.

Georgie had always been physically tough, biking long miles, slogging through hard labor, getting by on a few canned vegetables and not much else. But that fall she had a new, forceful intensity.

After Sommona's death, she felt numb and fatalistic. She could hike for miles without food or much water and think about nothing besides Sommona, like some kind of fever dream. It seemed like she was pushing herself just so she could feel something.

Harry had the same sort of frantic drive. River historian Renny Russell says they were two peas in a pod, at least at first. In a letter the next winter cajoling Harry into another river trip, Georgie called him the only free person she knew.

Their friendship was nonstandard, especially for the time. She said nothing romantic ever happened between them, and Harry was very clear in his journals to note that he wasn't messing around with a married woman. He noted where they slept: on opposite sides of the beach from each other. "They connected on a very deep level with wildness," Russell said.

She could out-hike anyone who showed up, which was a boon for him, and Harry was amenable to taking her places and teaching her how to navigate and run rivers. "He has more determination and sheer guts than anyone I know," Georgie said.

Movement, it seemed, was the only thing that could quiet her mind. So, at the end of that fall, when Harry took her to Lake Mead, and they looked up at the river, she started to get an idea about what might lie upstream.

She threw herself into the canyon with a bullheaded singularity and without seeming to care what anyone thought. She was in her mid-thirties by then, in the postwar era when women, even those who had worked in the war, were encouraged to be homemakers and mothers.

Georgie did the exact opposite. She ditched her job and her husband and every other responsibility to ramble around an unknown desert with two men who were basically strangers. Perhaps she could freely buck gender norms because she'd already burned through so many standard social markers. She'd been a mother but lost her child. She had been married twice, and was technically still married, although she and Whitey continued to struggle and drift. Georgie's social ties were already loose. She had already hit bottom. But as she spent more time on the river, she was still considered reckless and attention seeking. She was hassled for heading into the wild by reporters and other river runners because they didn't know what to make of her.

There was no great way to be a woman in the early days of river running. Mothers who spent time outside alone were called *negligent*. If you were childless and single, you were considered suspicious. Young, unencumbered women were threats or sluts or imbeciles. You can see it in how the other early female river runners were perceived. Actress Katie Lee, who sang in exchange for free river trips, was considered a vixen. When river runner Bessie Hyde disappeared in the canyon, people said she was in over her head, following a man. Botanist Elzada Clover, an older single scientist who conducted the first plant survey of the canyon, was definitely a witch. And her coworker Lois Jotter flirted too much. Georgie defied easy categorization but was similarly condemned, and many of those stereotypes still stand today.

Regardless of the pressure she might have felt, the swims clarified something for Georgie. She began to funnel her attention toward the web of streams that run into the Colorado River Basin. She was still working in LA, but she and Harry were sending each other fervent letters with plans to hike into the reaches of Lake Mead and Glen Canyon, upstream of the Grand. She was already thinking about their next river trip.

In 1946, as soldiers came back from war, and surplus stores opened to off-load military gear, combat-grade rubber rafts became available for civilian use. In LA, Georgie bought a 10-person raft, and Harry found a boat that could hold 7.

Harry knew that Amos Burg had run a rubber boat through the Grand Canyon in 1938, but before they pitched themselves into the Grand they figured they should try some smaller rivers first. On August 4, 1947, Georgie wrote to Harry, "When the rapids are mentioned I forget everything else. They cast a spell on me. Let's ride them all! Don't you think a large rubber boat can make it?"

In October they took their new rafts down Cataract Canyon, the tall-walled stretch of river upstream of Glen Canyon, below the confluence of the Green and Colorado Rivers. They were the first people to attempt the section in a rubber raft.

To this day, Cataract is a deceptive stretch of river. The first 50 miles are mellow until the Green River intersects with the Colorado River in what is now Canyonlands National Park. From there, Cataract holds some of the biggest, most treacherous rapids in the country, especially when the flows are high. The rapid names reflect the stress: Satan's Gut, Ben Hurt, Capsize.

Georgie and Harry came in from the Green River side, floating through the quiet water of Labyrinth and Stillwater Canyons, climbing up to carve their names at Bowknot Bend. That fall it was dark and cold in the canyon. River flows were low, but the rapids were complicated. They flipped early and then kept flipping. Georgie said they were so cold and uncomfortable that they spent most nights pacing the beach, trying to stay warm, waiting for the sun to come up so they could keep going.

But even in the exhaustion she was elated. The country was ruggedly beautiful. And once she warmed up again, she was already on to the next trip. In 1953, Georgie wrote to Harry, "Why did I leave a nice, safe job to do this and I do it every year? Just no accounting for human nature."

Georgie went back to LA after the trip through Cataract to dry out and start dreaming about other canyons. Those simple rubber rafts, which could withstand more abuse than a wooden boat, opened up a new kind of exploring. She would leave the raft rolled up in the back of her truck, so that if she found an interesting stretch of river, she could float it.

She went north, up to the Rogue in Oregon, and east to the other rivers that ran into the Colorado: the Virgin in Utah, Arizona's Verde and Salt. She loved those red-walled desert rivers, but she was omnivorous. During one big storm in LA, she launched her boat into a drainage canal in a neighbor's backyard and went rocketing down into the city. She said that she was scraped by barbed wire, and potentially trespassing, but undeterred. And when she'd had enough, she got on a public bus and headed back to her truck.

After the miserable Cataract trip, she and Harry slowly started to diverge. She was trying to explore as much as possible, while Harry was thinking about how to monetize running rivers. They also had differing philosophies about storytelling. Harry was strictly factual, while Georgie was prone to stretching the truth, spinning tales about how they never ran into trouble. He started to worry that her embellishment was cutting his credibility. Plus, he was invited on trips she wasn't. In '49, Harry went back to the Grand Canyon without her and ran his first raft trip there with experienced boatman Don Harris.

Despite those breaches, Harry and Georgie were still each other's best partners for harebrained expeditions. In the fall of '48 they traced the path of the 1776 Escalante-Domínguez expedition down the Escalante River, becoming the first people to float it. The next year they decided to do it again, and they brought a journalist, Randall Henderson from *Desert Magazine*. It was a disaster: There was hardly any water in the river, and they ended up pulling their boat for most of the trip, but the publicity boosted Georgie's standing as a river runner. In 1950, she was asked to help with a movie called *River Goddesses*, which was about five models on a river trip through Glen Canyon. She ended up in *Life* magazine as part of the filming story, and Irish McCalla, one of the actresses, said that's when Georgie started thinking about running her own rafting business.

Now, on the boat ramp at Lees Ferry, the start of every Grand Canyon trip, the shuttle van thermometer reads 100 degrees. The mercury will stay there most of our trip except when the monsoons break over us, blowing out the side creeks with runoff, and pushing us back upstream with unrelenting headwinds. Here, before my body has adjusted, the heat feels dizzying.

By contrast, the river comes out of the bottom of the Glen Canyon Dam 15 miles upstream at a frigid 46 degrees. It's clear, green, and devoid of most sediment, nutrients, and bugs.

I've heard that Georgie used to stand chest-deep in the freezing water and slowly drink a beer without shivering. Then she would challenge the firefighters she hired as boatmen to do the same.

I haven't hardened to that point, but I wade in to my shoulders to cool myself off as we do a final round of prep. We rig gear bags and fit life jackets and reapply sunscreen, and then we're gone.

The entry into the canyon feels shockingly fast. For the first 4.5 miles you float past places you've seen before, tracing the road in, but once you pass under the parallel Navajo Bridge—the ninth highest span in the country—you're in new territory, and there's no other road crossing until you hit the Hoover Dam, almost 350 miles downstream.

When we float under the bridges, Jeff, one of the guides, points up.

"Condors," he says.

In the '80s, the giant vultures were endangered; there were only 22 remaining in the world. They were reintroduced here in the canyon, and now their population is up to 500, but they still feel special and rare. "I can't see them," I yell back, but I keep looking, squinting up into the glare until I finally do, their 10-foot wingspans reduced to black dots.

If you were to look just at geographic stats, the Grand Canyon might not seem that grand. It's not the biggest canyon in the world, nor the deepest, nor the longest. It's not even the biggest canyon in its own basin. Desolation Canyon upstream on the Green is deeper. But here the razor blade of the river cuts through a billion years of rock, revealing all of human history and more. Even though it's not the most statistically impressive, the Grand Canyon is the pinnacle of American river trips for length and scenery and complexity. The Colorado River's basin covers 8 percent of the country, 246,000 square miles,

7 states, more than 30 sovereign Native nations, and this canyon is the crux of it all.

As we float downstream, immediate and geologic time feel like they're happening on the same scale. We move through the first 5 layers of rock in 16 miles, dropping through centuries as we do. That afternoon we hit the first significant rapid, Badger Creek, at mile 8. It's rated a 5 on the Grand Canyon rapids scale of 1–10, and from above it seems straightforward, just a series of wave trains down the gut. But I am unprepared for its force. As we drop in, the deceptively big waves stop the boat's momentum, and the powerful eddies at the foot of the rapid grab at the oars.

Everything is more here: deeper, redder, hotter, bigger. And we're not even in the heart of it yet. The first night we camp on a beach and watch the canyon turn gold and pink. In the crusty soil around the campsite, sacred white datura flowers bloom on glossy green stalks. I'm starting to see why Georgie could never go anywhere else, how no other rivers could compare.

Over the next few days, we slip deeper into the history and the landscape. We pass Georgie Rapid at mile 24—named for her after she passed away—and then the white water starts to come fast. We pluck a few apples from a tree that Shocklee says was planted and cultivated by Hopi, and we find an ancient mano and metate at South Canyon, where Hisatsinom communities, the first people here, lived.

Our days fall into a rhythm. I'm the bottom of the guide hierarchy, so it is my job to carry heavy things. There are Dutch ovens and dishpans and hand-washing buckets, a shocking number of which need to be perpetually filled up from the river. I am constantly reminded of the weight of water. I haul gear and unload boats and continually put things in the wrong place. I try to give in to the repetitive Zen of rebuilding our home on a different slanted beach every night. I try to be entertaining and helpful and also never in the way. When the real guides let me row, I get worked by the eddies. I get worked by the weight of the oars in my hands. Brand-new muscles deep inside my elbows ache, and my arms feel like half-cooked spaghetti, wiggly and dull against the sheer force of the water.

Georgie said that by the time she stopped rafting, people weren't as tough as they had been, and I believe it. I'm easily dehydrated, constantly smearing myself with sun block or body lotion, or draping myself in wet sarongs, perpetually chugging electrolytes and rubbing my sore shoulders.

I remember that water, paradoxically, makes you drier. My fingers and heels crack and split. I can feel a desiccated itch creeping across my back every time I get out of the river, dunking myself to relieve the heat. My hips cramp, and my shoulders knot from sitting for hours on the gear pile on the front of the baggage boat. But I also feel stretched, buzzy, springing. I sprint down the beach and wrestle the other guides. We swim in small rapids and explore side canyons.

I am, for the first time in a long time, actually paying attention. Soaking in the colorless predawn light. Noticing the hot midday blue, so high and clear, and the way the evening sky slips from golden blush to rouge to lilac before it goes indigo again. It changes so fast it's impossible to capture, even though I try with paint and photos and words. At night I sleep on the hatch of a gently rocking raft.

We're steeped in the whole wheel of known time, billions of years and countless generations. As one retired boatman told longtime guide Louise Teal, who wrote a book about women in the canyon, "When you stick your oars in the water, you're feeling the whole story. There's no words, but it's the full language of the formation of the earth."

In early summer of 1952, Georgie set her sights on the Grand Canyon again. Between Powell's 1871 trip and 1940, only 15 recorded groups or individuals traveled through the canyon. But then in the 1940s alone, there were 8 river trips down the canyon, and Georgie wanted in. As she rafted more, the canyon was always on her mind. This time instead of swimming, she decided to take the raft down. She brought along Elgin Pierce, who she'd known since her early Sierra Club days, and who had been with her when she'd sustained a head injury while climbing. She knew he was reliable in an emergency.

Their boat was that 10-person army surplus raft Georgie had salvaged after the war. Unlike today's Hypalon or PVC boats, which are self-bailing, rockered, multichambered, and balanced, the army surplus rafts were bathtubs made of rubber that felt like eczemic elephant skin. In addition to rowing and navigating, you had to bail the water you took on, but by using a rubber raft instead of a wooden drift boat, Georgie was predicting how the river running world would change.

I'm not sure how she convinced Elgin it was a good idea, but on July 11, they hauled the raft into the water at the mouth of the Paria River, just downstream from Lees Ferry.

Georgie and Elgin packed 3 weeks of canned food and planned to take turns rowing. To navigate they had a map of the lower canyon that Georgie had gotten from Jim Rigg, who ran Mexican Hat Expeditions, a fledgling guide company. He was planning to bring a trip down that month, too.

Georgie and Elgin successfully negotiated the first significant rapids, but at mile 77, Hance Rapid, things changed. Depending on the water level, Hance is an 8 or 9 on the scale of 10. As a rapid it's both technically challenging and powerful. The river constricts due to a debris flow, and there are huge holes on the upper left and lower right. The middle is unrunnable thanks to a massive rock. The move is to start on the right, grab a pocket of slow water behind the big rock in the middle, and pivot left, fighting through massive lateral waves along the way. From the scout point, you can visualize the line, but when you're in it, it moves so fast that it's hard to know where you are.

Georgie and Elgin might have been disoriented by the flush, or they could have gotten cocky after a few successful days on the water. Rigg had told them to run the rapid on the left side, to avoid the massive recirculating waves on the right, but Georgie said they'd had good luck running down the middle up until then, so they decided to try that. Elgin was flung from the boat almost immediately, taking an oar with him. Then the boat flipped. Elgin swam for shore, but Georgie stayed with the boat, trying to get on top of it as it flushed downstream.

Georgie held on to the upside-down boat but was swept through the Sockdolager Rapid 2 miles downstream. Below that rapid she pushed the raft into an eddy, exhausted. She said she was starting to lose her grip, about to give up, when she heard someone yelling upstream and saw Elgin running her way. Together they got the boat into a bigger eddy and pulled out the food bag. They spent another cold, wet night on the shore—which was becoming a Georgie specialty—and then were able to flip it over and keep moving downstream.

They stayed a night at Phantom Ranch, the lodge at the bottom of Grand Canyon, 88 miles down, to dry out and rebuild their confidence and then set off downstream again. They tried to drag out the days, because they knew that the Mexican Hat Expeditions trip was behind them, and they didn't want to navigate the biggest rapid on the river, Lava Falls, alone.

Lava, the rapid that gives guides stomachaches, is named for a 100,000-year-old intrusion of dark volcanic rock deep in the canyon. The rapid is deceivingly calm from above, but there's a massive ledge hole in the middle, which is hard to see over the horizon line, and once you're in the thick of the white water, there's much more to avoid.

After a week, the Mexican Hat trip caught up and together they lined the boats around Lava, picking their way over the sharp black rocks. Below the rapid, Rigg led the trip through an initiation: a slug of brandy and a bucket of river water to the face to signify that they'd made it through the rapids and could call themselves Grand Canyon river runners. It would become one of Georgie's signature moves. As they floated out through the remaining flat water into the head of Lake Mead, Elgin vowed he'd never do anything like the trip again, but Georgie was feeling reluctant to go home, already ready to get back into the canyon.

By the next spring, 1953, she was still living in LA and selling real estate with her sister, Marie, but when she could, she paddled the calmer waters of the San Juan River and Glen Canyon to prepare for her next trip down the Grand Canyon.

She decided the best way to do it was to find passengers to

share the cost of the trip. Through the Sierra Club newsletter and word of mouth, she wrangled a group of 6, including 2 women, Irene McKeown and Esther Flemmer. She brought along her brother, Paul, who rowed a second boat, and a reporter from the *Los Angeles Times*, who wrote about the trip.

McKeown fell in at Cave Springs Rapid, but other than that, Georgie's second run through the canyon was safe. The group swam in the clear water at Elves Chasm and Deer Creek Falls and hiked up to the ruins at Nankoweap. After Lava, Georgie gave the paddlers her version of the initiation Rigg taught her. She quizzed them on what they'd seen, dunked them in the river, teased them, and fed them brandy shots. She declared them *forever river rats*, a permanent part of the nascent community.

Other people, like Norm Nevills, who was considered the first commercial river runner in the canyon, and Harry Aleson, who had set his sights on running motorboats up the river, were trying to turn the river into a lucrative tourism business. Georgie's tack was different: She just wanted to be in the canyons as much as possible. Nevills's crew cooked dinner and set up camp for the passengers, while Georgie's guests hauled gear and worked hard. Dinner was usually canned goods warmed in a pot of boiled river water. The labels often washed off during cooking, so you got whatever you got. But the price differential was real, too. A Mexican Hat adventure trip cost $900, a small fortune at the time, while Georgie charged folks $250.

Those early trips established Georgie's philosophy: She wanted to make the river accessible to as many people as possible. But she also thought that life in the canyon shouldn't be a cruise. Over the winter, she bought three more surplus boats and started calling her company the Royal River Rats.

"Those years from 1945 to 1954 were very satisfying ones. I finally discovered something I really wanted to do, and every time I ran the Colorado River I simply wanted to turn right around and run it again," she said.

In the spring of 1954, she wrangled people for another Grand trip. Her husband, Whitey, was along for his first canyon trip, as was river explorer John Goddard, who had previously traversed the whole Nile and was planning to make a movie about the trip. Esther Flemmer, who had joined the group at Phantom Ranch on the last trip, was a repeat guest, the first of what would become a large group of Georgie acolytes.

From the get-go, the trip shaped up to be tougher than the year before. Both Whitey and Goddard wanted to row, but they were unreliable boatmen, and they both flipped early on, unsettling the group. The crew started portaging the rapids. Sometimes Georgie would guide the first boat through and then run back up the shore to pilot the other three. They still flipped and swam often, and the trip felt slow and frustrating.

By the time they got to Boucher Rapid, 97 miles in, Georgie was exhausted. She decided to lash the rafts together and run them through the rapids as a barge, to see if they might be more stable. She'd heard that Harry had experimented with something similar.

First, she stacked two rafts on top of each other and tied them together belly to belly. She figured that if one boat flipped the other would be upright. She and her brother, Paul, rode inside, in the dark. When it flipped—and it did—they had to somersault to stay above water, and they were mashed up in the gear and each other. They made it through the rapid, but the sandwich setup wasn't commercially viable. So on the next rapid she decided to tie three boats together side by side. She reasoned that if one boat got tangled up or flipped, the power of the other two would pull it through. Everyone else was skeptical, but the clunky three-wide boat, with a rower manning an oar on each outside boat, made it through the next series of rapids, the Jewels, and then all the way down to Lava without flipping. The group voted to portage Lava, but Georgie decided she was onto something with the massive boat.

Running the big rapids without portaging made passage exciting. She faced heavy skepticism at the time for her unwieldy rigs, but she set the bones for how many people run the Grand Canyon now, in big, hard-to-flip rubber boats.

She was solidifying the social side of river running, too. There was horseplay and heckling and singing on her trips. Practical jokes and long campfire nights where a bottle of blackberry brandy would make its way around the circle. In her later years, when Lew Steiger asked her what she loved most about being on the river, she said the people.

Once she had the idea of tying multiple boats together, she started perfecting her system. She got to work on what would become the G-rig, her trademark boat. She cut the bottom out of the boats and added an inflated oval sausage tube in the middle and strapped a 10-horsepower Johnson motor onto the stern. Rigging took multiple days. Ray Gorospe, a guide who worked for her later on, said that her system was constantly changing, and the guides spent hours yanking on hemp ropes and lashing down tubes. But the *Queen Mary*, as she called it, was stable in gnashing white water. It plowed through the crunchy holes of Lava and the big waves of Hermit and Hance.

To round out her flotilla for her 1955 Grand trip, she also set up what she called the triplet: the 3 smaller rafts tied together, with a rower on an oar on each side that she'd used the year before. Her brother, Paul, came along and ran a single-person boat, as he had in the past. Between the 3 boats, they carried 28 people, the biggest ever group to go down the gorge. Joel Sayer from *Sports Illustrated* was on board and reported that people liked the thrill.

In addition to tweaking boat design, she also started working the political system. The Park Service had been administering permits, trying to control and regulate the flow of river runners, but that year Georgie thought she was immune to the permit system because she'd invited Dan Davis, the Inner Canyon ranger, to come on the trip. He hiked in at Tanner Canyon and became the first Grand Canyon National Park employee to go on the river in 26 years since Miner Tillotson banned staff from going. Davis was interested in the river, and the park finally decided they needed a presence on the water.

In typical Georgie style, he didn't see any special treatment. Davis was put to work rowing. He saw the small boat flip and felt the violence of the river. He was, reportedly, overwhelmed by the beauty. He understood the appeal.

He also saw conflict between river runners; the companies had become competitive. Georgie's big motor trip was running parallel to a Mexican Hat Expeditions trip. Georgie's group rode through the rapids while the other group portaged, and neither liked the looks of the other. They battled over campsites, in part because Georgie wouldn't stick to her word about where she was staying, but also because they had very different visions for the river experience.

Aside from onboard entertainment from folk singer Katie Lee, Mexican Hat's passengers were promised a trip filled with wilderness and solitude. Georgie's raucous group, with their thrumming motor, was not what they expected.

The other group called Georgie's group *trashy*. Katie Lee started making up mean songs that their group would sing at Georgie's crew when they passed. Her lyrics about the triple rig went something like *There ain't no stern and there ain't no prow, it looks just like a garbage scow.*

The acrimony went the other way, too. Georgie's group called Mexican Hat the Brooks Brothers outfit, a fancy cruise for wimps.

Davis refused to get in the middle of the scuffle, but it was the start of a schism between engines and oars that still stands today. Purists who were still running wooden boats hated the triple rig, because they thought it undermined the adventure of rowing. They thought the rubber rafts were dangerous, even after stats showed they were safe.

"She didn't need much scrutinizing to raise eyebrows, but I wouldn't say she was the only one circumventing the rules," says river historian Tom Martin. "She was a person trying to get people through the Grand Canyon and have a good time, but she also had detractors."

The detractors must've noticed that she was starting to take more and more people through the canyon. She started making movies of her adventures, to show a wider audience that the river was fun and safe. She played the river films in her garage and then toured them around at boat shows in the fall and winter, telling stories about the thrill. She had a habit of leaving out bad parts when she told the story—she conveniently failed to mention flipped rafts, rancid food, and long rocky swims—but she was doing it to amp up the river's appeal. "The more I began to understand this and to feel the pressures of city life, the more I felt compelled to share this experience with others," she wrote.

She said she wasn't churchgoing, but river running felt religious, and she was evangelizing for the grace of being out there in the canyon. "From the moment I laid eyes on the Colorado River, I loved the raging water, and within a short time I realized that I was going to dedicate my life to this river and others like it," she wrote.

By 1957, she was rafting full-time. Stacking up trips all summer and then spending the winter traveling around to boat shows and film festivals, selling the idea of the Royal River Rats and the idea of herself. You could see the evolution of her identity written on the sides of her massive boats. In 1955, the boats read *J R White*, claiming Whitey's name even though he had minimal involvement. By 1956, the boats said *Geo White*, and in the 1957 season, and for the rest of her career, the boats had the same thing painted on them in blocky red letters: *Georgie Woman of the River.*

On the river, the changing rock walls of the canyon mark our progress. On day 4 we transition from Redwall Limestone into the Tapeats Sandstone where the rock reveals weepy, white trails of salt. The Redwall is what it sounds like: big rosy columns, the kind of grandeur that Jeff says makes him feel like he's really coming into the Grand Canyon. We dip into the lighter Bright Angel Shale above the multicolored Nankoweap granaries, where ancestral Puebloans stashed food around 1100 CE. From the river we see the trail up to the granaries baked in the sun.

Ten miles below Nankoweap, we stop at where the Little Colorado River runs into the Colorado. The inflow is ecologically significant; the confluence is home to one of the last viable populations of endangered humpback chub, but it's also, crucially, sacred for 11 Indigenous tribes including the Hopi and Navajo, whose historic homelands include the Little Colorado, and who have been fighting for their right to the river—and to their most important religious sites—for decades. The ties go back an eternity. For generations, tribes have dryland farmed the river's banks and made pilgrimages to the salt mines along its shore. Hopi believe that life started at a spring near the confluence, the Sipapu. "It is a place of emergence, and the place we go home to. That's why Sípàapu is so important, it's a gateway to a spiritual world," says Vernon Masayesva, a former chairman from the Hopi Tribal Council and the executive director of the environmental-advocacy group Black Mesa Trust. "When your body passes away, your spirit travels down into the Grand Canyon."

When we get there late in the day, the beach is open. We tie up the boats and walk upstream.

Even if I didn't know the history, even if I wasn't already overwhelmed by the beauty of the whole canyon, the walk up the Little Colorado would be shocking. Rivers reflect their carried content. The eponymous red of the Colorado comes from the sediment and sandstone, iron-rich. In contrast, the Little Colorado is fluorescent milky jade, somewhere between turquoise and teal. It seems sage or silver or aquamarine depending on the angle and light. The water feels thick and soft. The texture and tone come from the high concentration of calcium carbonate, which coats the rocks and the shoreline with a slippery talc-like layer. At the campsite that night, we will wash the chalk out of our skin and hair, sloughing away reminders of the Little Colorado.

We walk up to a lucent pool where the guides let the guests float through a rapid in their life jackets. They are laughing and trying not to swallow too much river water when they do. After I swim through the rapid a few times, I stand on the shore with Shocklee and Evelyn, another guide, who tell me why they both think it's so special.

Shocklee says it's healing. Evelyn says it brings you in tune, that it keys you into everything you might need. I'd initially felt a little weird about taking tourists to splash in a sacred place. But I also know that play is a kind of ceremony, that it can feel important and imbued with respect. That feels true here in the whole canyon. I wonder if Georgie felt that, too.

We are 4 days in. Many river trips I've been on end somewhere around here, 60 miles deep. But we're barely breaking into the trip. I'm starting to settle into the physicality and the people, the reverence and the rawness.

Georgie said she'd always been restless before she found the Colorado. "This characteristic of the river, even today, satisfies my basic need for constant change and challenge," she said. I wonder how she felt at this point in any trip. If and when she started to settle.

As the sun sinks and the swimmers get shivery, we plod back to the boat beach. When the chain of hikers slows and gaps, I drop off the end of the group and sneak back upstream to say thank you. I'm trying to be grateful, trying to take it in. I'm surprised when my throat gets tight with tears.

I catch up back at the boats, and we slip downstream, coming around the corner to set up for the night at Crash Camp. The Little Colorado is an origin story, but it also marks the end of Marble Canyon, the first piece of the trip before we get deep into the gorge. Coming out of the eddy, Cole, one of the guides, turns back and yells, "Hey, we're in it. We're in the Grand Canyon now."

WE DON'T HAVE CATHEDRALS, BUT WE HAVE THE GRAND CANYON

The pot of coffee water goes on the blaster around four in the morning. It's too dark for me to see my watch, but I hear the propane tick on and see Shocklee's headlamp flashing in the kitchen. We're on today. Our crew of 8 rotates through cook teams of 2. That means that every 4 days, when the boats hit the beach in the afternoon, you set up the kitchen to your liking so you can start making dinner and appetizers. In the morning you wake up well before first light to start prepping breakfast. You boil massive pots of water for coffee and hot drinks. Trying to be silent, trying not to burn yourself as you pour coffee from the huge pots into the insulated tubs, because on the river, every task involves carrying heavy things. Then it's on to chopping fruit, forearms still sore from yesterday's rowing and hauling. Still a little shaky from staying up too late listening to and telling stories, looking at stars and naming the constellations.

If you're not cooking, you get the grace of sleeping until the water boils. But once the coffee is up, you're on boat rigging, endless dishes, groover duty, and making sure everyone gets their shit together on time. We've got miles to make, and there are a million things to do, but it's also someone's vacation, so being a river guide means threading a needle. You have to be precise, always on-clock, while also seeming effortless and cool.

Only a small part of guiding is navigating rapids. You also need to be familiar with natural history, emergency medicine, cooking, thermodynamics, boat repair, bartending, babysitting, oration, costume design, anthropology, geology, and therapy. The day-by-day, minute-by-minute entertainment and maintenance and social awareness is necessary to ensure that humans who aren't normally in this rugged, removed landscape—and who have paid a lot of money to be here—aren't endangering themselves or having emotional breakdowns.

Some days we move downstream fast. Some days, like the one where we slog through the slow water of Furnace Flats, the wind blows directly upstream, making headway painful. Between hikes into green grottoes where native fish circle our toes, I watch the guides clean and dress wounds, bake birthday cake, and explain the entire geologic history of the world. Jeff plays the flute every morning at first coffee call to wake the camp up with a melody.

Underlying everything is the knowledge that so much can go wrong so quickly—and that we're our own best rescue. One day at lunch I tie the raft to a solid-seeming clump of tamarisk roots. I think nothing of it until I hear Kelly, another guide, yelling, and see her standing waist-deep in the river, holding on to the raft for all she's worth. The rest of the trip I triple-check all my knots, haunted by the idea that I could have lost the boat with all of our cooking supplies with one slip.

The details are different from Georgie's era. Today the production starts in the boathouse, where we load massive coolers with fresh veggies, fancy cheese, and dry ice. There are huge sides of salmon. Ice cream. The coolers are so heavy that we place them into the rafts with a forklift. Then the rafts are so heavy that they have to be winched onto the trailer. We go through a gear checklist, everything from extra oars to art supplies. We go through a medical roster, and a list of dietary restrictions. We learn who has a deadly peanut allergy, and who is casually gluten free. On the river we have to keep up that vigilance. One afternoon, when we're pulled up at Stone Creek Falls camp, we get visited by the Park Service health inspector, who examines everything from our egg-packing technique to the pH of our dishwater. He has a serious military haircut and a knuckle-breaking handshake, but, because we're in the canyon, his painted toenails peek out of his Chacos. Since the Georgie days of early rafting, there have been a slew of added rules and regulations, and most of them came into play because something went wrong in the past, from diarrhea to death. By bleaching the dishwater and double-checking the med kits, we are trying to hold a tricky tension between wild and tamed, trying to take care of ourselves and the place.

Stone Creek Falls flows through a red gash in the rocks, the water clear and cold. Its cove is lined with bright green moss and catches the light. Writer Terry Tempest Williams, who comes here as often as she can, wrote that she sees the falls as a woman wrapped in a veil of water and maidenhair ferns. This rangy, rugged landscape is an idealized portrait of what nature *should* look like. You can stand on the edge of those falls, spattered by icy spray, and feel like you're in a wild, lightly touched place. But everything down here, from the beaches to the bugs, has been changed by people. We are between two dams. We can hear the buzz of helicopters overhead. We are in a kind of paradise, but even when it feels wild, it's carefully constructed.

It's not just remarkable landscapes like the Grand Canyon where you can feel the changing importance of outside places and our place within them. The drive to control our experience in nature goes back to the beginning of human history. And it's intertwined, like I guess a lot of things are, with God, morality, and power. You can track it back to the Old Testament. Formal religion has never been a big part of my life, but I still know the story of Adam and Eve and their fall from grace. Eden was a garden paradise, and when they were cast out for sinning (Eve's fault, of course), men would ever after have to work the land and women suffer the pain of childbirth. From the beginning of storytelling, morality was tied to the landscape.

In ancient Rome, around 30 BCE, the poet Virgil codified the idea of what an ideal landscape should look like: controlled, pastoral, and safe, tended by diligent shepherds. It makes sense that early civilizations wanted peaceful places, ones that were productive and nonthreatening, when weeds or wolves or windstorms could be the breaking point between life and death. Nature was already testing them enough.

Far before we got to capital-*W* Wilderness—the federal landscape designation that came into play in the 1960s—the idea of small-*w* wilderness tended to connote danger. The Oxford English Dictionary first found evidence of the word *wilderness* around 1200 CE in the Trinity College Homilies, some of the earliest written Middle English. The word was used to define land *not* used for farming. Unlike high-value, human-managed pastoral landscapes, wilderness was scary.

During the enclosure period in Europe, most wilderness was split up, managed, and owned by the wealthy.

When white settlers came to America, those ideas came, too. Colonists set out across the country driven by puritanical work ethic, a desire for independence and new beginnings, and the moral imperative to remake the wilderness into gardens for God. They took over the land and violently pushed out Indigenous peoples. They were turning the continent into a fertile garden with no regard for the natural balance of an ecosystem. That fervent frontier-claiming also set up a fake, dangerous dichotomy between settlers and First Peoples: that white people lived in civilization and so-called savages lived in wilderness. As European settlers spread out toward the Pacific, pushing the edge of what was considered the frontier, even the arid desert canyons and wide Midwestern grasslands were reformed into the shape of pastoral gardens. Beavers were turned into hats, and old-growth forests were turned into fields. Manifest Destiny problematically implied that these changes were the God-given right of white men. Historian Adam Sowards told me that he also thinks it came from a sense of optimism and exploration. "Maybe this is a time where they thought they could do it all. The population is small; the continent feels vast," he said.

That period of colonial exploration was shockingly short. By the 1890s, the frontier was considered closed because of increased population density. But as European settlers pushed West, they created an idea of what America—and an American—was: someone rugged, independent, and brave, who could thrive in the wild lands that had become synonymous with the country. "One of the things you see in the record is that Americans are fairly culturally insecure in the nineteenth century," Sowards told me. "We don't have cathedrals, but we have the Grand Canyon. Those become a cultural answer to Europe. We find these monumental landscapes as part of a cultural heritage." By the end of that century, stories about sweeping landscapes, and the bravery it took to live within them, had become a part of the national identity, even if most of the population was pushed up against the coasts and, increasingly, living in cities.

Maybe that's why I'm so obsessed with stories of people like Georgie pushing into wild places: I want part of it, especially when it feels like so many places are picked over. I still hold on to the problematic myth of individualism, and the idea that toughness is the best quality you can have. I've felt that perverted sense of American exceptionalism play out in my own body. I moved West after all, chasing exhilaration, trying to come into a country of my own.

The romance around wild places only grew as America became more urbanized. "Appreciation of wilderness began in cities," historian Roderick Nash wrote in *Wilderness and the American Mind*. In the US, urbanization increased rapidly in the middle of the nineteenth century, after the industrial revolution and as more people moved to cities to live and work. As populations spiked, people needed more resources. Cities demanded vast quantities of timber and coal to keep them going, which led to deforestation. The wilderness was shrinking, and a scarcity mentality around access to wild places took hold. The wilderness evolved from scary to enticing.

At the same time, new modes of transportation made it easier to travel, which also led to shifting attitudes around scenery and wildness. Outdoor places began to represent an escape from urban life.

As technology changed, many people also moved away from religion as the central tenet of their lives to new organizing principles: industrialization, sciences, rationality. Romanticism, the artistic and intellectual movement that began in the early 1800s, glorified our relationship to the outdoors. German artists like Caspar David Friedrich popularized atmospheric landscape paintings, while poets like Samuel Taylor Coleridge and William Wordsworth wrote dreamy verses about the Lake District of England. By the middle of the nineteenth century, the movement had made its way to America, where it took on a particular bent toward nationalism and nature.

In 1832, a disenchanted young minister from Massachusetts, Ralph Waldo Emerson, set off on a trip to Europe, where he met Coleridge and Wordsworth. He came back ready to channel their ideas in ways that aligned with his ascetic New England Unitarianism and the growing American identification with open space. Once back home, he started talking about the tenets of what would become Transcendentalism, a philosophy that elevated the power of intuition, nature, and spirituality.

It became the bones of his treatise "Nature," which honed his idea that everyone should develop their own personal understanding of the universe, in part through their individual experience with nature. He said you could go out, pay attention, and become transformed.

Emerson was a part of a group of Transcendentalists, including Margaret Fuller and Henry David Thoreau, whose work anticipated what we might now call *nature writing* and reflected social change. "In wildness is the preservation of the world," wrote Thoreau in his essay "Walking," a statement that has been co-opted and rehashed so many times that it now feels empty.

But his words did have weight. When Thoreau cataloged the seasonal shifts at Walden Pond or wrote about testing himself on the knife ridge of Mount Katahdin, he was talking about the value of wild space, which to him was an expression of the beauty and goodness of God, as well as a place to find yourself. Nature, with its beauty and burden, was where you could burnish your self-resolve, shore up your spirituality, and find truth.

I come from the same place they did, the uptight academia of Cambridge and Concord, so I understand, at a gut level, the need to explain and intellectualize the feeling of being outside. For me and, I think, for uptight thinkers all the way back to Fuller, Transcendentalism gives the limbic desire to touch grass an idealized point.

Out of that idealism emerged a modern sense of outdoor recreation. Historian Adam Sowards says that people tend to flock to nature after major conflicts. Rafting and what we now think of as camping culture ramped up after World War II. In that postwar period, as men came back to their communities, many were craving the connection and structure they found in the military. In *Camping Grounds*, historian Phoebe S. K. Young says that in the postwar outdoor boom, recreational campers wanted human connection, leisure, simplicity.

William H. H. Murray, a nineteenth-century minister, said being in nature was both good for your physical health and a balm for spiritual unease. His wildly popular 1869 book *Adventures in Wilderness; Or, Camp-life in the Adirondacks* helped spark the camping craze in the US and reframed being outside as an act of devotion. The book sold hundreds of thousands of copies—the publishing company ran eight printings in the first year alone—and unleashed a flood of other publications and periodicals, like *Outing* magazine, which started in 1882 and covered biking, hiking, and camping. Those stories expanded Murray's framework and attempted to smooth over the past, with its violent reality of frontier rampage, by creating a new image of how to be outside. Young says camping was meant to be simple and not too luxurious, but not so rough that campers could be confused with a "bum" or "tramp." It should hit a carefully prescribed balance between comfort and freedom. Living outside was considered healthy—but only if you were someone who fit a certain social, racial, cultural standard.

But that standard was expanding, at least by some metrics. In 1868, Congress passed an 8-hour workday for federal employees, and that practice, along with the 5-day workweek, trickled down (slowly and painfully, with many labor strikes) into other fields until President Franklin D. Roosevelt signed the Fair Labor Standards Act of 1938, giving workers those parameters, along with overtime pay.

These new boundaries gave workers time off for leisure and vacation. "Tourism met other psychic needs in fin de siècle America. Especially after the pronouncement of the closing of the frontier in the aftermath of the 1890 census, Americans yearned for a salve for their sociocultural wounds, the malaise that defined their condition," historian Hal Rothman wrote in his book *Devil's Bargains*. "In the spectacular vistas of the West, in a growing obsession with native peoples and their arts, Americans used a geographic place as mythical space to work out tensions."

As more people traveled to remote, wild places, it became harder to divorce land use from land policy. Starting in the mid-1800s, the US government began setting aside public land for what people in power considered public good. It was an idea that had only really happened at scale before in Mongolia where the Bogd Khan Uul protected area was established in 1778. In 1872, President Grant signed the Yellowstone National Park Protection Act, making the geyser-studded grizzly range the first national park. In 1890, Congress designated two more: Yosemite and Sequoia National Parks.

In 1903, President Theodore Roosevelt took a 3-day camping trip into Yosemite with John Muir, who would found the Sierra Club that would eventually provide Georgie with a path to wild places. They slept under giant sequoias and weathered snowstorms. Roosevelt, who had been an asthmatic, myopic kid, found his footing in nature, claiming it toughened him up. He felt he was of a generation that had missed out on the pioneering challenges of their parents and grandparents. He wanted adventures and believed in what he called *the strenuous life*, the idea that you should work hard and take in wild places to develop tenacity.

When he came to the Grand Canyon, the same year that he visited Yosemite with Muir, those ideas of wildness were on his mind. The canyon was still a big blank space on the map, rugged and harsh, but miners like Louis Boucher, who had failed to make good on their mineral claims, started bringing visitors to the rim to take in the vistas.

"The Grand Canyon fills me with awe," Roosevelt said after that visit. "It is beyond comparison—beyond description; absolutely unparalleled throughout the wide world . . . You cannot improve on it. But what you can do is to keep it for your children, your children's children, and all who come after you, as the one great sight which every American should see."

In 1906, on the strength of the brand-new Antiquities Act, President Roosevelt created the Grand Canyon Game Preserve and laid out a runway for conserving more public land, a path that enabled Georgie 40 years later.

Roosevelt's claims about the importance of the outdoors for developing connection and grit feel prescient today. A 2017 Yale study found a widening disconnect between people and nature, which led to decreased awareness of ecosystem values and of the simple pleasure of being outside. According to a 2021 Bureau of Labor Statistics survey, only 4.3 percent of American workers spend most of their day outside. Public land like the Grand Canyon, which sees about 500 million visitors a year, is one of those crucial places where people can feel the connection and pleasure.

Of course, the history of human use in the Grand Canyon stretches back much longer than recreational history. In the Grand Canyon's 2 billion years of geologic history, there's concrete evidence that people were there around 12,000 years ago, dryland farming, making art, mining salt. Hopi say that a boy named Tiyo, who was searching to understand the river, was the first person to travel down the San Juan and Colorado Rivers, into the Sea of Cortez. He returned with the story of the rain dance and helped break drought.

The first documented trip through the Grand Canyon by Westerners was the Powell geographic expedition of 1869. Before Major John Wesley Powell led a group of 10 men down the Green and Colorado Rivers, the canyon was the last great undrawn section of the country's map. No one had reportedly made it through alive. Powell made it back with maps and stories but lost three men along the way.

From the time Powell made his first Grand Canyon trip until 1956, when Georgie was running her early motor rig, just over 200 people traveled through the canyon. But by 1960 that number nearly doubled, and by the '70s, 10,000 boaters had ventured through.

The numbers were so low for so long because the canyon is harsh and remote. Before the Glen Canyon Dam was built, the river vacillated between 125,000 cubic feet per second in the spring and 3,000 c.f.s. after runoff season. Navigation was variable and tricky at best. And the land didn't align with Euro-American ideas about using resources: It wasn't great for irrigation; it was hard to dam; and mining, with the exception of uranium in the mid-twentieth century, was never very fruitful. For a while the most valuable thing coming out of the region was bat guano, which was pulled out of a cave in the low-walled western reaches and used for fertilizer.

After the Grand Canyon became a national park, the scenic views were considered valuable in their own right, but below the rim, the vacillating river was still a menace, unpredictable and inconvenient for the arc of irrigation. In 1920, Interior Secretary Franklin Lane wanted to dam the whole Grand Canyon, and the USGS began to plan a survey of potential dam sites.

In 1922, the seven states along the river signed the Colorado River Compact, which determined how much water each state was allocated, and the nascent Bureau of Reclamation was tasked with making the arid West workable for farmers. Essentially, Reclamation was—and still is—responsible for dams and water storage west of the hundredth meridian, the line of longitude that drops down from North Dakota and demarcates the less-wet left side of the country. Over the next half century, Reclamation would dam and divert almost every major water system in the West. And the reservoirs on the Colorado were their biggest. The Grand Canyon became the heart of a fight over public resources and how to balance recreation, wildness, and use.

People were also starting to think about running the river for pure adventures. In 1927, Clyde Eddy made it down the river with a crew of 9 college students and a bear cub named Cataract. He'd hired petty criminal Parley Galloway, the son of a boatbuilder, as his guide.

That same year, Miner Tillotson became superintendent of the park. After a few high-profile deaths, including the disappearance of newlyweds Glen and Bessie Hyde, he attempted to prohibit all rafting expeditions. In October of 1928, the Hydes had come down from Idaho to try to set a speed record and cement Bessie in history as the first woman to raft the entire canyon. It was their honeymoon: They'd married the previous spring, the day Bessie's divorce from her first husband went through. In December, when they failed to show up in Needles, California, Glen's father rallied a search party. Their boat was found, fully upright, with all their gear in place, around mile 237, and Bessie's journal noted that they'd made it through the rapid at mile 231. Their bodies were never found, and after Georgie's death, there were rumors that she might have been Bessie, because a copy of the Hydes' marriage license was found in Georgie's underwear drawer, and because Georgie had never been transparent about her past.

I think the story is too tidy. It smashes together the lives of some of the few women on the river and conflates them. But whatever the truth, Tillotson was distressed enough to try to shut down boating right as river running was gaining popularity. Brothers Frank and Bus Hatch became the first people to charge for river trips on the Green River through Dinosaur National Monument in 1936, the same year the Hoover Dam was completed. Just like in the wake of the industrial revolution, as dam building ramped up and untouched rivers became rarer, there was a burst of desire for wild places.

One of those people spearheading rafting on the San Juan River was Norm Nevills, a failed actor and geologist from Mexican Hat, Utah.

Nevills took his wife, Doris, down the San Juan River in a modified horse trough for their honeymoon in 1933, and that trip sparked the idea of running commercial expeditions. The next year, he started taking people on trips through Glen Canyon and down the San Juan. One night in a bar in Mexican Hat, he was talking up his rafting ambitions to traveling botanist Elzada Clover, who wanted to catalog desert plants in the canyon. They started scheming up a plan to go down the Grand Canyon, starting in Green River, Utah, finishing in Lake Mead.

Clover brought along her coworker Lois Jotter and a male scientist because two women alone wouldn't have been proper. Nevills, who talked a big game but had never actually seen the Grand before, tried to recruit boatmen. He wrangled any able-bodied guy willing to go, but a number of them bailed at Lees Ferry after Cataract Canyon shredded their nerves. Nevills had to scramble to find more rowers before they went down the Grand Canyon.

When they made it to Lake Mead in August 1938, Jotter and Clover became the first women to run the canyon, and the trip marked the beginning of Nevills's decade-long domination of rafting on the Grand. In the 1940s, there were 8 total river trips down the canyon, 6 of them by Nevills. In April 1947 he was given the first National Park Service permit to raft the Grand. All the Park Service units with major rivers, like Big Bend on the Rio Grande in Texas, and Dinosaur in Utah, only gave permits to people who had been down the river before, even though fewer than 100 people had ever boated the entire canyon. "The way I see this time, it's the beginning of the commercialization of the river," historian Tom Martin says.

In the same period, loving rivers started to feel complicated. Beginning in the 1930s, the federal government kicked off a four-decade mission to build major dams across the country. By the '50s, boaters began to question the validity of large-scale engineering. In 1950, writer Bernard DeVoto called out the Bureau of Reclamation and the Army Corps of Engineers in *The Saturday Evening Post.* He wrote that by damming and flooding rivers, specifically the Yampa and Green Rivers in Echo Park between Colorado and Utah, the feds were shredding American cultural heritage and their children's ecological future.

The fight over Echo Park became a flash point. Over the next few years, conservation organizations like the Wilderness Society, Sierra Club, and Audubon Society coalesced around fighting the dam, because they worried it would be the first of many if it was allowed to be built. Rivers became one of the first big battlegrounds of a growing environmental movement. And in the midst of that, in 1952, Georgie first launched her boat into the stream at Lees Ferry.

One morning the boats drop us at Tapeats Creek for a hike. Away from the river, the air feels scorching and heavy. The thin riverside rim of green fades into scratchy barrel cactus and spiny brittlebush. The trail winds up and over a skinny ledge where we have to shuffle over an overhang. The river below us is 76 feet wide. We're in the narrowest part of the canyon, and the water is terra-cotta-colored cream.

We drop into a hidden valley hundreds of feet above the river where red ledges are worn slick by the clear water of a side stream. The water has carved out curves in the canyon, so smooth they're almost soft, and the sun filters through the lush green trees, illuminating a perfect swimming hole. This place has been important to the Southern Paiute forever. The waterfalls below hold sacred stories and it's long been a place to gather plants like willow and watercress. Other tribes call it crucial, too. In the days since rafting exploded in popularity, tourists have started calling it the Patio, because it's a near-perfect place to lounge. We slip off our packs and slide into the cold water. I lie back in the cobbles, letting the water run through my hair. Cottonwoods twist above us, and below you can follow a weaving trail along the canyon's rim back down to the river.

After we swim and eat our sandwiches, Jeff turns to Lilah, Nolan, and me, the three members of the crew who haven't been here before. "Do you guys want to go for a run?" he asks. "I want to show you something." I am wearing Chacos and a bathing suit, not ideal running gear, but I say yes, because I want to see everything.

We follow a stream, hopping over cottonwood roots and chunks of Tapeats, and then we cut up the canyon, through bushy overgrowth, eyes on the ground for snakes. We reach a rocky opening, and then we're at the cataract of a waterfall. Hidden in the canyon's overhung cove, someone has built a series of chairs out of stacked sandstone. It looks like some kind of ancient living room, carved in pale red. "Welcome to the

Throne Room," Jeff says as he takes a seat. He says guides—he doesn't know who—built this place over the years. It's been here as long as he's been coming through the canyon.

Back at the river, Evelyn points me to another secret. She sticks a note and a beer into an empty tin of Gatorade powder and then tells me to follow her up the rubble pile above the beach. Hidden in the ridge there's a triangular slot that serves as a riverside mailbox. She's leaving the note for her fiancé, who is behind us on another trip. He'll be in this exact spot in a week or two. In the cave there are envelopes and packages and nips of booze. Warm beers and love notes. Someone named Colter has several of the latter. I love knowing that the canyon has many secrets to reveal, and that I'm in on some of them. I love the petroglyphs and the hidden mailboxes but I'm still wondering which human traces add to the history and which are harmful.

Georgie, too, faced this dilemma when she lost one of the big fights to preserve the river. In October of 1956, President Eisenhower pushed a button in his office in the White House, detonating the first charge of dynamite in the construction of Glen Canyon Dam. The dam sits at the head of the Grand Canyon, and once it went in, the canyon was irrevocably changed. The wild spring flows were tempered, and the water, which had been silty and warm, turned clear green and cold. Bugs, fish, and many other species were stopped by the concrete wall. Sand didn't transport. After that, every trip downstream was different.

Georgie was livid. "I opposed the dam vigorously and always urged anyone who came in contact with me to write to senators and congressmen in protest," she wrote.

For her, part of the river adventure was the variability, the vacillating flows, and the way a wild river was different every time. The dam made the river more predictable, but it also changed the ecosystem. "The dams have really destroyed the entire Colorado adventure as I used to know it and have changed the entire complexion of river running everywhere, forever," she said.

HERE COMES THAT CRAZY WOMAN

Through the late '50s and early '60s, Georgie crammed in as many river trips as she could. She brought repeat customers back to the canyon and took journalists and filmmakers down the river. She made first descents down international rivers and paddled major rapids across the Western US and Alaska. By 1961, Georgie had brought more people down the Grand Canyon than anyone in history. And over the next few years she kept up the frantic pace.

"I guess you might say I receive the same satisfaction running rivers that an artist gets from expressing his feelings on canvas, or that a pole vaulter feels making a high jump without disturbing the bar," she wrote in her memoir. "I shall never tire of this feeling, and no matter how many times I've run the Colorado River, the challenge of reading the currents and running the rapid just right will always excite me."

Like many of the boaters at the time, she took risks, but as she spent more time in the canyon, she started to gain a reputation as being loose and dangerous, one that didn't seem to stick to any of the men who were also making history. In 1957, when the river was high, she and another boater both had trouble at the Granite Narrows. Some of her crew fell out when her boat got sucked into a whirlpool, while her male counterpart flipped. Yet she was judged much more harshly. Historians and fellow boaters considered it a mistake on his part, while it was seen as proof that she was dangerous.

She said she would walk into the Temple Bar Marina at the top of Lake Mead and hear veiled whispers. "Oh, here comes that crazy woman!" She laughed about it, or tried to flip it to her advantage, shrugging it off as tough women often have to do, but *crazy* is a belittling, gendered word, and it got under her skin. Especially because the other outfitters, particularly Norm Nevills, would cut her down. "Norman would never quite believe that a woman could tackle the Colorado River. I understand that he was quite upset when I started running rafts through the rapids while he was still lining or portaging his boats through most of them," she said.

The budding rafting scene was competitive all around. "All the original outfitters didn't like each other much," said longtime guide Brian Dierker, in a podcast with Lew Steiger. "They were stubborn old goats." But as a woman, Georgie faced added hostility. "They weren't easy on her," said Dierker.

And even if they were competitive, those dudes bonded together and started sharing ideas. In 1954, a group of Green River guides formed the Western River Guides Association, a trade group to support the burgeoning river running business. In less than 100 years, the canyon went from largely untouched to crowded enough to necessitate permits and a business association. But even though Georgie was already gearing up to lead more trips and guide more people than almost all of the men in the WRGA, she wasn't welcome in the group.

In 1968, Ken Sleight, the longtime river guide who gained

notoriety as the model for Ed Abbey's character Seldom Seen Smith in *The Monkey Wrench Gang*, says Georgie's application was rejected because "she was a woman and got too much publicity."

Georgie was making films and showing slideshows about her river trips to try to drum up business. As she did so, the business association said she tried too hard. By keeping Georgie out, the guide association drew boundaries around what a river guide looked like: not a woman; not a promoter. Or at least not a woman promoter.

On a drive through Utah, after my trip through the Grand, I stopped at the John Wesley Powell River History Museum in the town of Green River, Utah. The museum, full of wooden boats and river detritus, is home to the River Runners Hall of Fame. Georgie is one of three women there, along with Elzada Clover and Lois Jotter. Compared to the other plaques, hers is spare, just five sentences. One cites Harry Aleson, one talks about her first husband, one calls her *reckless*. Even when she's being celebrated, it feels like she's reduced to a novelty.

By the time we pull up at Trinity Camp, the sky is mackerel spotted, then massive with rain, breaking the heat. The light turns blue, and the wind rails as we put up a tarp and tie down our loose things. The inner gorge is tight at Trinity Camp, so steep you can't see the rim, constrained by the hard basement rocks. Black Vishnu Schist bleeds into blood-colored Zoroaster Granite veined with mica flecks. Metamorphic into igneous, the ancient heart of the earth.

The storm makes me antsy, full of electric energy, and when I've determined the risk of flash floods is minimal, I decide to climb up the creek-bed canyon behind camp, eager to explore.

I scramble up steep ledges, looking for footholds, following the path the water has carved. I'm sure a million people have been up this creek before—we're staying at a common camp—but after being hemmed in with people for so many days, it feels good to be on my own, gripping the granitic crystals with my fingertips when the rock gets slick. Alone I am constantly keying into the angles of the rock and the temperature changes, noticing every little difference.

Down here, my body is a tool. It carries me up side canyons and moves through the daily grind of dipping oar blades in the river over and over again. It knows the exact moment to jump from the boat to the shore. I understand why Georgie craved that feeling. But even if your body is a tool, it comes with a specific pressure when you're a woman. You can't separate yourself from your body, and you can't separate your body from the culture it swims in.

Our crew is evenly gender-split, but the trip leader and two of the three guides are guys. On the other end, both of us unpaid swampers are women. Evelyn, the sole female guide, who is a knot of muscle with a long braid and a big laugh, says this is the most women she's ever worked with on a trip. Everyone has to help with daily chores and maintenance—it's part of the deal—but I watch Evelyn hold all the meal planning in her head, and Kelly, a gear boater who has been guiding across the West for decades and has a no-nonsense toughness that belies her big heart, obsessively cleans up after everyone. Lilah and I fritter around trying to fill any unfinished chore. We step into female-oriented housekeeping tasks, even when there's no house to keep. It's not that the guys don't help, it's more that we have an embedded sense of noticing, even here. There's a subtle difference in our extra work. Like Georgie, we want to be judged on our capability, but we're also culturally conditioned to perform a gendered role.

To understand why I didn't have female outdoor heroes, I wanted to dig into the gender divide, even though it felt complicated. Parsing the differences can take you down some dangerous lines of biological essentialism and the flattened, often-weaponized ideas that gender is binary, and that we have innate, immobile ways of being.

So yes, there are some generalized physical differences between men and women. At elite levels, male athletes are 9 to 12 percent faster and stronger, particularly when it comes to sports that require explosive strength. Men tend to be bigger, with more muscle mass. But I see little girls tumble boys their age, and older women win long races. I feel my endurance and my toughness increasing as I age.

And sure, testosterone is a performance enhancer. And muscle mass makes a difference when it comes to physical tasks like pushing boats. But I don't think a black-and-white gender divide really exists when it comes to being capable in the outdoors.

Where that gender difference *does* matter is in how we're socialized and in how society treats us. The gap in how women are perceived outside, and in so many traditionally male spaces, is an ideology gap, not an ability one.

TA Loeffler, a professor of outdoor education and recreation at Memorial University of Newfoundland, studies gender roles in outdoor spaces. When I first called her, she couldn't talk. She was leading a sea-kayaking trip off the coast of Baja. But when I finally got her on Zoom, she explained that she's been working for decades both on identifying the gaps in how women and nonbinary people are perceived outside and on trying to close them. Starting with her dissertation in 1988, she's homed in on the factors that make it difficult for women to thrive in the outdoor world.

First, there's history. Leadership and power in the outdoor world has historically been male dominated, and those men tend to bring in other men. That could be hiring rookie male guides, or inviting guys on a climbing trip, or taking young boys camping and leaving their sisters at home. "We call that homologous reproduction. We like to surround ourselves with people like ourselves, and that makes it harder to break in," Loeffler says.

That means many women aren't given opportunities, formal or otherwise, to learn or engage in the practices of being outside. It's particularly relevant in activities that are skill- or gear-heavy, like rafting. We have fewer chances to casually try skills or to develop muscle memory for tying knots or feeling ourselves fall.

Karen Warren, a professor who long ran the outdoor program at Hampshire College and has published widely about women in the outdoors, calls this the *myth of square one.* We don't start from the same place. Boys and men often get signals that they're welcome in an outdoor space, that they can mess up or fall down or get messy or try and try again. Girls often won't try a new physical skill until they're confident they can do it.

Technical or strength-based skills are "hard skills" ("Hard not to think about male anatomy there," Loeffler laughs) and often male-coded, whereas interpersonal skills, like conflict resolution, are "soft skills." Hard skills are often given higher value in a professional or leadership context. To get hired as a Grand Canyon guide you have to prove you can handle a flipped raft, but no one is evaluating how you entertain guests in the 200 miles of flat water or how you deflect conflict around the campfire when everyone has had a few drinks. The soft stuff is mutable, trickier to evaluate, and trickier to do well. Loeffler says those interpersonal skills are crucial. I saw that in the canyon, where Evelyn tracked that we had enough food to see us through and monitored a million other tiny details—vigilant for things that could go wrong.

That focus on skills that are male-coded and often taught by mentorship creates a competence gap, both real and perceived. "Women doubt their competence more than men," Loeffler says. "And they often don't have an accurate assessment of their own technical skills because of that." Research shows that both men and women favor male leaders in the outdoors. Women like Georgie, who do break in, must be exceptional to be perceived as on par.

Warren calls that the *superwoman myth*. It's the perception that you must be flawless, better than the men, to belong in any male-dominated context. That any failure isn't just a momentary miscalculation, it's proof you're not strong or smart or savvy enough. It can feel like the credibility of your whole gender rests on your shoulders as you're rowing into the maw.

Another factor: The stories of women who have gone before us can be hard to find, even if they've always existed. It's what Karla Henderson, a professor at North Carolina State, calls the "invisibility and distortion of the female experience."

Georgie's story is a prime example of both that invisibility and distortion. I didn't know her story until late in my time on the river, even though, for decades, as rafting the Grand Canyon became more popular and mainstream, she continued to be one of the busiest, boldest guides on the river. Other outfitters started running motor rigs like she did, but a Georgie trip was special. People would come back year after year to run the river with her. She'd take them hiking into hidden grottoes and hold talent shows around the fire. She'd steer her boat right into the gut of the biggest rapids, standing them straight up on end. One passenger said she could read the river the way other people could read *TV Guide*. She was constantly reminding her guests to look around, to remember that they were in the Grand Canyon.

Despite her experience, Georgie was still shunned, both on the river and off. One time when she was visiting Desert View, the South Rim watchtower where you can spot rapids like Tanner, she mentioned to the man standing next to her that she was running boats down there, and he silently walked away. "I got that a lot, people say 'You must be dreaming or something,'" she said.

By then, Georgie was a scraggly, scrawny, middle-aged woman with cold blue eyes and wild hair. She did not look the traditional part of the river hero. "I look like someone's secretary," she quipped about herself. That misperception fueled her.

To gain credibility and drum up more business, she courted the press. *Sports Illustrated* and *Desert* ran stories about her trips, but she said that reporters tended to twist the narrative or reject her invitations. "I had one reporter tell me to my face that if I were a man a lot of people would be interested. But since I was a woman he just wouldn't run the story," she said.

Georgie was never one to hew to honesty; she lied about her personal history to make it seem more exciting and about her safety record to entice people into the canyon, but she said journalists were not accurately capturing the magic of her river runs. She once called out well-known adventurer John Goddard for perpetuating false stories. "When I asked him why, he said flatly, 'I don't want other people going on the canyon. I want pictures that nobody else has. If everybody goes, then I won't be doing anything different.'"

She felt like they were challenging her livelihood and perpetuating exclusionary practices. The best way to set the record straight, she decided, was to go on TV. She made several appearances on the Art Linkletter show, *House Party*. In one episode, after showing a few river clips, Art asked, "Georgie, tell me, aren't you even afraid?"

"Yes I'm afraid, but not on the river," she answered. "I feel water is my friend. But when I get on the freeway and someone else is driving, then I'm scared to death." She leaned into her scrawny secretary look and made people laugh, diffusing their anxiety. But behind the jokes she was hustling.

That hustling took a toll on her, and in 1971, nearly 30 years after she first found the river, she sent a letter to her river rats—the moniker she'd given her guests—about the stress she was enduring, both professionally and personally. Her brother, one of her main boatmen, died from complications with an ulcer, and she divorced Whitey after she learned he'd been selling her boats to other outfitters for booze money. It felt like everything was going sideways. The Park Service was trying to cut back the motor trips that were her livelihood, and the river world she'd helped create was changing around her once again, becoming more commercialized and crowded. By the early '70s, more than 15,000 people were rafting down the Grand Canyon each year.

Georgie needed to adapt to the growth and expand her

business. To do so she found an unusual source of boatmen: LA firemen. Her friend Pete Thompson mentioned that the firemen he knew were trained in first aid, they could handle stressful situations, and he was pretty sure they would work for free. That started a pipeline from LA County to the canyon. For the rest of her career, a coven of men would come out to run rapids with her each season. Many of them called her Mother. "When I think about her life, I'm always in awe," Ray Gorospe, one of those firemen, told me.

It was a clever move. She was trying to grow her business by playing on those gender norms, trying to walk the line of being exciting without being considered too crazy. "Georgie was a wild card. There's always room for a wild card as long as it's not the whole deck," Liz Hymans, the third-ever female Grand Canyon guide, said.

She leaned into the wild-card image. On the beach, Georgie would stand around in her lacy underwear as she set out cereal and hard-boiled eggs. At some point, her sister, Marie, got sick of Georgie staining all her clothes with motor oil and river silt and suggested an animal print might hide the wear. Her signature outfit became a Frederick's of Hollywood leopard-print catsuit.

Her boat ran a leopard flag, and she found a leopard tablecloth to set out on the portable dining table she started bringing after the Park Service insisted that she couldn't just make guests eat out of an inflatable kiddie pool—her original method for serving meals. She'd prank her burliest fireman guides, pulling down their pants and wrestling them to the ground, but she'd also sit with small girls and braid their hair. She was perceptive: On hikes, if someone was moving slow, she'd stop to take a picture, to give them a breather. On her trips there were mud fights in the morning and music in the evening at dinner.

"My experience of her is passing her at camp drinking a beer, talking to passengers, surrounded by enthralled listeners: kids, young women, grizzled men," Becca Lawton, a Grand Canyon guide and river ranger who started in 1976, told me.

Storytelling is a big part of river running. At night we sit around recounting screwups and close calls, rivers we've seen, and people we used to know. One evening the female half of the crew is sitting on a smooth rock for happy hour, and when I mention my tired arms, Kelly, who has been a guide for decades, jokes that young men row with their shoulders, and women do it with their brains. Finesse versus brute force. She's been giving me tips about how to use my body efficiently, pulling me into the lineage of women down here, but it hasn't always been like that.

"You know who was the big exceptionalist was Georgie," Becca Lawton told me. "She never acknowledged me. She looked over my head." She said that Georgie's defensiveness made it harder for other women to get in. By then, there were a handful of other women guiding, and it felt like they had a mission: They were groundbreakers, trying to make room for each other. But Georgie pushed back because she felt like she had a tenuous hold on being the singular superwoman. "She was the exceptional woman, which can do terrible things to you," Becca said.

Georgie brought other women down the river and forged long friendships with several of them, but she was in charge, and her openness didn't extend to employment or mentorship until late in her life. Georgie explicitly said she wasn't a feminist. She discounted and opposed other women in the industry as she fought hard to gain a foothold in the canyon.

Her livelihood was based on being *the* Woman of the River, singular. In part, I think, because she felt like she had something to protect.

Maybe it's helpful to remember that women weren't even able to vote until Georgie was 10. She came of age when the outdoor world was inaccessible to women. In 1923, the president of the men-only Explorers Club, Roy Chapman Andrews, said that women were not suitable for exploration and shouldn't be mixed in with men.

In the war era of the 1940s, when Georgie was working at Douglas Aircraft, she was part of a wave of women moving into jobs like manufacturing and engineering that had been historically male dominated. That flood of work brought women money, independence, and some inklings of sexual freedom and racial integration. Childcare was nonexistent, wages were abysmally skewed, and sexual harassment was rampant, but the change proved a broad, hard-to-negate point: Women were just as capable as men.

After the war, as men returned to domestic life, the social pendulum swung back toward conservatism. Pop culture pushed pictures of suburban housewives with several children. Ads for everything from Coke to cleaning supplies promoted the idea that women should want to be at home. The term *nuclear family* gained traction during the Cold War. The proportion of women attending college in comparison with men dropped from 47 percent in 1920 to 35 percent in 1958. Marriage rates were at an all-time high, and fewer women—especially well-off white ones—worked outside of the home. When Georgie was recruiting river rats to come down the canyon, the vast majority of her peers were popping out kids.

The narrative said that the country wanted stability after

economic depression and war, but in her seminal 1963 book, *The Feminine Mystique*, Betty Friedan found that women were actually frustrated by their limited options. The book largely focused on middle-class white women—Friedan's peers—but it set off a cultural spark and underscored that women wanted more. Georgie was living that out, even if she wasn't part of the social movement.

In the '60s, the growth of second-wave feminism was a rejoinder to postwar conservatism. The first wave of feminism in the late 1800s emerged from equal rights and antislavery work and the idea that suffrage should be for everyone. The second wave, in the 1960s and '70s, led to the Equal Pay Act of 1963, Roe v. Wade, and 1972's Title IX, which was written to bring equity to education and, with it, sports. The second wave tapered off when the Equal Rights Amendment failed to pass, and when culture took another conservative turn in the '80s.

But that idea of equal rights and opportunities seeded deep in the brains of the next generation. And in the outdoor world, where power figures once said women couldn't be explorers, it set off a slow move toward openness. In 1973, 28 years after Georgie first swam the canyon, Marilyn Sayre, became the next woman to guide the canyon. By the end of the '70s, there were 15 woman guides.

The canyon changes and changes again. By the time we get into the Lower Granite Gorge, close to Diamond Creek, nearly 2 weeks into the trip, it feels like we've been to the center of the earth and back. Skinny young bighorns line the high ridges, and tadpoles, first cousins of trilobites, nibble at our toes. We are deep in it now.

After lunch, a storm starts to sulk into the canyon, bruising the sky and dialing down the thermostat. It turns the sky to chalk and the river to blood, making us all jittery with electricity. We've been sliding through a mud pit on the beach, and by the time we load up the boats everyone is loopy. Kelly rescues a watermelon shell from our compost and straps it to her head like a helmet. We are already giggly, and this gets us over the edge. "Let's go, girls!" Kelly yells at us, channeling Shania Twain, and Lilah and I hop onto her boat as she pushes it into the flow.

We are picking mud out of our teeth and fruit out of our hair. The storm starts to crash and build, making the air crackle. Side streams rush into the narrow canyon, flash floods sending silver sprays of waterfalls out of the rock, cascading and flying.

Kelly in her melon helmet is fighting the wind, and we are all laughing so hard we can't breathe, singing along to made-up songs, dancing on the bow of the boat. These are the parts I feel like I can't get anywhere else, loose and goofy and unselfconscious. But that looseness can be a tricky line.

Every evening before dinner the crew circles up on one of the boats. We have a drink and a snack and talk about the day and the guests and tomorrow and whatever else is on our minds. At one meeting, at Bass Camp surrounded by dark rock and prickly pear, watching thunderheads build in the distance, I ask about the darkness beneath the fun. Everyone in the circle has stories: running trips with known harassers or creepy longtime guides who keep coming back. The women have more personal stories: off-color comments, lingering hands, being asked to not make a big deal out of something, worse. The rafting world has a bad track record of sexual harassment and abuse and an even worse one on the line between joking and offending.

That complicated joking has long been caked into the culture of the canyon. "I have over the years developed a kidding relationship with the men who are my boatmen on the river," Georgie wrote. "Frequently they will make a joke in front of others about taking me off somewhere and giving me a sexual thrill. I always tell them that anytime they can equal the experience of running Lava or Crystal Rapid—I'm ready." You spend day and night next to people and you learn things about them, you get close. There's an intimacy that doesn't come a lot of other places. But it's slippery.

Often we can identify the bad, but the middle ground is blurry. Even here on the river we have our own off-color jokes. In the machismo culture of the outdoors, part of the deal is that we're subversive, funny, and loose. Sometimes I feel like I have to double down on grossness because I'm a woman. It feels like a part of the superwoman thing: immune to the ick, dishing it out as hard as you're getting it. I'm sure that's why Georgie was throwing it back at the boys.

As TA Loeffler has found, a lot of social capital is rooted in the theory of fraternal bonding. It's the idea that men connect through shared experience and humor, and often that humor is "generally sexually aggressive, and frequently consists of sexist or racist jokes," she writes. I think that's true everywhere, but it's unavoidably true in outdoor communities. That's why we have mountains called the Grand Tetons.

Sometimes it can be funny, but sometimes when you're not in a position of power, it can feel safer to go along with the joke, even if it feels bad, because if you don't you might get ostracized. Or because the people joking might be in charge of things like your safety and your food. Or because your boss, who is responsible for your money, hints at what you could do for a raise or holds back work when you don't give them attention.

The term *sexual harassment* wasn't even coined until 1975, and the idea of consent came into the public eye around the same time, when a survey by *Redbook* magazine found that 80 percent of respondents had been sexually harassed at work.

In a 1995 study, Loeffler found that more than half of women who worked in outdoor leadership had been sexually harassed. More recent studies, like a 2017 survey from *Outside* magazine, found similar numbers. Fifty-three percent of respondents said they'd been sexually harassed while recreating, and 66 percent said they'd felt unsafe outside.

In the outdoors, where we tell scary stories about animals and accidents, statistically the biggest danger is men. And the Grand Canyon in particular has been a cesspool for harassment and assault.

It came to the public's attention in 2014, when 13 people who had worked for Grand Canyon National Park filed a letter to Interior Secretary Sally Jewell, saying that they'd suffered discrimination, sexual harassment, and retaliation at the hands of male boatmen and supervisors in the Grand Canyon's river district.

In 2016, an Office of Inspector General investigation followed up on the statement and found that everything in the letter was true and worse. They looked back over 15 years and found 35 incidents of harassment, from one senior boatman withholding food from women who rebuffed his sexual advances to cases of groping and trying to take pictures up a woman's shorts to unreported rape. There was violence—one woman was threatened with an axe—and denial of duty. The perpetrators tended to be supervisors or trip leaders. One of the women said she and others were afraid of retaliation or inaction. If they spoke up, they might get harassed more, in different ways.

Follow-up reports found that similar transgressions were happening across a wide range of national parks. There had been a history of sweeping sexual harassment and assault under the rug.

It was bad at a federal agency, with mandated harassment policies and HR people. In less formal rafting companies and on private trips, where participants didn't have the benefit of government oversight, it was often worse.

When the investigation came out, so did the stories. An unwanted coworker crawling into your bed when you were passed out on the boat. A client making a comment about you being down on your knees when you're pulling their beer out of the cooler. Of course, sexual harassment shows up everywhere from Hollywood to high school, but the river world has a toxic combo of isolation and partying, permissiveness and power.

Men's transgressions were often forgiven if they were good boatmen, or powerful, or fun—which they often were. Women were bullied if they brought something up, continually harassed if they didn't. Heather McLaughlin, a sociologist at Oklahoma State University who studies gender inequality, found that women in power positions, like Georgie, were harassed more.

She also found that in a sample of 364 women, nearly 80 percent of the women who had been harassed at work quit their jobs. *If you don't want to get harassed, don't show up* was the solution. That means women wash out because they're exhausted by the emotional energy of trying to fight a skewed system where the bad guys keep gliding through. That's hard on the women, who often have to start over at the bottom of a new business. They also report losing the joy and confidence that comes from being outside, and it's hard on the industry and the people who remain.

Around the circle in the boat, we all know the score. The dudes acknowledge that they have to be allies and call out the shit when they see it. We know it, but it still happens. At least we're talking about it, but it's still deep and dark, still harmful, still not changing fast enough. We still shiver at the creepy stories. "You know what you also have today is the language," Becca Lawton told me about what she thought was different. "We didn't have exceptionalism and patriarchy. We just said *fuck him.*"

SOFT FASCINATION

Teresa Yates Matheson says she knew Georgie was testing her the first time she took her to the river. Once the boat was in the water at Lees Ferry, Georgie turned to her. "She grabbed a beer and said, 'Let's go stand out here in the Ferry and hang on to this boat,'" Teresa tells me. She found a Pepsi and followed Georgie into the flow. They stood chest-deep in the 40-degree dam runoff. Teresa listened to Georgie tell stories about past trips, trying not to shiver or cave first.

Georgie didn't take on many female guides, but she saw promise in Teresa. They stayed close until the end of Georgie's life.

Teresa had reached out to Georgie first. In the early '80s, when she was in her twenties, she and her husband bought two military surplus boats in hopes of learning to raft. She'd found Georgie's book *Thirty Years of River Running* in the library and wrote her for advice. Georgie responded, and after a few notes back and forth, Teresa and her husband went to a boat show in Sedona to meet her. Georgie invited them both to be swampers. They sold their house-cleaning business in Phoenix and headed to the river. For Teresa it would become a yearslong love.

Georgie was 75 at that point, but she was still lugging

around generators and motors. Teresa says they'd be lying next to each other in their sleeping bags, about to fall asleep, and Georgie would start doing sit-ups.

Teresa thinks Georgie initially accepted her because she was tall and tough. By the end of that first trip, Georgie was teaching Teresa to drive her boat—a skill she hadn't taught many of the firefighters. "I came out of that trip, turned around, and went on two more in a row," Teresa says. "I was falling in love with the Grand Canyon."

Maybe Georgie saw some of herself in Teresa: in her toughness, as well as her connection to the canyon. "You never get to see Mother Nature like you do down there. The stars and moon, the colors and the lighting," Teresa told Lew Steiger. "I was more at peace, more comfortable, calmer and at home there, and I think Georgie was, too."

Teresa tells me that what drew her in was the silence and the solace, the way worries stayed on the rim. "At that point in my life when I found the Grand Canyon, I was looking for healing. I really felt the therapeutic value of being in the canyon," she says.

Georgie, for all her toughness, felt that, too. "She loved what being outside did for you, and she felt like the more that people could see and experience the place the more it would be protected," Teresa says. As the '80s wore on, and Georgie got deeper into her seventh decade, she didn't shy away from the big rapids, and she was still cavalier and unreliable about her safety record, but she softened socially. She'd take help, she loved having kids along on the trips, and above all she wanted her rafters to care about the canyon. "That's where the river rat initiation came in," Teresa says. "It's an oath to a way of living your life after a river trip."

•

One morning we walked into Blacktail Canyon, at mile 120, in silence, listening to our steps echo off the striated rock. Blacktail holds a broken gap in the rock layer that geologists call the Great Unconformity. Twenty-five percent of the earth's geologic history—more than a billion years of time—is missing between the 1.7-billion-years-old Vishnu Schist and the 550-million-year-old stacked Tapeats Sandstone on top of it, with no good explanation. Blacktail is also said to be haunted. If you stick around after dark, you'll start to hear ghostly drumbeats getting closer in the perfect acoustics of the cavern. During the day, we sit silent and let time go. If you concentrate hard enough, or don't concentrate at all, you can feel a kind of looping rhythm echoing off the stone.

That healing Teresa talks about, I get it. In the canyon, you become close to yourself, stripped down, exposed, sensitive to light and heat and wind. This is the sensation the Transcendentalists were chasing, a version of divinity that shows up when you get out of your own way and feel the place around you. After a few days, your eyes change, your focus softens. At some point, once you get used to the sand in your sheets, you start sleeping better. Your heart rate drops, and so do your cortisol levels.

The benefits of being outside are immediate, but they also get better over time. Researchers have found that even just taking your lunch break in a city park can improve memory and mood, but being immersed in nature for an extended period amplifies those good impacts. In the '80s, psychologists Rachel and Stephen Kaplan introduced what they call Attention Restoration Theory, which posits that being in nature, where we're immersed in patterns, restores our ability to concentrate and pay attention. When you're on a river, for instance, the movement of waves washes out distraction; it gives your brain the message to relax and absorb your surroundings instead of being hypervigilant. The Kaplans called it *soft fascination*, and it increases your resilience and capacity for joy. Since they introduced the theory, decades of research, including EEG studies of brains outdoors, have confirmed the idea.

Time in wilderness gives us simplicity, physical hard work, community—all things we need to feel existentially healthy. It's what psychologists call *eudaimonic well-being*, a sense of connection and purpose, beyond the ephemeral rush of hedonic experience.

Our brains stretch when we see beauty. A 2018 study from UC Berkeley found that awe, more than any other positive sensation, gives us a full-spectrum sense of well-being, which can help people recover from PTSD, anxiety, and a range of other stressors. That's particularly true when it's combined with soft fascination. Those Berkeley researchers monitored the stress hormones of veterans and at-risk teens who spent time outside and found their levels significantly lowered on river trips. I think something deep and old pushes us there when we need to heal. I know it does for me. It's probably why Georgie craved the canyons after Sommona's death.

English fails here, but other languages do better. In Finnish, *sielunmaisema* means a landscape you carry in your heart. In Spanish, it's *querencia*, from *querer*, to desire, to love—the place where you feel rooted and claimed. I felt that the first time I launched into the glassy gray-green water of the Kennebec in Maine.

For Georgie that came in the canyon. "When I first seen

[sic] the Grand and went swimming, it had everything I wanted: It was beautiful beyond words, like nothing I'd ever dreamed of; and it was wild; and at the same time you had the parts that was peaceable; and last but not least, there's no mosquitoes," she told librarian Karen Underhill in a 1991 interview.

"I'm the lucky one," she said. "No one will ever have the freedom I had."

In a lot of ways, she's right. No one will ever swim down from Diamond Creek on undammed flows again or have the same kind of wild peace that comes from being off the map. But in that freedom, she learned that if you love a place that deeply, you're going to get your heart broken.

The four-plus decades that Georgie was in the canyon might have been the biggest period of change in Western American river systems in recorded history. In the span of less than half a century, dams and recreation—two lines of dominion—changed the Grand Canyon forever.

Georgie had helped drive the change. She'd gone on TV, hustled for customers, and brought down more people than almost anyone else, but as it changed, she felt the damage. By the time Glen Canyon Dam closed its gates in 1963, severing the river's flow, it split Georgie's heart. "It was a dormant river after that," she said.

Dams don't just stop water, they fundamentally change the composition of a river. Georgie said she wouldn't have swum the river if the dam had existed when she did it—even though the river levels were lower after and there was less driftwood and debris—because the water became too cold. Georgie said the real river rats used to drink straight from the river, wood chips, silt, and all. But after the dam went in, Georgie stopped drinking river water because it started smelling like gasoline and rot.

Before, the river had a yearly ebb and flow. It would flush high in the spring, then run slow and turgid by the end of the summer. The cycle was ideal for fish. Today, those native fish have disappeared. The clear, consistent water erodes beaches, scraping away potential camps. Early on, Georgie saw that change. "You're going to have problems because the camps will slowly disappear one by one," she said, prescient.

But the clear water and predictable flows kicked the commercial rafting industry into high gear. "A few years before, when I mentioned wild rivers, everyone looked at me like I was crazy. Now, I had become a hero to certain groups of people, as river running became a very popular outdoor sport," Georgie wrote. "The days of river pioneering in North America are really over."

In the Grand Canyon alone, passengers increased from 70 in 1955 to over 1,000 in 1966 to 16,000 in 1972. More people and more desire for wildness put more pressure on remote places. Before the dam, the high spring flows would wash away the previous year's catholes or fire rings. But the dam diminished the high flows, and more people were coming through using the same camps, shitting, and burning driftwood and leaving trash. After a few seasons of experimenting with assigned catholes and installing latrines, the park mandated that every trip bring down a portable toilet. They also put into place fire regulations and sanitation checks. So much of how recreation is now organized and regulated—from permitting to pooping—spun out from those years in the Grand Canyon.

Georgie worried that the rules, even if they might have

been necessary, diluted the experience, particularly her own. For 25 years, she'd been minimally regulated, doing whatever she wanted. But things changed. This is one reason why Georgie feels complicated to me. So much of her ethic comes from a selfish bent: She wanted freedom over everything else, and even if it came at the expense of the collective good.

Despite her disillusionment, Georgie kept initiating new river rats. Lew Steiger said she had more repeat customers than anyone else because she intuitively sensed what people craved in a river trip. Her prescient ideas, like rubber boats and motors, shaped the way other companies operated. "They all giggled and rolled their eyes at first, but then they started doing what she was doing," he said. She implanted a kind of toughness on the people who were there with her, and even though she couldn't show them the canyon before the dam went in, she could show them a good time.

She would throw people's wristwatches in the river at Lees Ferry and watch them sink. She'd give you a sleeping bag, but no pad. She expected people to be able to operate on canned soup and hard-boiled eggs. Nothing was luxurious. "That's what I remember from her trips—no camping gear whatsoever. That was part of her adventure: It's not an easy trip, it's not Disneyland, it's not everything done for you," Teresa says. Georgie's real focus was on the rapids.

Even at breakfast the energy is different on big-rapid days. And day 12 is one of those days. The air feels keyed up after the storm, the river redder, thicker, warmer. Every day the group switches boats, rotating who they ride with, and today the three youngest boys, an unruly group of cousins, decide they want to ride alone, without their parents, in Evelyn's boat. The crew huddles in a circle on the beach like we do every morning, making plans for the day.

"Will one of you ride with me, so I can have another adult?" Evelyn asks Lilah and me. I tighten my PFD and wedge myself into the boat beside the boys. Over 6 fast miles, we hit three of the biggest rapids of the trip. Granite and Hermit come quick below camp, less than a mile apart. They're both a series of mangly wave trains, thick with the muscle of the river. Granite is steep and choked with teaming lateral waves. Hermit is just huge. Huge. Heavy enough to stop a boat and flip it end over end. Long enough that it's hard to hold your momentum as you row through the compression. Brute force is the one thing that will get you through.

We move through them clean, nerves jangly, breathing deep because we know Crystal is coming. While Hermit is a pulsing roller coaster you want to hit hard down the middle, Crystal is the opposite. Instead of force you need to rely on finesse as you avoid two huge, boat-flipping holes, fighting all the river's energy as it pulls you toward them. Below them, the current splits around an island, which can make for a nasty, rocky swim. If you lose someone off the side of the boat, they can get sucked down the wrong channel and dragged over rocks.

We clamber up to the scout point on Ego Beach. I have busted toes and bruised shins. Grit in my scalp and peeling heels. Evelyn points out the skinny line between a reef of rock and the edge of the hole, barely a boat wide. "You have to wait in the current till it pushes you past the rocks and then pull like hell away from the hole," she says. I can see the tension in her jaw. Jeff is standing next to us, moving his hand in the air, tracing the line he wants to run. There is no other good option besides the sneak. Shocklee tells us he ran the left side once by accident and ended up flipping his dory and getting stuck in the river with it overnight.

Crystal wasn't always like this. In 1966, a thousand-year flood ripped a ridgeline of rocks down into the river, forming a new rapid that is long and mean. It became Georgie's favorite rapid, but she didn't take the sneak line we'll be taking. She ran right through the meat of the white water in her big boat, sometimes disappearing for a while in the hole, the G-rig bucking and rolling in the water.

Back in the boat I chide the boys to hold on tight, channeling my own nervousness, knuckles white. We cast off into the current, and at first we seem good. We're right on line until we grab a corner of slow current, and suddenly we're sideways and dropping toward the hole. Evelyn pulls like hell. "Oh fuuuck," says preteen Leo as the boat starts to highside. I fling my body across, pinning him down, pushing my weight into the wave. The boat tips precariously. Suddenly I'm looking down into the trough of the wave, near vertical. Evelyn yanks on the oars, everything stops for a slow, slow second, and then we're spinning out of it, backward but upright. It's a while before I remember to breathe again.

On Tuna Creek Beach, below the rapid, we compare our runs and make celebratory tuna sandwiches. Evelyn is giggling, tension released, and as we chop veggies and fruit she tells the story of another Crystal run: one of Georgie's.

In 1983, a stormy winter led to high flows, and the rocks in the rapid moved, creating new hydraulics, bigger than anything river runners had seen before. In late June, after a death in the rapids, the Park Service ordered commercial trips to walk around Crystal Rapid. They told boaters launching at

Lees Ferry and dropped notes by helicopter to the trips already in the canyon. The warnings were tied to a sandbag with red streamers. "Camp high, don't run Crystal," the note read.

Georgie put on the river in mid-June, so she must have gotten the note, but she said the river was moving so fast that she didn't realize how far downstream she was until she looked up mid-snack and realized the boat was right above Crystal, floating in.

Instead of stopping to portage, she gunned through Crystal instead. Actually, reportedly she didn't gun it. Above the rapid, she shut the motor off, hunkered down in the motor well, and aimed straight for the middle.

Her 37-foot-long boat stood straight up before getting sucked back into the hole. It came up again, spitting out 5 passengers and assistant guide Daryl Bates before dropping back into the hole for another round where it threw off the rest of the passengers and all of the baggage. By the time the boat washed out of the hole, heading for the gravel bar below, the only person still on board was Georgie.

From shore it looked like a maelstrom. A group of rangers who had pulled off to scout and plan their route through Crystal watched Georgie's boat come through. They were slack-jawed as they watched the carnage, straps popping, people flying. "And we had to run it next," said scientist Nancy Brian, who was on a trip with her husband Terry, a National Park Service ranger. They had no choice but to get in their boats and chase Georgie downstream, trying to pick up people and gear in the fray.

Bates said it felt like being whitewashed in the ocean: He thought he might never come up again. When he surfaced, he heard Georgie yelling at him to grab one of the other passengers, floating a few feet away, but the current was so strong he couldn't. It took them 45 minutes to get the boat to a beach, collect all their passengers, and assess the damage.

When Terry Brian caught up to Georgie, she had all her people and was bemoaning the loss of her lucky horseshoe, which was in one of the dry bags that had ripped off. When he asked her what happened, she famously said, "Well, I told them to hold on. They just don't make passengers like they used to."

This is where Georgie gets tricky for me. She was known to disregard rules, even when it put others at risk. "She was not a safe boater," Becca Lawton told me. "We really pushed for her to lose her permit."

Georgie didn't lose her permit, but she did commit acts that called her judgment into question. She was considered an uncouth scavenger after she let her passengers hunt for wreckage at the site of the 1956 TWA/United Airlines crash, a midair collision over the canyon that led to the forming of the Federal Aviation Administration. In 1981, she was reprimanded for camping at the sacred Hopi salt mines, a place considered off-limits by the tribe. But her safety transgressions were worse than her social ones, and she didn't take responsibility even when she was asked point-blank. "Have you actually ever lost anybody on your trips? Has anybody died while they were with you?" Karen Underhill asked her.

"Heart failure," Georgie said, without blinking.

"Heart failure?" Underhill asked.

"Uh-huh," Georgie said.

That was patently untrue. She'd lost several people on the river, including some of her closest friends. In 1973, Mae Hansen, who had been on more than a dozen trips with Georgie, died after getting trapped under the boat at House Rock Rapid. In 1984, another one of her longtime guests, Nori Abrams, died after getting sucked overboard along with her husband when the boat hit the ledge hole at Lava. When Kim Crumbo, the ranger on duty, helicoptered into her camp to handle Abrams's death, Georgie had the body wrapped in a tarp. "I don't want you to scare people. Get this body out of here," she told Crumbo, according to Becca Lawton, who was also a ranger in that era.

"You want me to hide it?" Crumbo asked her.

"Damn right," she said. "I want you to take it out."

Her callousness peaked in 1989, when one of her closest boatmen, Marty Hunsaker, flipped his raft in Crystal after his motor conked out. Marty's assistant guide, Tanya Wilcox, saw him float by and almost grabbed him, but she says he waved at her to grab someone else as he was swept downstream. By the time Tanya and the passengers got the boat to shore, Marty was missing. A trip from Hatch Expeditions, another big rafting company, came down an hour later and found him floating face down in an eddy, ice-cold.

Georgie was already downstream with the big raft, and when the Hatch boatman, who knew Marty and knew how much he meant to Georgie, caught up to her and told her Marty had died, she barely flinched. "Well, he was a smoker," she said.

The Grand Canyon is a harsh place. An average of 12 people die on river trips each year. It's not that it's out of the question that bad things happened, but I think it's out of the range of morality not to own up to it, like Georgie did. If she had been honest and taken responsibility, I would have fewer questions.

It wasn't just Georgie who was taking chances on the river, although she might have been particularly prone to risk. Adrenaline-chasing is what drives a lot of the outdoor world.

Some people need that chase more. "When she hits the rapids and starts splashing people, her face lights up with pure, evil joy," passenger Norma Hansen once said about Georgie.

But for a lot of people, especially those like Becca who were on the river with her, that lack of accountability became Georgie's legacy. I wonder how much of that is due to a double standard and how much is due to her own defensive posturing.

Lava Falls is the last big rapid on the river and it hangs over everything else. There's an adage in the Grand Canyon that you're always above Lava. Even off the river.

It has been holding space in my mind as we drift downstream, and then suddenly we are above it. Scouting the rapid, I watch the water pile up over the thundering ledge hole before funneling toward the Big Kahuna wave and slamming the Cheese Grater rock on the right. Some of the famous rapids in the Grand aren't tricky, they're just big, but Lava is both technically difficult and huge. You can feel the force from shore. And you have to make it through Lava to make it through the canyon. "If you get off-line, things can get sideways real quick," Shocklee says when we scout, his usually laconic voice tight.

We run left at Lava, hitting the edge of the guard wave and skirting the huge central hole. Kelly pushes hard on the oars, punching through the huge, sloshing waves until we come out clean. I ride the bull on the nose of the boat, clenching the chicken line with both hands, screaming-laughing in the troughs of the waves.

And then, just like that, we are above Lava again, regrouping on the beach below, already thinking about next time. Buzzing down to our toes.

•

Georgie was 72 in that big water year, and through the rest of the 1980s she kept rafting, cementing herself as a sharp-eyed matriarch of the river. As years went by she became almost part of the canyon herself; her early stories, even the reckless ones, became river lore. On November 10, 1990, the crew at Hatch Expeditions planned a celebration for her eightieth birthday.

Hundreds of people in tight jeans and faded flannels circled around drinking beer and telling stories. They hung balloons and streamers in Georgie's favorite color—red—and someone constructed an enormous cake that looked like a G-rig. It had a trapdoor, and later in the night when it was rolled out, long-time guide Brian Dierker jumped out of it wearing Georgie-style leopard tights and a red cape.

Georgie almost bailed on the party. After decades of feeling like an outcast, she worried no one would come, but it turned out to be the biggest celebration of river people to date. Five hundred people signed the guest book. Photographer Don Briggs shot shaky video of the whole thing and interviewed people on film. Those conversations became the bones of the Grand Canyon River Guides River Runners Oral History Project.

Kenton Grua, who set the speed record in the canyon, said the party felt like a validation of what their community had created together. "We all came because Georgie is kind of our hero," he said. "But we're also kind of all our own heroes."

Georgie seemed a little dazed at the party, mouth open in a silly grin, those piercing blue eyes a little hazy, like she was surprised that everyone showed up. She felt vindicated. "For years people have chuckled at how she does things, but it works, and then they were doing the same things. People respected her by the end," Grua said during the party.

As guides swilled cold Coors and danced, the band thumped out classic rock hits until four thirty in the morning. Georgie swirled in the center of the dance floor in Brian Dierker's red cape and a red rain hat. "I like it a little rough, it gets people away from their everyday lives," she told Briggs when the camera was on her. The next year would be her last one on the river.

Every bit of being a boater is physical. It's not just the time on the water in the rapids, it's running up beaches, hauling cooking gear, cinching straps, and carrying water. Using your body and your mind. On the river I can feel my stiffness and my age, and I'm as young as Georgie ever was in this canyon.

She was always tiny and stringy, and when she started to lose weight in 1991, she blamed the Park Service regulations, which had just banned guides from drinking on the river. But the beer was a cover-up. By December, she had a terminal cancer diagnosis. "The doc said, 'We can give you a good five years if we operate,'" her friend Roz Jirge told me. "And she said, 'Five years of what? I need to be on the river.'"

Georgie was embarrassed by her decline. She'd always considered herself tough enough to handle anything that came her way. She tried to isolate herself so no one could see her fail. But people from the community she'd built came out for her at the end, and despite her outward toughness they were tender with her as her body gave up. "She really was treated like an angel when she got ill," Roz said.

In April, a couple of her boatmen brought her down to Lees Ferry in a motor home, so she and Teresa could sit with her favorite river ranger, Tom Workman, and tell some stories. Workman said that he was shocked at how frail her body looked but that her voice sounded the same. She died of stomach cancer that May.

Georgie asked Teresa to keep flying her leopard-print flag after she died. She wanted her story to endure after she was gone. Teresa made her next trip a memorial to Georgie. "I got two ice chests full of roses and gladiolas, and we wore red and leopard print," she said. "We had a long chat above Crystal, and then everyone threw the flowers in the rapid and watched them go."

Roz went on a mission to name a rapid after Georgie after her death. She said Georgie really wanted Crystal to be renamed after her: Georgie's Crystal Rapid. But it's nearly impossible to get the major rapid names changed, so instead they settled on something upstream. "Teresa and I picked 24 mile," Roz told me. "It wasn't what she wanted, but it does do something she loved to do—kick you in the butt once you're through."

After Lava, the river becomes languid and thick. We still have several more days, but it feels like the pace is relaxed. We cliff-jump at Pumpkin Springs and go into the grotto of the Travertine Falls, where the water feels soft and clear.

The trip, which felt so long at the beginning, now feels like it's slipping by. There were points, a week or so in, when my hair felt itchy and the wind railed and I could have tapped out, but now I'm used to the grit and the ache. I'm already thinking about coming back.

At the last camp, we try to stretch out the evening, drinking the end of the boxed wine, watching a storm come in. The colors get deeper and softer as the sun dips. Purple washes over everything. I can hear the wind and a two-note birdsong.

The trip reaches an anticlimactic end as we float into the dull brown layers of Lake Mead. At the takeout the shore is littered with human detritus, dog bones and cut bait, single shoes and rings of ash. No birdsong, just the hollow lap of lake waves on sandstone.

I'm jealous that Georgie got so much time down here. I'm jealous of how wild it seemed. I watch grainy videos of her river days, and I get an ache for a time I didn't live through. Georgie's story hits something in me that is spiky and lonely and looking for a rush. She chased what she loved, and she trusted that feeling. She didn't compromise, even when the canyon began to change.

But it can't all be beautiful, and Georgie still feels complicated for me. Her selfishness still gets under my skin, and so does her recklessness. I hate that she hamstrung other women. I came into this thinking about heroes, and I'm still not exactly sure what I found. But I realize a canyon is a container, constrained. So I'm heading into another landscape to see if the chase to be outside can take me deeper.

ANNE LaBASTILLE

THE WELLSPRING

Halfway up the lake I see the loon. Body black on the dark water, the only thing out here but me. No one knows where I am except the stranger who lent me the boat I'm in, and I have no real reason to trust him except for the small kindness of giving me a kayak and a paddle and pointing me up-lake when I blatantly trespassed onto his land, asking about Anne LaBastille.

I had been lost, wandering around the lake. Plus, how do you find someone who never wanted to be found, and who is dead besides?

I am trying to locate the footprint of a cabin built half a century ago by a half hermit, hidden by the dense Adirondack forest, because I have an idea that being there can help me understand why I'm drawn to woods like these and to the idea of being out on my own.

The loon lifts off, white belly rising, heading toward the shore where a woodswoman once wandered.

That morning I'd driven past the map dot of Big Moose, New York, with its boat shop and shuttered breakfast spot, open weekends only. I'd turned onto the cracked dirt road toward Twitchell Lake and rattled over the washboard, driving slow. I had come to the Adirondacks on a mission to try to find Anne's cabin. I'd followed the Hudson north, past small, one-gas-station towns, into the Adirondack Park. It's the largest park in the contiguous US, nearly 3 times the size of Yellowstone—a fact that surprised me when I first learned it. The park sprawls across most of the top of New York State, and it holds a density of old-growth forests and boreal birds. It's a perfect place to disappear if you're looking for solitude and space.

Anne, a wilderness guide, wildlife ecologist, and early climate scientist, moved to an off-the-grid cabin on Twitchell Lake in 1964, partly out of desire, partly out of desperation, after her marriage to a much older lodge-owner crumbled. In a time when women still couldn't get home loans or credit cards, she became a specific archetype of independence. It was an ideal she intentionally cultivated and shared through her *Woodswoman* book series, in hopes of inspiring other women.

She conducted groundbreaking research about endangered species and environmental pollution, and in certain small circles she became emblematic of a kind of Thoreauvian ideal that encouraged self-discovery through solitary outdoor exploration. But unlike Thoreau, Anne wasn't a short stroll from town, and the act of living solo in the wilderness was only a piece of her philosophy. She built a remote homestead, and she fought the elements to live there, drinking the water straight out of the lake, chainsawing her firewood, and avoiding predators, including the human kind, because she wanted to live out her work as a scientist.

I grew up in Massachusetts, not far from Thoreau's home on Walden Pond, so I was immersed in his environmental awareness and asceticism early, but when I found Anne through the first *Woodswoman* book, she felt deeper than Thoreau to me, and less self-involved. She had Georgie's grit and drive to explore, and she wanted to be deep in the woods, but she also thought about the integrity of those woods beyond her own desires. Her time alone at the cabin was the root of her ideology, so I wanted to go see it.

Anne was notoriously reclusive, and she tried hard to keep her cabin's location a secret until her death in 2011. In 2015, her friend Leslie Surprenant, who became the keeper of her estate, had the cabin hauled off and rebuilt at the Adirondack Experience Museum on Blue Mountain Lake before donating the land to the state, so I figured it was okay to visit the spot where the cabin once stood—I just had to find it first.

The night before, at a cheap motel on the shores of the Fulton Chain of Lakes, I sat on the empty, spiderwebbed porch and tried to triangulate where her property might be. I overlaid Google Maps with clues from her writing and my feeling about what it might look like. I couldn't pinpoint it, but I figured I could go try.

A low, humid fog is rolling in as I arrive at Twitchell. The lake is different than I'd pictured. Smaller, stiller, rimmed by summer houses and floating docks. One cabin has a floatplane tied up out front. I wasn't expecting that kind of fanciness. I have to remind myself that stories and reality don't always align, that it has been years since Anne struck out for the homestead, and that this landscape, even when it's preserved, has been used for vacation homes for nearly 150 years.

The lake is built-up, but there are no roads around it. I park at the dock and load a backpack with rain gear and snacks, feeling a little creeped out, unsure of what is private property and of what, exactly, I am doing. In her books, starting with *Woodswoman II*, she talks about unwanted visitors showing up to find her. She's long gone, but now I'm one of those people. And I have the unromantic benefit of maps on my phone. I start walking past the scattering of cabins along the lake, and when the road dead-ends, I check my map and then walk down a faint trail tracing the lakeshore, quickly immersed in deep woods. Someone has placed boards on some of the swampiest sections, and eventually I pass a tidy boarded-up cabin with a path down to a dock. Then I pass another that looks equally abandoned but far more ramshackle, with junk on the porch and windows gaping.

Leslie later told me that some residents keep those camps looking unruly on purpose to keep people away. They want the same kind of solitude Anne craved. But the woods here also want to reclaim anything new or unnatural. It takes work to keep the cabins from decomposing. Moss creeps over the roofs; everything feels like it's being absorbed back into the woods.

By the time I pass the third dock, the trees thin out, and I can hear the hit of hammers on solid wood. Small buildings emerge through the trees. I have stumbled into a compound.

"Hi! Hi!" I say, raising my voice, trying to sound harmless, aware of the tension of trespassing, and of the *Don't Tread on Me* flags I'd seen on the road in.

As I get closer, the hammering stops. An older man in worn-out double denim comes down the woodchipped trail. Squinting, inscrutable, maybe ready to murder me. Hard to tell.

"Hi. I'm so sorry to show up like this, but I'm looking for Anne LaBastille's property," I blabber. "Am I on the right track at all?"

His blank-eyed stare breaks. "Hmm, yeah, let's see." He looks in the direction I've been heading. "You can . . . Actually, let me just lend you a boat. That will be easier."

We walk down to the lake, where he pulls a sun-punched yellow kayak off a rack and finds me a paddle and a faded blue life jacket with a whistle wrapped around one shoulder strap. His name is Dan, he says. His family has been here a long time. And then he points me up the lake, telling me where I should see her dock.

Once I am in the water, it doesn't take me long to paddle up to the point of rock where he told me to start looking for her dock. The lake is tannic and dark near the shore, with a lattice of roots and plants under the surface. When I started paddling, the lake was still, but in the hour that I'm out the glass breaks up. Maybe it's the wind or the morning rev of still-docked motorboats. Or maybe I'm the disturbance. The surface ripples and chops, refracting the sky.

Before I reach the shore I stop paddling and let the edge of the blade drip. I eat my granola bar, looking out for the loon again. Feeling the slight pull of the wind. Feeling alone and alert, aware.

I'm probably not the only lone woman Dan has seen stumbling out of the woods, looking for the way to Anne's cabin. I was taken in by the straightforward way Anne explained her life at the lake in her four *Woodswoman* books, which outlined her decades of living alone at Twitchell, which she called Black Bear Lake in the books, and which inspired a cultish following. I loved the way she calmly addressed storms and fear and wilderness, and the way she set up the life she said she wanted: writing, dipping in the lake, hiking far into the surrounding mountains. She said she felt calm at the cabin. It was the place where purpose and personality aligned for her.

When I first came across Anne, her story seemed dreamy. I loved the idea of living alone in the wilderness, self-sufficient and strong, tapping out stories on the dock in the summertime sun, backpacking to barely touched lakes, seeing how resilient and close to the land you could be. It felt like a hero's story worth absorbing. Before I found rivers, and before being outside became my job, I was sneaking off to the woods by myself. Trail running turned down the anxiety in my brain; breathing hard made me feel calmer. I know all the research about how nature settles us down and brings us back to ourselves is true because I've felt it in my body. Being out alone was braided into my idea of toughness and release early, in part because it came with the relief of avoiding the world's gaze, of only answering to myself. Anne's story struck a tuning fork inside me. It got at a visceral desire.

And then as I started to dig in, it felt deeper and more aligned. She had the same independent, physical streak as Georgie, but for Anne, being outside was also tied up in a fierce desire to protect the places she loved.

She complicated the idealized vision of being a hermit writer, but she made it richer, too, by expanding the question of how to make an independent life in the wilderness.

If Georgie is intensity, a twitching muscle, Anne is slower, stiller. Tough in a totally different way. That self-sufficiency and solitude is what made her semifamous, but she didn't just stick it out on the lake alone for the sake of the solo skinny-dips.

Anne wasn't just a hermitic writer. Her sphere of influence extended far beyond her stories of life at the cabin. She was a wildlife biologist, a wilderness guide, a land commissioner, a climate advocate, and the first female professor in Cornell's Department of Natural Resources. She tried to do it all from Twitchell, where she felt the most in touch with the environment. At home in the woods by herself, she was constantly torn between emergence and retreat. Being a hermit in the woods means tying your health and your heart to those woods, and that was hard as those wild woods felt threatened by big climatic forces. Like Georgie, she was controversial. Anne had rabid fans, but she also had haters, especially here in the northern mountains, where conservation work was sometimes viewed as an attack on personal freedom. I wanted to see how she worked through that all.

Time feels slippery when I paddle over to her property. Her dock is slightly rusty at the cleats, but otherwise sound. I tie up the boat, stash my borrowed PFD and paddle in the bushes, and walk up the gravelly path, past a firepit ringed by moss-slicked half logs. The ground springs under my feet, and I have to adjust my eyes to try to picture where the cabin might have been.

A line of gravel leads from the dock to the sloping house site, where the cabin once sat, facing the lake. Everything else is dense, but you can pick out ghost trails if you're paying attention. Skeletons of some of the outbuildings are still standing between the trees, and the bush maple is already starting to redden, even though it's the end of June.

I notice the ping of frogs like a guitar string twang, the scratchy call of red-eyed vireos, and the distant vibration of boat motors. Aside from the lull of the engines, I am seeped in soft fascination: the rhythm of animal sounds, the patterns of light on the lake. Those background sensations, I learned from my time chasing Georgie, are part of why it feels so good to be in nature.

I start snooping, wandering, picking through the overgrown woods. Once I'm in deep enough that I can no longer see the light on the lake, I startle at a branch that looks like the antlers of a moose ready to charge.

I am not scared, exactly, I am just alert, all my senses firing. The trails are overgrown, but I can find the path easily enough. The landscape isn't hostile, just indifferent. I'm insignificant, and that feels good.

I find a plaque at the edge of the former cabin site that reads: *The cabin is the wellspring, the source, the hub of my existence. It gives me tranquility, a closeness of nature and wildlife, good health and fitness. A sense of security, the opportunity for resourcefulness, reflection, and creative thinking.* Red columbine and clover bloom around the plaque, and a water bowl for dogs sits next to it.

As I go back to the lake, I stop for a minute to slug water and look around. It's still quiet, early in the day, early in the season, but the neighboring homes are close enough that I can pick out the chairs and toys on the docks. I can see how she felt encroached upon.

But I'm here, and I can't see anyone else around, so I figure I should try to be a little more like Anne.

I shuck off my clothes and slip into the water. It feels cool and soft. Anne drank straight from the lake the whole time she lived here. She called this lake *wild water*, before she learned that acid rain and neighboring sewage were starting to seep in. I let myself sink under the surface, and lean back, feeling the chill.

I pull myself out and dry off on Anne's dock as the wind pricks up goose bumps. I wonder if the neighbors can see, because they don't seem so far off. I wonder if this is normal, just another naked lady on Annie's dock, looking for clues about how to live right.

THE HEROINE'S JOURNEY

Mariette Anne LaBastille was born in New York City in 1933, but once she made it to the woods, she kept her age and given name a secret. The details only came out in her obituary. She was secretive about much of her past, perhaps because there wasn't much in her early life that would point her toward the north woods. She was the only child of a suburban New Jersey opera-singer mother and an automobile-industry-executive-turned-academic father. She was actively discouraged from going outside.

Her parents, who met at Illinois State University, both had unconventional upbringings. Her father, Ferdinand LaBastille, was born in Haiti and moved to Brazil as a young child. He'd spent a lot of his twenties skipping around South and Central America, working and traveling. Her mother, Irma Goebel, came from a family of academics. Her father was a controversial Stanford professor, Julius Goebel, who was fired for spying on the university president at the behest of Jane Stanford. Irma spoke 3 languages by the time she was 8 and became a world-renowned concert pianist at 15. She studied music at Illinois State, and she kept performing for the rest of her life, but she also worked as a journalist for *The New York Times* and *The London Times*.

Irma was obsessed with Indigenous folk songs and folktales. When Ferdinand got a job as a sales executive for General Motors covering Latin America, the couple moved to Argentina, and while Ferdinand worked, Irma collected stories and artifacts. According to the University of Miami, which holds her archive, she became a member of the Society of Women Geographers and an official consultant on Latin American music and allied arts, as part of the US State Department's Office of Inter-American Affairs.

They traveled across South and Central America, but they must have felt some sort of pressure to settle down. By the time Anne was born, they were back in the States, setting up life in Montclair, New Jersey.

Anne was an only child, in part because Irma was a reluctant mother. At a different time, she might not have had a child, and even though she did, she was still focused on her work and passion projects. Anne was alone a lot as a child, and she didn't get much attention, although Irma pushed her to play music and tried to shape her into a smaller version of herself.

Anne had a range of nonstandard, international experiences as a young person, which revolved around her parents' interests. The LaBastilles, especially Irma, were still devoted to exploration. When Anne was 5, they took her on a 25,000-mile research expedition through South and Central America. Anne's first writing, a daily journal, showed up on this trip. But instead of international culture, she kept finding herself drawn to nature, even if it was just the woods of the golf course behind their house in Montclair.

"I yearned for a tent and a pack," she wrote in *Woodswoman*. "At Christmas, I asked my parents for stout boots and a .22 rifle—only to receive silk stockings and a dictionary. I dreamed of running away to become a wrangler out West or a trapper up North. But when a strong-willed mother states, 'Girls can't go camping,' or 'You mustn't walk in the woods alone,' what's a 16-year-old to do?"

Linda Powers Tomasso, a researcher at the Harvard School of Public Health, says that there's both a nature and a nurture aspect to wanting to be outside. Part of it is what you're exposed to, but studies from the University of Queensland found that 46 percent of our desire to be outside is genetic. Tomasso says that those who center their lives around nature tend to describe it as a calling. "These people knew simply that they wanted to follow their spirit outdoors, [and] they felt like they were denying or limiting who they truly were if they didn't," she told me. Those people tend to rank high on what's called the Connectedness to Nature scale, a test developed by two Oberlin psychology professors that quantifies how close you feel to nature by running through a series of statements like *I think of the natural world as a community to which I belong.* I took the test and scored 4 on the scale of 1 to 5. I'm guessing Anne was a 5.

Tomasso also found that shy children were more likely to gravitate to the outdoors. "They could get out in nature and overcome that sense of self-consciousness," she says. Nature becomes a refuge.

My family spent a lot of time outside, and my parents are both competent and comfortable in wild places. They showed me how to backpack and breathe between ocean waves. I had the nurturing, but I also feel an innate desire to be outside. I grew up in an urban neighborhood, on an alley, but even there I could find little pockets of wild places where I didn't feel watched. I spent a lot of time climbing the trees that marked the boundary with the Catholic school behind our house. I'd sit on their sturdy branches with a book or a notebook, spy on the neighbors, make up stories. I was a squirrelly, socially anxious kid. I often felt judged, or like I had to be alert, to try to read the signs to fit in. But in the trees, I could be the observer, a part of the landscape. Anne said she felt similarly.

As Anne got older she was more constrained by the propriety of her all-girls school, by her mother's rules, and by social pressure to pursue polite indoor activities. As we age, girls are less encouraged to be physical, tough, and competitive. According to 25 years of research from the Women's Sports Foundation, preteen girls drop out of sports at twice the rate of their male peers. By the time they're 17, more than half of young women have dropped out. That's because of social stigma, because of twisted messages about body image, appearance, and ability, and because the girls' sports are less resourced, less role-modeled, taken less seriously. We aren't taught to push our bodies in dangerous ways. If we want to do it, we have to learn it on our own.

I stuck with organized sports through college, in part because movement has always helped calm me, but I was always cautious about pushing myself too hard. I sometimes wonder if I would have been braver and less scared of bruising—or falling or looking foolish—if I had been told my body was tough, instead of being told to be careful. Or if I hadn't felt pressure to suck in my stomach or blend in. It was harder to try to unlearn those parts later when my body—and my brain—was less flexible.

In high-school pictures, Anne is smiling, carefully groomed, careful-looking, her hair neatly parted and pulled back. As a teenager she was picked up on the street to model for Conover, and in the pictures from her modeling portfolio she's dreamily smiling off into the distance, slightly vacant-eyed and ladylike in a picture-perfect 1950s way. The shots don't suggest anything of the barefoot woodswoman she would become.

Anne's parents divorced when she was 16. She stayed with her father in Montclair until the end of high school, cooking dinner and taking care of the house, because her father didn't know how to.

After high school, she moved to Miami, where her mother had established herself after the divorce, to start college. When Anne was still in Montclair, she wrote her mother letters asking if she could paddle into the Everglades, dive for treasure, and wear shorts when she came to Miami. Her mother had other ideas.

In Miami, Irma had changed her name to Kate Thornhill, because she wanted a new persona, and took on a series of different careers. She still performed as a concert pianist, but she also took on odd jobs to support herself, including as an assistant to famous herpetologist and alligator wrestler Ross Allen. Anne remembered going to feed the reptiles at night, after her mother's concerts, dropping mice into the dark alligator tanks, still dressed in the evening's crinoline and taffeta.

Her mother eventually found a place where she could run the show: the Miami shipping docks. Kate learned to drive a tugboat and started a business shipping racehorses overseas, earning her the nickname Tugboat Kate. She was the only female stevedore boss in Miami—and likely in the world, at the time. Her linguistic fluency came in handy. She could swear in multiple languages, and she wasn't shy about bossing men around, but she expected Anne to be formal and polite.

They were both strong-willed and trying to figure out their

roles in a male-dominated world, but Kate kept Anne on a tight leash. She forbade her from driving or wearing pants. But she also showed her how to be tough and independent, and she inadvertently nurtured Anne's love of the outdoors. She spearheaded a cleanup of the Miami River, inspired in part by her friendship with journalist and conservationist Marjory Stoneman Douglas, another strong-willed woman who was pivotal in saving the Everglades from being drained and developed. When Anne was 17, she took her on a canoe trip into the Everglades and into Seminole territory. The experience was formative for Anne, who decided to study marine biology at the University of Miami.

As a freshman, Anne met "Major" Claude Vernon Bowes, a naturalist 17 years her senior. Major was making seasonal swings between Florida, where he worked as a guide for the Audubon Society, and upstate New York, where he owned a historic lodge on the edge of Big Moose Lake called Covewood. He offered Anne a summer job at the stables. She'd never heard of the Adirondacks, and Major was still a stranger to her, but she was sick of being under her mother's thumb, and she liked his offer.

Her mother, who didn't think running a stable for a strange man was appropriate, forbade her from going. But indomitable Anne played her divorced parents against each other and made a covert plan with her father. She booked a flight to Newark and snuck out of the last day of classes with a summer's worth of clothes in her bag without saying goodbye to her mother. Her father met her at the airport, and they headed north, to the mountains.

To see what it might have first felt like for her, I follow Anne's route to Covewood, where the lodge is still open, and Major's family is still involved. It has been raining too much this spring, and everything is spongy when I park on the soft, overgrown grass near the sport court. I find some gardeners on a sandwich break and ask them about the history of the lodge and if they know anything about Anne. "You should go ask Diane about the stories," one of them tells me. "But maybe don't mention Anne, at least not at first."

They tell me Diane, Major's second wife, who still runs Covewood, should be in the main lodge, so I wander that way, past a stack of old canoes and up a grand porch. Many of these old lodges seem dark and hazy inside, even in high summer, and I feel the temperature drop as I walk in. I find Diane in the office in the middle of the lodge, and she gives me the rundown of the history as she walks me around.

Covewood, which was built by Earl Covey, was listed on the National Register of Historic Places in 2004 for its impressive regional architecture. Earl, a self-taught builder and the son of renowned Adirondack guide Henry Covey, began construction in 1924. He had no blueprint, just grand ideas of big timber and stone. He sheathed the lodge in silvery vertical split logs, a local signature he used in all his buildings, and searched out massive river rocks for the multistory fireplaces. The sweeping stonework feels like the vestige of a bygone time when nature was for the taking.

Covey got sick and sold the property in 1938. In 1952, Major, who had just graduated from the Cornell University hotel school and was looking for a project, bought it and turned it into a modernized guest lodge.

Diane tells me that many families have come back year after year for decades. She shows me massive, time-swollen photo books of past guests. Covewood is still solid, if weathered, and elegantly shabby. It feels like it's been there forever, greened over and softened. It's not accidental. These lodges were designed to hit the careful margin between wild and tamed, comfortable but still close to the edge. It's a controlled fantasy of wildness, and here everything tilts toward the lake.

Anne was stunned by her first sight of the lodge. "After an interminable drive up old Route 9, I arrived at the rustic lodge where I would be working," she wrote in *Woodswoman*. "Strolling down to the dock, I stopped transfixed by the dazzling blue lake and the backdrop of forested hills. Only a few cottages and boathouses broke the shoreline. There were no other signs of civilization."

But she wasn't there to be transfixed. She was expected to work every single day from July Fourth to the fall, slopping dishes, saddling horses, and catering to the guests' whims. But for the first time in her life, she had unfettered access to the outdoors and freedom from her mother's expectations. She took the horses on rides and started hiking farther and farther into the woods. She eased around the edge of the lake in a canoe, exploring. I wonder what she fell in love with first, the person or the place.

In the first *Woodswoman* book, Major is initially portrayed as a mercurial mentor who encouraged her to take her first solo camping trip over Labor Day.

The trip was a veritable disaster. She only brought dried soup, and she shivered all night in a bunch of blankets safety-pinned together, chomped by mosquitoes and no-see-ums, drinking tannic swamp water. But by the end she felt victorious. She felt like she had been in dialogue with nature, and she liked the way time slowed down. She said Major looked at her differently when she came back. She talks about him with some distance, but it seems like he might have had his eye on her from the start. She'd already decided to transfer to Cornell, to be closer to the Adirondacks, and presumably to him.

In the fall, Major invited her on another camping trip, but this time he chartered a Cessna floatplane loaded with supplies and brought a nicer menu of roast beef pie and fresh-baked bread. After the plane dropped them off on the idyllic beach of Deep Lake, they set up camp under a stand of pines. Major was capable and kind. He made the backcountry seem luxurious.

They cooked dinner and sparked the campfire. The air was charged. "I've been watching you all summer," he told her. "Like I said before, you're different from most who come to work at my hotel. You really love nature, and that's a nice trait to find in a woman."

At first, she refused to sleep in the tent with her older boss—it seemed inappropriate—so she rolled her sleeping bag out on the ground. But then it began to rain, and then she started to shiver, and then you can probably imagine the rest.

In the morning, she was elated. Another storm was rushing in, so they decided that she'd hike out and get back to class while he stayed to wait for the floatplane. She set off, picking out the trail through the tamarack groves, everything Technicolor with feeling. "In my state of heady exhilaration, every color, every scent, every sound seemed intense and beautiful even in the pouring rain. Fallen leaves formed a carpet as polychromatic as a Persian rug—colors as warm, wet, and rich as finest wines and brandies—burgundies, clarets, and rosés, peach, apricot and plum," she wrote. "I hummed and skipped over those five enchanting miles, soaked to the skin but glowing warm, in love with the woods, with life, with [him]."

I think this was part of her fantasy, both being the hero and being with the hero. Major taught her how to build fires and read maps. He gave her the confidence to explore alone. She loved all of it. "Camping has become one of my most beloved pastimes," she wrote. "I take fierce delight in swinging a pack onto my back or into a canoe and heading for the hills and lakes."

Major started one of the first ecotourism companies in the US, and by the time they got married in 1956, they were operating the company together. They bought a 57-foot boat called the *Snowbird* and spent winters living on it while they ran bird-watching tours through Central and South America and the Caribbean. In the spring, they would head back to Big Moose Lake to open the lodge and then work unceasingly until they went south again. Anne learned to fell trees and split wood, and she took on plenty of the physical work of running a lodge, which she loved. It was a good life, but it wasn't exactly hers. She had been under her mother's thumb, and now she was under Major's.

Anne liked being outside, working hard, but what she really wanted to be doing was research. At Cornell, she became the second-ever woman in the natural resources department and the only one in her class. Although the school, which was conducting innovative work in forestry, wildlife management, and biology, was open to women, it wasn't particularly welcoming. She wanted to be out in the field doing research, but at Cornell she was told that it was inappropriate for women to do fieldwork and that she'd become a *neurotic old maid* if she did.

She was able to fight to do it, in part because she had support from professors like Lawrence Hamilton, a widely beloved expert in ecosystem management who focused on Latin and South America and supported her interest and history there.

Despite the support, she knew she was missing opportunities because of her gender. "She watched her male friends and students go off to become forest rangers and wardens, and the only forestry job she could get was behind a desk," Leslie says. Leslie, who was tasked with dealing with all of Anne's papers after her death, found her college diary and was amused by her conviction. "In her diary, she said that her life's fight was for her and other women to have outdoor careers. She would fight and win or die trying."

Anne also faced flak from her fellow students. They lodged complaints against her because she was wandering around campus barefoot in jeans, carrying her books in a pack basket. They argued it was inappropriate and distracting. When they brought it to the dean, he said she was getting straight A's, so he didn't see the problem.

After she graduated, and shortly after she and Major were married, she took a job in Florida at the Audubon Society working the front desk—the only forestry-adjacent job she was offered. Once she was there, she worked her way up and became the first female National Audubon Society tour guide, leading people into the Everglades looking for birds. As a guide she protested having to wear skirts and loafers instead of pants and boots, like the other male guides. She changed the dress code and the standards, paving the way for other women to feel comfortable through small fights like those.

She never forgot what it felt like to be marginalized, so she tried to hold open doors. Decades later, when Leslie, fresh out of college, was struggling to get a job, Anne opened her Rolodex and gave her a pile of contacts. Leslie became a backcountry ranger and then spent 35 years as a fisheries biologist and ecologist for the New York State Department of Environmental Conservation—the kinds of jobs that weren't available to Anne.

The year after Anne and Major married, she went back to school to get her master's in wildlife management at Colorado State University. She'd applied to 12 schools, but only CSU would allow her to do fieldwork. In 1962, she became the first woman to work in a US Fish and Wildlife Service research unit, where she was studying mule deer migration.

The field of wildlife ecology was still relatively new—it had come into fashion in the '30s—and ecology as a whole had only been a concept since the 1860s. For Anne, ecology and outdoor recreation were intertwined. Guiding gave her research real-world context, and her education brought depth to her time in the woods. She could see the interdependencies, particularly in the ways people impacted places. She started honing her own theories and observing the ways people impacted wildlife in particular. But when she submitted her research papers for publication, they were categorically rejected. Assuming gender bias was at play, she decided to resubmit the same papers under the name Al LaBastille. They were accepted.

She was trying to carve out space for her research, but while she was in school she was also helping Major run Covewood and their winter tour business in Miami. She was guiding trips, hosting a new load of guests every week all summer, and promoting the business. There were no breaks, and that wore on her and on their marriage.

She wanted to be a scientist and a writer, not a tour guide, and that desire was making her fingers itch. She had started a weekly column for the local *Adirondack Echo*, "Women in the Woods," and while she was able to devote Sunday afternoons to the writing, she wanted more. She was trying to find a story for herself, too, to align the ecology and science with adventure and exploration.

Writer and academic Joseph Campbell, who studied mythology and philosophy, coined the concept of the hero's journey in his 1949 book *The Hero with a Thousand Faces*. In the common narrative arc, a hero heeds a call to adventure—maybe to slay a dragon or protect their homeland—then they cross a threshold into the unknown, where they face tests, conquer a big challenge, and come home with a lesson or a prize. They've grown and learned and made things better. They get the girl; they save the castle. They are often a guy.

In the '80s, Maureen Murdock, a Jungian psychotherapist who was a student of Campbell's, came up with an alternative plotline, which she called the *heroine's journey*. She found that in her therapy work, the hero's journey arc didn't encompass everything that her patients—particularly women—were going through.

Anne was bumping up against those ideas, too. She'd seen herself as a hero from the beginning, but now she was stuck in someone else's journey, playing a sideline role. She wanted her own quest.

Like the hero's journey, the arc of the heroine's journey comes in stages. The heroine starts by rejecting feminine values because she hasn't seen a way to be fulfilled as a woman. She begins to identify with masculine ideals and external visions of power, like being the fastest, toughest person on the trail, because that seems like a clear path to success. Then, like on the hero's journey, she faces tests and trials; she finds success and slays dragons. But that's where the arcs start to differ.

Murdock says that at that point, on the outside the journey might look good, but on the inside you feel hollow, and not true to yourself. You start to get the feeling that your life isn't quite right. You've achieved and achieved and you still seem unsatisfied. She calls that a *sense of spiritual aridity.* You feel oppressed, but you can't find anyone oppressing you besides yourself. You might fall into crisis, even though you've achieved what the world said you should. That's the stage Anne was in, working at the lodge with Major.

From there, the heroine has to recalibrate and align the ideals she was chasing with the things that feel true to herself. Murdock calls this "healing the mother–daughter split," and "healing the wounded masculine." I see it as trying to square the pressure of achievement with what feels core. It's Anne both wanting to be a respected scientist and wanting to live alone in the woods.

The last step is acknowledging that the real work is setting up your life so it works for you. There's never really any dragon or any perfect pinpoint when the journey ends.

Murdock found that arc resonated with many of her patients. But when she brought it to Campbell in the early '80s, his response was "Women don't need to make the journey. In the whole mythological tradition, the woman is there. All she has to do is to realize that she's the place that people are trying to get to."

When I found Murdock's ideas, as I was scrambling to put a finger on why a fulfilling path felt so elusive, for me and for Anne, it made me realize I'd been chasing a masculine conception of adventure, even when it didn't exactly feel good to do so, in part because I didn't see other paths to follow. I think Georgie was stuck in the hero's journey, unable to sink deeper into an honest sense of self and fighting to justify herself in a male space. Anne was struggling with that path, too. In 1964, her father died, and her marriage was falling apart. She'd long ago distanced herself from her mother, proved herself as tough and masculine. She'd gone through trials, in work and in school, and found some success in a male-dominated world. But she was still searching for a concrete sense of meaning.

In the end, Anne's vision wasn't compatible with Major's life. That spring, Major filed for divorce. "We had had very little privacy and a great deal of work in our married life. Perhaps this combination had gradually eroded our love," Anne wrote. Major told her she had to be out before the guests came in for the summer because he couldn't handle the distraction of their discord.

Leslie says that even before Anne's divorce she'd long dreamed of building a remote cabin and having a place to write. But Major's ultimatum set the clock ticking. That spring she found property on a lake in the western Adirondacks, owned by an older woman named Beatrice Nobel, who was breaking up a wide swath of property into smaller tracts. The parcel Anne bought had no electricity, no running water, no road in. In the winter, the fuel truck would drive out onto the frozen lake to deliver supplies, but in summer everything had to come in by boat. There was one other year-round resident on the lake. She would be out there alone.

She broke ground in May of 1964 and hired a crew of carpenters and friends to help build the log cabin she envisioned. Major helped, too, because he wanted her gone.

She moved into the cabin on July 4, the same day that Henry David Thoreau moved into his cabin in Concord. Independence Day.

ALONE IN THE WILDERNESS

Once I'd seen her land, I wanted to see Anne's cabin, safely installed at the Adirondack Experience Museum on Blue Mountain Lake. The museum hugs the elevated shoreline of the lake and sprawls into the woods. It holds art galleries and recreated guide shacks, a boathouse, and a grand pavilion. It almost feels like one of those great camp compounds, man-made but mimicking the twiggy density of the woods, bigger than I thought it would be.

In the Bull Cottage, an old log-skinned structure facing the lake, I meet Penny Harr, a museum clerk who has been working on a biography of Anne. We wander onto the deck, away from other visitors, and she tells me that Anne is controversial around here. Penny is a seventh-generation Adirondacker, and she says that for a long time, like a lot of locals, she thought of Anne as a weirdo and a fraud. She had her pegged as an opinionated outsider who was trying to impose rules about wilderness. "I heard her name in a negative light, all growing up," Penny says. "But I read the *Woodswoman* series and loved the books and thought, 'There's got to be more to this woman's story.'"

And, of course, there was. Penny loved Anne's stubborn focus. "She basically bucked the system at every turn. I think that's why she resonates: She had the guts to do what she wanted to do," Penny says, the fire building in her voice. Eventually, visitors start to swarm with questions so I let her get back to work, and I go hunting for Anne's cabin.

I thought it would be prominently displayed, but after a couple of laps, I still can't find it. I wander through the buildings, past endless murals and installations. I learn more than I planned about hunting camps, and I catch a glimpse of Anne in a video about logging, but I still can't find the cabin.

Finally I ask someone. It turns out the cabin is deep in the back corner of the Life in the Adirondacks building, beyond a guide boat and an exhibit on the rise of auto tourism. Part of that might be because the 12x12 cabin is small enough to fit there. Laura Rice, the museum's curator, says that taking care of old, historic buildings can be problematic. They put Anne's cabin inside so it would last longer, out of the elements, but I feel let down by the lack of fanfare.

The cabin feels like a rugged dollhouse staged with Anne's belongings. Snowshoes and a guitar hang on the walls. There are books stacked in the opening to the loft and piled on her desk next to a typewriter. Red curtains and woven rugs from her time in South America accent the room, and a moka pot sits on the stove. It looks idyllic, simple but chocked with character. Exactly what you'd think a hermitic writer's cabin would look like.

A team from the museum spent the winter of 2015 carefully taking the cabin apart, labeling every beam and truss so they could put it back together. They sledded the parts out over the frozen lake and brought them here. Structural preservationist Michael Frenette says they didn't see anyone the whole time they were dismantling it. He says the original structure was beautiful—and that by re-creating it, they're channeling a collective nostalgia for a bygone era of life in the wilderness.

But while that image is nice, it's not entirely accurate. Sure, those were all Anne's things, but they're only a piece of what Anne's life looked like. Leslie says that in reality, Anne was a pack rat, and the cabin was stuffed with papers and slide film and bent-spine copies of field guides and poetry books. The storage under the porch was overflowing. Over the years, she built additions to the cabin and outbuildings for guests, creating a slapdash compound around that original building. The exhibit is sanitized, missing the elements and the context of Anne's life. She moved into that isolated cabin to evaporate the barrier between herself and the place she loved. And while the cabin is important, to understand the full story I had to go back to the lake.

I knew that Anne wanted to be alone in the woods to write, to watch wildlife, and to live simply. She wanted to set her own equilibrium. After years of hosting and guiding, she wanted to be able to shut the door on other people. She was aching for some space of her own.

Alone in the wilderness, you either learn to survive or you quickly fail. Bravery and desperation can sometimes look the same. For Anne, in the aftermath of her crumbled relationship with Major, they were intertwined. "Intuitively now, I made my decision," she wrote in *Woodswoman*. "I would build a log cabin in the Adirondack wilderness. I hoped that a withdrawal to the peace of nature might remedy my despair. I reasoned that the companionship of wild animals and local outdoor people could cure my sorrow. Most of all I felt that the creation of a rustic cabin would be the solution to my homelessness."

She bought the place on intuition, too. She motored up to the property for sale in her skiff one warm May day, soon after Major had told her that she had to get out. She found a shaded sandy cove for swimming and a balsam-scented evergreen forest that morphed into hardwoods farther away from the lake. The neighbors were beavers and loons. By the time she pulled her boat out of the water that evening, she had an idea of where and how she might build her cabin there. "Even without a house to live in, I'd found a place to go," she wrote.

Two days later she bought the land in one bright streak. She took the midnight train to New York City, signed the papers, and then split back to the mountains before dinner. Even that purchase was bold. Women couldn't get home loans until the 1974 Equal Credit Opportunity Act, so she bought the 22 acres with cash she inherited from her father, free and clear.

In her mind, she began calling the cabin West of the Wind, and she had a vision for what it would look like. It would face south and west, to catch the sun, and be set up on a rocky knoll, crowned with a slanted, snow-shedding roof. It would need to be small enough to build in a few months, for cheap, before Major kicked her out at the beginning of July. Every piece of the construction would have to be done by hand or with portable generators.

Anne had never built anything before, but Leslie said that once Anne got an idea in her head she stuck to it. She vowed not to log any trees on her own property, because one of the things she liked best was the intact, old-growth forest. She committed to a simple, rustic design that would require no unnecessary resources and leave no outsized impact on the forest around it. She'd have no electricity or phone.

Based on her rough calculations, she haggled with a local lumberjack named Pierre for forty-five 16-foot-long spruce logs. He dropped them in the water at the Twitchell boat ramp, and she dragged them up the lake behind her motorboat.

Penny told me that one of the things people disliked most about Anne was based on a widespread rumor that she lied about building her cabin alone. But she never said she did. It's a misconception started by some of her neighbors who were trying to discredit her. She makes it clear in her book that she had help building the cabin. Major pitched in, and she hired a couple of contractors, Bob and Dave, who brought the necessary tools and skill set, and who talked her out of building an expensive, time-consuming hand-hewn cabin. They helped build the floor and framing out of commercial lumber, and they notched and set the log walls. She cut doors and windows and laid the floor while they built the roof. They were all racing to build something livable by July that aligned with her ideals. To me, that doesn't diminish her credibility. Part of growth is learning to trust people. Even hermits don't have to do it all alone.

Once the structure was up, she had to figure out the practical details: heat and light, how to cook, where to sleep. She framed in a loft for a bed and boated in a 300-pound Franklin woodstove, along with a gas-powered oven and fridge, big windows, and a writing desk. It took 4 people to wrangle the stove up the slope from the lake.

She put balsam branches under her mattress so she could smell the woods all night. The first evening alone she ate dinner on the dock bathed in the golden July light. But she quickly realized it wasn't always going to be idyllic. In her rush to build, she hadn't completely read the covenant for the land. In August, a lawyer came knocking with a notice that she'd violated regulations. Her newly built cabin, which was 38 feet from the lake, needed to be 50 feet away. She had until November to tear down her cabin or move it back 12 feet to comply with the legal document she'd skimmed when she signed.

It seemed impossible. The cabin weighed 14 tons and was pinned to the ground with iron and concrete. But visiting friends came up with a plan to jack it up, skid it back 12.5 feet, and use the old base as a deck. Anne spent the next month digging new foundation holes, cutting down trees, and finding grease to skid the logs. Starting on Labor Day she and the friends took 5 days to move the cabin and resite it, higher on the hill. The move taught her that life in the outdoors required frequent pivots. She'd learn that over and over again.

In those northern latitudes, seasons come through fast. At the end of summer, you notice the dip and change of birdsong first. You hear beavers cracking limbs, otters eating bullheads and crunching bones. You feel the water temperature drop. Once the motorboats are pulled out for the season the soundscape changes even more.

Autumn is about taking stock, checking the pipes and the chinks in the logs. Laying up wood. The geese are gone, and skeins of ice start to skate across the lake.

When Anne first moved to Twitchell, that was fall's biggest task: waiting for the lake to solidify so it was safe to traverse. In the 1960s, a propane truck could drive over the lake midwinter to resupply. By the time she left in 2008, the surface wasn't reliably thick enough to hold a snowshoer. Anne noticed that erosion; she was paying attention.

She had to. Her life depended on it. In her first few years on the lake, she learned that surviving alone takes focus, particularly when your easiest path to more food or more fuel is across a not-quite-frozen lake, too tender to hold your weight. That in-between space, when the lake started to get thick and sludgy with ice in the fall or when that ice started to fragment and get fragile in the spring, was when things were most fraught.

Alone, she had to be hyperaware of risk. She worried about appendicitis and about falling and freezing to death. She worried about frozen waterlines and fallen trees crashing through her roof. All her fears and challenges were amplified in the winter, when help was harder to get and the weather was harsher. Sometimes people would sled over the lake for frozen picnics or to watch the aurora borealis, but largely she was alone, taking in the immense silence. Winter, in its eerie, lonely beauty, made it clear how fragile her existence could be.

After the first few years, she'd usually travel for most of the winter, but she'd be back at the cabin for spring, when rivers swell, the sun comes back, and the lake ice starts to break up. "The breakup is a prelude to spring. The breakup is a prelude to comfort. The breakup is a prelude to companionship. Through it the lakes, ponds, and rivers are loosed from winter's rigid fetters—the ice," she wrote.

After the ice broke up, she'd wait for the lake to get to 50 degrees, and then she'd start swimming again. In the summer, she set her own rhythms, beginning with a dip in the lake, followed by a morning of writing. Sometimes she wrote in the sun on the dock, or in the woods with her typewriter on her lap, or in a canoe on the lake itself. By lunchtime, she'd grow antsy and set out on a hike with her German shepherd or take on some of the chores necessary to keep life in the woods on the rails, like chopping wood and caulking seams in the cabin. In later years, she might paddle across the lake to a friend's house where she kept a phone line hooked up to an answering machine to check her messages. In the afternoon, she'd take another swim, drying off on the dock, watching the brook trout rise, before evenings on the water, where she could walk down to the dock with a pot of spaghetti, a bowl of salad, a shortwave radio, and an ice-cold beer. She'd set cushions in the bottom of the canoe and float out, cracking the beer, turning the radio to a Beethoven symphony, the chords reverberating in the metal canoe, the dog sitting calm between the gunwales, the pasta still warm.

Summer turned to fall turned to winter back to spring. She lived through the freeze-up, then the break-up on the lake again. She became a woodswoman over time, learning more as the years came around again.

It didn't always run smoothly. She was constantly working to keep back the creep of the forest: repairing the roof, draining the water system, felling dead trees. Her learning curve was steep and inconsistent, and her methods were often sketchy—Leslie has pictures of Anne running a chainsaw barefoot in a bikini—but she learned to trust her own work. "The first thing was to convince myself that I could handle anything I had or wanted to," Anne wrote. "The time-old excuse of being a woman, hence frail, dumb, afraid, in need of protection and a man's assistance, has no place in an isolated and rustic lifestyle."

She learned that the stereotypes that had stopped her when

she was younger weren't real. "Some of the fictions I had to overcome had been planted in childhood and perpetuated in early adulthood. I learned that I would not damage my 'delicate internal organs' by doing hard work. I discovered that calluses, firm muscles, or a smudge of grease on the nose would not make me unfeminine," she wrote.

Megan Mayhew Bergman, a Middlebury College professor who studies and teaches Anne's work, says that was one of the many ways Anne was subversive, in her time and now. She countered those stereotypes by learning the skills she needed to build and live at the cabin, one sketchy chainsaw swipe at a time.

Anne said that the decision to buy the land and build the cabin was rash, but really she'd been moving toward it for years. She'd long been frustrated at her lack of autonomy and had spent years learning navigation and backcountry skills while she worked with Major. She says she wanted space and time to write and research in nature. But what she also wanted was liberation, and in trying to define that for herself she was part of a mounting wave of women who were trying to figure out what that looked like for them.

The Feminine Mystique, Betty Friedan's book about the deeply frustrating limitations housewives were facing, and the meager options women had outside of the home, came out the year before she bought the property and the same year President Kennedy signed the Equal Pay Act. The baseline for second-wave feminism, focused on women's liberation, was building. Anne's path toward solitude and purposeful work was part of that reframing. Now, when many women are guides, and single women are more likely than single men to be homebuyers, it might seem small, but at the time living and working alone, especially in a remote place, was radical. She had property, which gave her safety and space, and she also had time. She could make her own schedule and life. That was her version of freedom.

It's part of my version, too, which is one of the first reasons I was drawn to Anne's story. I also have a fantasy of living in a remote cabin, where my life depends on the seasons and self-reliance, and where I can prioritize writing and being outside. A part of me wonders if my life would be simpler and clearer off the grid. But I also know that being a hermit is hard to pull off. I look at Anne with some awe because she went beyond a thought experiment. She built the life. The execution is the interesting part.

I love people, and I think Anne did, too, but I understand that breaking point. I often feel like I have to be on and performing, in a way that can be exhausting. I need space and solitude to recalibrate, to breathe and think. Alone in the woods she could devote her time fully to writing and try to reach a wider audience with her research. Organizational behaviorists at the Johns Hopkins Carey Business School found that being alone, and even feeling social rejection, can lead to inspiration. Van Gogh, Emily Dickinson, and Harper Lee all hew to that line. When you're alone, there's less distraction, and there's also more space to write in your own voice. You can hear this in Anne's first book in particular. *Woodswoman* feels unconstrained, a little wild and unruly. Her later books seem more self-conscious, aware of an audience.

Virginia Thomas, a solitude researcher at Middlebury, found that being alone in wilderness in particular can get us out of our own heads. "Research has shown that we're least likely to feel lonely, and more likely to feel spiritually connected, when we're alone in nature, compared to being at home by ourselves or alone in a public place," she wrote in *Psychology Today*.

That connection was what compelled Anne the most. There's a Welsh word, *hiraeth*, that loosely means a desire for a landscape that feels like it should be yours. One translation calls it *a longing to be where your spirit lives*. Similar ideas show up in different cultures, too. Anne said that going to the cabin felt like going home. It's a feeling geographer Yi-Fu Tuan calls *topophilia*, the symbiosis between us and a particular landscape.

The Adirondacks aren't my place, even though I find them beautiful and deep, but I am starting to feel that sense of topophilia in the landscape I've chosen for myself. The mountain that stretches behind my house in southwest Colorado is filled with pinyon, scrub oak, and sage. In the spring, the columbines come in slow, then all at once. Half-witted deer wander through the alleys into the hills, and mountain lions are up there, too. The dogs can tell when they're out.

When I let myself slow down and pay attention, I start to notice new things. Walking the chalky social trail after breakfast, I say the names of plants out loud, committing them to memory. Over time, I've learned when the winter light hits the ridge, and where I've seen mountain lion tracks. It's a direct kind of knowing that comes through extended contact. It's similar to how Georgie saw the beaches in the Grand Canyon change over time. You mark somewhere in your mind, and then notice how it oscillates and varies, how it might diminish. I think a sense of home comes from paying attention.

At the cabin, Anne would walk to the nearby lakes and swim out to the rocks where the otters and loons would rest.

It became the baseline of her ecological research, but she was also learning the texture and rhythm of that specific place, the continuity of the landscape and the way it connected and sprawled out. She was ahead of the culture of what we now call *forest bathing*, the act of immersing ourselves in nature, which has a host of physiological and psychological benefits, both personal and reciprocal. Forest bathing combines parts of what biologists call *phenology*: the study of the cycles of the natural world, which comes from deep, long-term knowing. "Phenology requires a complete immersion in place over time, so the attention, the senses, and the mind can scrutinize and discern widely the dates of arrivals and departures, the births, the flourishing, the decays and the deaths of wild things, their successions, synchronicities, dependencies, reciprocities, and cycles the lived life of the earth," author and mountaineer Jack Turner wrote in *Deep Ecology for the Twenty-First Century*. "To be absorbed in this life is to merge with larger patterns. Here ecology is not studied but felt. You know these truths the way you know hot from cold."

That felt sense of ecology was the core of Anne's work as a scientist as she tracked the demise of endangered species and the rise of environmental pollutants, and it was also the heart of her life philosophy: that being in wilderness helps us understand the world.

I learned about the science later. The thing that first grabbed me about Anne was that she lived in the cabin alone. Before I found her, I got sucked into stories of other solitary people, like the saga of Chris McCandless, the fraught hero of *Into the Wild*, who went out into the remote Alaskan bush seeking independence and adventures but only lasted 4 months in his broken school bus before he starved to death. The idea of being a hermit fascinated me; something felt pure and focused about it.

When you think of a hermit, you probably think of a man alone outside, maybe lacking social skills, probably on some kind of moral bent. That's my first image. That's because the vast majority of self- or society-identified hermits are just that.

The root of the word *hermit* comes from the Greek word *eremos*, which means *desert* or *wilderness*. Historically, hermits were solitaries who cut themselves off from society and went to wild, lonely places largely for religious reasons. Third-century Christian hermits Saint Paul of Thebes and Saint Anthony the Great, who lived monastic lives in the Egyptian desert, were considered some of the first intentional hermits. It wasn't just Christianity that engendered hermits. Laozi, who founded Taoism and wrote the *Tao Te Ching*, lived as a hermit, as did many other religious leaders.

But over time, hermits weren't just religious ascetics. After the Enlightenment, when religion wasn't the main source of meaning for many people anymore, hermits struck out looking for different kinds of meaning, derived from nature or the depths of their own psyches.

Men who chose to live alone were often valorized, but the earliest female hermits were considered weirdos, witches, or social pariahs. While some, like the thirteenth-century female Zen master Mugai Nyodai, sought solitude for religious purposes, tales of reclusive women are fraught with negative depictions. From the child-eating witch in "Hansel and Gretel," and Baba Yaga, and Dzunuk'wa, the giant ogress of Canadian First Nations tradition, to Cailleach, the Gaelic crone who brought winter, women who opted out of a traditional family dynamic were often considered evil, demented, or damned.

That's in part because until quite recently, it was difficult for women to have the physical resources or social ability to live alone. Until 1974, women couldn't even get credit cards in their own names. An independent life in any form would have been logistically and financially challenging. It was also socially challenging. We have plenty of stories about men going out to live in nature alone but very few of women, especially ones who committed to isolation for the long haul, and who removed themselves from social strata to follow their own intellectual and physical desires. I think that's because in being alone to think or write, you have to believe that your thoughts are worth prioritizing.

Those negative assumptions were grafted onto Anne as well. She was accused of being a witch more than once. Choosing to be alone, particularly in a wild place, is a break with a certain kind of conventional expectation of what women want and what we are like. Penny Harr says Anne was a pariah for living at the cabin, but that she was judged for other choices, too. After surviving three winters on the lake, she started spending the colder months in South and Central America, conducting research on endangered birds. Because of that seasonality, she was accused of being a fake hermit by the same people who say she lied about building the cabin alone. Yet compared to Thoreau, who only lasted 2 years and who lived within walking distance of his mom's house, Anne's homesteading feels hardcore. Nor did Anne deny or fight the accusations that she wasn't on the lake all the time. In her later books, she called herself *half a hermit*, possibly to counter the harassment.

I think some of the people who are still railing on her even after her death see her lifestyle as opportunistic. With her books she was, of course, trying to capitalize on her hermitic life. But plenty of other hermits, religious or otherwise, wrote philosophical treatises. Thomas Merton, the hermitic Catholic monk, wrote 50 books.

Virginia Thomas, the solitude researcher, found that loneliness can spark creativity. Anne went to the woods in part so she could write. She scrawled stories longhand on yellow legal pads, then pounded out drafts on her manual typewriter, sometimes carrying it onto the dock so she could soak up more sun while she worked.

This is part of the hermit dream for me. I have this idea that, in solitude, I would be able to write clearly, that I would have more self-control and depth. Of course, some of that is fantasy—I'm prone to procrastination wherever I am—but Anne said some of that was true. "When I can write it makes me feel better, I can balance the stress of being out in the world," she wrote. "It makes my life balanced." Being alone to write honed her focus; it gave her space to research and drum up stories and, ultimately, make a living.

Unlike Thoreau, who puttered on *Walden* for 12 leisurely years while he lived off income from his family's pencil factory, Anne had to work to support herself. Over the next 40 years, she wrote more than a dozen books and hundreds of articles and scientific papers. She worked on federal conservation projects and local political initiatives, and she lectured and taught.

At first, her work consisted solely of academic articles. But while she wrote them, she was also recording the details of her life on the lake, the seasonal swings, and the work that went into living simply in the cabin. She started chipping out the story that would become *Woodswoman*.

The book is a memoir about living alone, a work of popular ecology, and a screed against change. Sometimes her writing is stilted and stuck in academic phrasing; by other turns it's too intimate. But the book feels real. It's loose and earnest. In *Woodswoman*, she was trying to both make a record of her time there and etch out a blueprint for other women, a path through the woods that someone else could follow. The best parts of her books aren't the sentences but the stories themselves: sparkly winter picnics in the middle of the lake, autumns spent stowing away firewood and watching migration, spring white-water races down swollen rivers.

As a woman writing about ecology Anne gets likened to Rachel Carson—one of the only women to have written widely in that space and broken into the canon. But while Carson had help from E. B. White, who championed the story of *Silent Spring* and plugged her into the New York publishing world, Anne had no writing mentors. She pitched the book to a publisher, Dutton, without an agent, and despite her lack of polish they bought the story. And when it came out in 1976, it hit the zeitgeist of coalescing social movements.

The year before, the UN had declared 1975 the International Year of the Woman, and *Time* magazine's Man of the Year Award went to "American Women." Second-wave feminism was peaking: Roe v. Wade had just passed; the Equal Rights Amendment was on the table; and women were gaining ground on social, political, and sexual liberation.

The environmental movement was also gaining steam as a flurry of federal policies around pollution, species conservation, and land preservation passed. More people than ever were going outside to recreate as infrastructure and awareness built up. The number of hikers and backpackers in the US more than tripled between 1965 and 1977 from 9.9 million to 28.1 million. Anne's story underscored the importance of wild places and refuted the idea that you had to be a grizzly, old guide to be competent outdoors.

That's because she put herself in the scene, skinny-dipping or slicking on pink lipstick as she ran a chainsaw, struggling with cabin maintenance. When she wrote about her divorce, and how it catalyzed her transformation, she tapped into something that resonated with women who felt trapped and misunderstood by their relationships or families.

As the book became popular, it made her a figurehead, which inevitably exposed her to more scrutiny. Leslie said that Anne embraced being a role model, but it conflicted with her quest for solitude. What began as a trickle of fan mail turned into a flood. Fans wrote letters about their own divorces, their desires to live alone. She got half-baked novels and bad poetry. After the book came out, she taught her dog, Pitzi, to go to the dock and get the bag from the mail boat, but by the next summer it was too heavy for him to carry. Some of the letters were missives from admirers, some were quasi-obsessive screeds from men and women confessing crushes, some were menacing or blatantly threatening. She got postcards inviting her to go bear hunting, and others that called her a bitch.

Then people started showing up at her cabin, declaring their love or asking for tips about how to live alone. They came in the middle of the night; they showed up at the boat launch offering gifts of watermelon and whiskey; one man walked by while she was in the outhouse; one woman set up camp on her property for weeks when she was out of town. "Other dreamers feel they own me and my cabin after reading my book," Anne wrote.

Anne fed the attention to a degree. She answered fan mail, she held public appearances, she continued to write, but Leslie said she became anxious, even though the fanfare was helpful, financially, to promote her books.

Sometimes the trespassers were misanthropes who wanted to set her straight. Anne began sleeping with a gun. The overzealous trespassers were predominantly men, perhaps not aware that their presence broke down the barrier of solitude that they claimed to love. Maybe part of why we haven't had many woman hermits is because people won't leave them alone. More than once she pointed her gun at trespassers who showed up uninvited.

That's one of the things that Caitlin Kelly, a young outdoorswoman in the Adirondacks, says she admires about Anne. She wasn't a pushover. She swung from sensitive to steel. "What really spoke to me was her bravery and tenacity. She didn't let people fuck with her, even if that meant going out with a shotgun," Caitlin told me. "I struggle with that as a woman, but when I've been at a big crossroads, I've thought, 'What would Anne do?'"

Soon after *Woodswoman* came out, critics began comparing her to Thoreau. Anne felt ambivalent. "I feel extremely flattered at being compared with the man who gave early America the first strong guidance toward ecology, animal rights, peaceful civil disobedience, and love of nature," Anne wrote, diplomatically, but she felt squeamish about his legacy and how it compared to her desires.

She read his work—carefully and frequently—because there were ideas to glean. She liked his push toward simplicity, and she followed his low-budget ideas about building. She noted that she and Thoreau were both water signs: She was a Scorpio, he was a Cancer. His style of observation slipped into hers when she monitored the minute details of change around the lake, tracking when the ice froze up or the loons came home.

But she wasn't impressed by his prose, and she chafed under his joyless asceticism. She said their reasons for going to the woods to live deliberately were different. Thoreau was a dilettante who was supported by his family, couldn't hold a job, and would walk home to do laundry. She was a scientist, escaping social pressure, and supporting herself. She identified more with Merton, who wrote, "I live in the woods, as a reminder that I am free."

Still, *Walden*, his book about living alone on the edge of Walden Pond, has become shorthand for a certain kind of American purity. "*Walden* is a work central to national self-mythologizing," wrote Kathryn Schulz in *The New Yorker.* But, as she notes, it's full of all those transcendental, postfrontier fantasies of trying to hold on to wildness, false ideals about our roles in the American wilderness, and the broken bootstraps idea that being impressive meant figuring everything out on your own. He harped on honesty and truth, but he was creating a false image of himself as an isolated ascetic.

Even his time at Walden was a bit of a sham. Emerson lent him the land. He lived there for a little over 2 years, then spent the next 10 years writing *Walden*, which was published to middling acclaim. After Thoreau died at 44 from tuberculosis, Emerson upsold his book, which is part of how *Walden* became classic high-school canon. It fits a neat narrative about America's perceived, idealistic relationship with nature, one that is heavily male. Bergman, who teaches a class on environmental writing that includes Anne, starts by asking her college students what nature writers they've been taught, and when they collectively write out the names, they're shocked to realize it's all Aldo Leopold and Wallace Stegner and other men. Maybe they get some Rachel Carson, most likely they get Thoreau. The bookshelf is narrow. Like Anne, many of the students have to actively unlearn to look at male heroes or find ways to slot themselves into stories that don't quite fit them.

I read *Walden* in high school and took pieces of the myth to heart, but I was less enamored with Thoreau than with the pond itself, which is near my childhood home. It's where I learned to pay attention, to notice how the seasons blew through and when the water temperatures changed. I learned all the ways my body might have power through teenage skinny-dips and long runs around the spiderweb of trails that encircled the pond, beating my brain quiet through motion. I loved the place before I loved the idea of being alone, and before I dredged my way through the self-conscious prose of Walden. I liked the bones of his ideas about self-reliance and paying attention.

It's why I understand how Anne came into the Adirondacks and never left, how you can imprint yourself into a landscape and try to hold on to its shape, even as it changes.

Anne liked the bodily autonomy and edge of brutality it took to live in the woods. She liked the rhythm of days and seasons swinging by. At the cabin, she had a sign that read *LaBastille, you can handle anything.*

But no one can handle *everything.* Committing to solitary life in the wilderness comes with costs. It might have suited her, but that doesn't mean that it wasn't hard. Alone on the lake, especially after a long day of work, when the light got low and the peepers started to sound particularly mournful, she thought about what she didn't have. "Everyone gets lonely. It's the human condition," Anne once told another writer. "The whole problem with American life is we're brainwashed to think we should always be happy, we should always be fulfilled, we should always have a beautiful partner, we should always have all these wonderful, good things, but life isn't that way. When you don't have those expectations, it's easier."

Anne said she was lonelier in her marriage than she was alone at the lake. When people started to come looking for her, as they did after *Woodswoman* was published, she said they were so often looking for identity, purpose, and connection and self-reliance—those things she was seeking when she moved to the lake and committed to being a hermit, and claimed power over that aloneness, like the kind of self-reliance those visitors hoped to acquire from her.

But there were no quick tips. Along with bucket showers and a frozen outhouse, Anne dealt with isolation and loneliness like any other factor of her existence.

She valued her independence, but on those solitary nights at the lake she wanted a partner, too. She had a web of friends, near and far, some who might come up from the city to visit, some locals who popped by to help, some she would write letters to. But they tended to be weak ties, nothing close and singular. Leslie says some man from the Northwest was periodically trying to spirit her away on a yacht, but Anne struggled to find a partner who fit her lifestyle. The logistics of her cabin life were hard on their own, but it was even harder to find a man who was comfortable with her power and skill.

Her independence, the trait she was proudest of, pushed people away. "The process of learning how to cope as a woman alone had backfired to an extent," she wrote. "The more competent I became, the more insecure certain men acted, or the more aggressive others behaved toward me."

And unlike Georgie, who could joke about being married to the river, Anne wanted love. Leslie says there's a draft of a romance novel, deep in the bowels of the Cornell archive, that Anne wrote but never published. She periodically tried to go to New York and Washington, DC, to meet people and to have a relationship outside of the woods, but it never felt like she could be herself. And even when she met someone who supposedly loved the north woods, it wasn't easy to make their lives align.

She'd known Nick before. He'd come riding at the Covewood stables, but when they reconnected on a chance meeting during a hunting trip, she fell hard. He was outdoorsy, handsome, capable, and purportedly excited about her life on Twitchell. He'd come up to the cabin on the weekends from his job as a professor in Albany. It seemed like she could be independent and still have companionship. They set off on long hikes; he took her flying over the Adirondacks. I think it felt good to have butterflies again, to shake off her identity as a washed-up divorcée in the woods.

But there was some sourness under the surface. Though he'd initially admired the life she'd built at the cabin, as they spent more time together he began to resent the isolation, the inconvenience, and the fact that Anne had stronger backwoods skills than him, even though she had spent years building them.

"I was constantly faced with a choice," she wrote. "To go ahead and act competently and independently, as I had been doing, thereby alienating the man I cared for. Then I was forced to handle the situation in a most careful and diplomatic manner. Or, to act like a 'dumb blonde' or 'helpless female' to build up my man's ego. Then I compromised my integrity. This conflict, I often reasoned, must be a basic concern of women's liberation. It certainly was of mine."

It was a rift in both logistics and ideology. And the deepest divide was her commitment to the place. "Somehow I sensed that Nick resented my deep attachment to the cabin, this piece of land, the mountains," she wrote.

They made it work for several years, and when he was offered a teaching job in Alaska, he asked her to join him. It was a warm summer afternoon at the lake when he opened the offer letter, and Anne froze, mind already drifting outside to the woods, the birds, the soundscape of her home. When they went down to the lake to think about the choice, she swam out far and dived under, holding her breath for as long as she could until she came up with an answer. "I knew in that shimmering second between gulping air and water that I would stay and Nick would go."

That kind of break would happen in all of Anne's romantic relationships. Megan Mayhew Bergman says she thinks those kinds of choices were among the most liberated, most modern ones that Anne made. She might have been lonely and looking for companionship, but ultimately she decided men were less important than her mission.

Anne's desire for solitude got stronger as the place she loved became more crowded. By 1984, when wild-eyed fans were creeping her out and the near-constant thrum of motorboats on Twitchell started to drive her crazy, she'd had enough. She went half a mile into the woods away from the lake and built another, more isolated cabin, on the edge of boggy Lilypad Lake. It was over a ridge, back in a spruce grove, meant to be a retreat.

She'd been reading Thoreau again, and she explicitly took her inspiration from *Walden* when she built the next cabin, which she called Thoreau II. She cut logs on-site, and over the course of the summer friends came up to help carry timbers and cut posts. The finished structure was 100 square feet with a sleeping loft and a hand-me-down stove. She was proud that she spent less money, adjusted for inflation, than Thoreau. She had three chairs, like he did, but unlike him she stocked up on shampoo and soap. She finished it the year I was born.

Thoreau II was taken down after her death because it was on the land that Leslie donated to the state wilderness after Anne died, which meant there couldn't be a permanent structure. But I'd heard that the state had done a hack job of deconstructing it, and that you could still find the remains of the foundation at the site. I wanted to see it for myself, and so on one visit to West of the Wind, I start heading for the back of the property, picking my way through overgrowth and underbrush.

While I wander, I am guessing, checking Gaia maps, looking at my phone for clues, but I have a feeling about where it should be, and when I finally look up, at the back of the property there's a faint path that keeps going, just barely visible through the understory and regrowth. There are a few limbs that I can tell have been taken out by a chainsaw, and so I follow the trail looking for other signs.

Up over a rise I find the edge of Lilypad Lake, and in a slightly overgrown clearing I start to see evidence of the cabin. I find the remains of the former toilet first, tipped back at the base of a tree, and then I notice logs and siding and scraps covered in moss and brush. There are glass shards, some chunks of concrete blocks, and scorched wood. It all feels less reverent than the main site by the lake, less special, even though it was more of a sanctuary for her. I will come back again, with Leslie, who will encourage me to take a bit of wood or siding for a souvenir if I want. She says that eventually it'll all be gone, given back to the wilderness.

When I think about my particular fantasy about being a hermitic writer in the woods, what I really want is what she called *fierce delight.* It's the uninterrupted mornings on the lake or the freedom to strike out on a hike and keep going for as long as you want, feeling strong and long-legged, rambling around as the light filters through the trees. It's the moment of the moon landing, when so many people were in thrall to technology, watching it on TV, while Anne was out solo canoe camping, looking at the moon and the stars directly, from her tent site, on the edge of an empty lake.

FOREVER WILD

To get to the Adirondacks initially, I drive out the Mass Pike from my parents' house. I turn up the Northway, heading deeper into the biggest stretch of wilderness east of the Mississippi, parallel to the Hudson River running down from the mountains. I am still shocked at the scope of the Adirondacks. The park is bigger than Yellowstone, the Everglades, Glacier National Park, and the Grand Canyon National Park combined. It was created in 1885 by the New York State Legislature. It's public land with private inholdings, a patchwork of political jockeying and long-held history. It's still very possible to get lost within those boundaries. This isn't a place I know very well, even though it's only a morning's drive from the city where I grew up. Even as I approach the edges I am surprised by how rugged it feels.

One of the last times I made this drive, out the Pike and then up toward Albany and across, I was moving west. I was fresh out of college, trailing two friends, hatchback fully loaded. I was trying to find a landscape that fit my idea of wildness, a place to stretch out and see what I was made of. It was an ideal largely conceived from books, grown through a few summer vacations, and made real because I bought into the American myth of going West. In the process, I somehow skipped over places like this.

Anne loved the rangy expansiveness of the Adirondacks. Part of why the area has been so well-preserved is that it's geologically wild, rugged, and dense. The Adirondacks' highest mountains are hard domes of anorthosite, a billion-and-a-half-year-old igneous rock more common on the moon than on earth. The peaks were pushed up from the center of the planet by plates colliding a billion years ago, then carved out by more recent glaciation in the Pleistocene. They're new mountains eked out from old rocks.

There are traces of Indigenous groups in the region dating back 10,000 years, before the mountains were carved out by the glaciers, when the Champlain Sea covered the area. In more modern eras, back to some 4,000 years ago, the Six Nations of the Iroquois or Haudenosaunee and the Algonquin tribes, particularly the Mahicans, were active in the area. The Adirondacks were a common hunting ground, and while the tribes were often in conflict, the area was considered *a dish with one spoon*, a peacekeeping concept that meant multiple groups could make use of it.

The first European to have significant impact on the area was French explorer Samuel de Champlain, who came through in 1609, looking for resources and new territory to claim. He immediately got into a fight with the Mohawks, who were members of the Haudenosaunee, a rival of the French-allied Algonquin from the south, who were looking to assert themselves in the region.

The mountains were hard to navigate, especially without local knowledge, and Europeans found the wilderness scary and intimidating, but cash was a powerful motivator, and the Adirondacks were rich in resources like timber and fur, which sparked the beginning of the Beaver Wars. The tribes were pulled into conflict between the French, Dutch, and English over trade routes and trapping territory.

The tribes were decimated by smallpox and measles brought by the Europeans and then by the bloodshed of the trade wars. Their experiences were subsumed and twisted in stories like James Fenimore Cooper's 1826 tale, *The Last of the Mohicans*, which took place during the French and Indian War, and which shaped a specific, wild image of the place, flattened the Indigenous characters into caricatures, either savages or saviors, and gave the settlers narrative power.

The area continued to be a hotbed for conflict between European nations. The British gained legal rule of the area in the French and Indian War, but tensions remained high because the Crown was still taking a cut of the beaver trade, which led to anger about taxations without representation among the English colonists. The Adirondacks became a battleground in the Revolutionary War. French settlers fought alongside the colonists because they were still angry about English rule.

When it was over, in 1783 the government of what would become New York State was given ownership of the former Crown land. But the nascent government was still reeling from war debts and losses. The state needed money, so it sold off most of the initial public land for pennies an acre to lumbermen who deforested 7 million acres of spruce and white pine. By 1850, New York had become the number one lumber-producing state in the US.

As timber production ramped up, Adirondack locals started to worry about erosion and overuse, and visitors started to think differently about what the dense, wild mountains meant to them. After the Civil War, the Adirondacks became a hub for recreation.

Remember that guy William H. H. Murray who seeded the idea of camping? His love for it started here. Every year along with his wife and friends, he would come up from Boston, where he was the pastor at Park Street Church. They'd set up camp at places like Osprey Island at Raquette Lake, where Murray started writing essays exalting the region's natural beauty. He compiled them in his hugely popular book *Adventures in the Wilderness.* With his stories about the virtues of living outside, Murray had tapped into a deep, emotional vein.

By 1869, a flood of campers had found the Adirondacks. In places that might have previously seen a hundred visitors over the season, thousands showed up. Murray's book release aligned with an economic boom, which meant the middle class had more time off and more money for things like books and vacations. By that summer, railroads and telegraphs were also expanding across the Adirondacks, making the region more accessible.

Murray was a minister who underscored the spiritual side of going to the woods. In a time when the country was reeling from division, death, and deep technological changes, he imbued camping with a sense of pilgrimage and purpose. He piggybacked on the practice of outdoor spiritual revivals and meetings, which had sprung up in the middle of the century. In Boston, he overlapped with Emerson and the other Transcendentalists. He internalized their ideas that nature was a version of God. He blamed cities for a rash of social ills and said people should go to the woods to purify their souls, that camping could solve anxiety and achy hearts.

He opened up access in other ways, by including women in equal measure, which was highly progressive at the time.

"Of all who go into the woods, none enjoy the experiences more than ladies, and certain it is that none are more benefited by it," he wrote.

Murray's work reflected a sea change. Wild places could be more than the sum of their extractable resources. They could be places for respite and growth regardless of gender. They could have intrinsic value on their own.

Yet those with access to the benefits of wilderness were often those who needed it the least: the wealthy beneficiaries of industrialization. As urban areas grew denser and more expansive, wild places became rarefied and alluring. Those who didn't need to work the land were drawn to it as a proving ground. By the end of the 1800s, the Adirondacks became a Gilded Age destination.

To get to Great Camp Sagamore, I turn off Highway 28 onto a gravel road lined with boggy woods. On the approach I navigate a wooden bridge, barely wide enough for my station wagon. The stream below splashes over smooth rocks, and once I'm across, it feels like I'm in a different time. I can't keep my Roosevelts straight from my Vanderbilts and Astors, but as I get into the Adirondacks, I know I'm heading deeper into robber-baron country.

Great camp is code for *a Gilded Age mansion in the woods*. The Sagamore compound of 27 buildings sprawls over a point of land projecting into Sagamore Lake. There's a boathouse, a bowling alley, a playhouse, and a dining hall with two massive stone fireplaces. The main lodge is a Swiss-chalet-style behemoth made of rough-hewn logs. Its iron-studded door looks ready for a medieval battle. A servants' compound hides uphill.

I am here for a writing weekend in honor of Anne. She

would lead women in wilderness workshops here when she was alive, taking them canoeing, showing them how to start fires, and sharing stories of her time at the cabin. That tradition still stands after her death, and I'm curious about how her legacy transmits.

After I get settled into my room, I learn about the lodge's history. The previous owners, the Vanderbilts, brought their wealthy friends here by the steam engine. Sagamore is just one of the dozens of great camps that were built at the end of the nineteenth century when the nation's wealthiest families began shaping nature to their own tastes.

Credit for the great camp idea goes to railroad baron Dr. Thomas C. Durant. In 1871, his Union Pacific Railroad completed a train line to the Adirondacks, making the wilderness more accessible at a time when cities were getting particularly polluted and grim. He and his son, William West Durant, thought they could capitalize on it by selling the idea of wilderness retreats. Dr. Durant was a known swindler and schemer. He bankrolled his takeover of the Union Pacific Railroad by smuggling Confederate cotton during the Civil War. In luring the wealthy toward the Adirondacks—and using his own transportation to do so—he turned another profitable scheme.

William started building sprawling complexes where members of polite society could come up from the city and live out their wilderness fantasies in the luxury they were accustomed to, with elaborate meals and ornate places to stay. It was a kind of cosplay of life in the wilderness, similar to the dude-ranch experiences emerging at the same time in Wyoming, where wealthy East Coasters would ride horses and round up cattle. Those same people came to the northern woods to spend their summers at great camps. They hired locals to take them to hunting grounds and bait their fishing hooks.

The New York State Outdoor Guides Association officially formed in 1891. Locals found that they could make a living off showing city people outdoor skills. The early days of guiding in the Adirondacks became the bones of the outdoor industry, which is now a trillion-dollar economy supporting 7.6 million jobs, according to reports from the US Department of Commerce. Recreation jobs are still some of the most viable in the Adirondacks, especially in the places where development is banned. To Anne, it felt like a way to be a part of the area's history and future, and a way for her to support her life outside.

In Anne's first years at the cabin, she met a neighbor named Rob, a licensed New York State guide. Anne was curious about his career and wondered what it would take to get licensed. She had guiding experience from Audubon and from working with Major in the summers, but she wanted to learn the skills necessary to being a traditional Adirondack guide.

Rob started taking her along to check traplines and suss out remote trails. They spent the next few summers hiking hundreds of miles into the Pigeon Lake Wilderness, climbing the Adirondack High Peaks, and tracing the edges of the park's many lakes. "She was learning her territory," Leslie said.

Anne was also learning how to survive outside. Rob taught her trapping and trail knowledge, how to carry gear, and how to rig a boat. He also taught her how to bring other people into the process, the core skill of being a guide.

For Anne, that mentorship was crucial. Now there are formal tests, but when Anne got her guide badge in 1970, Rob had to vouch for her in front of the association. That year, there were about 250 licensed guides in the state, and while there had been female guides as early as the late 1800s, when women like Julia Burton Preston were licensed, there had never been more than a handful of women at any given time. Anne said she was one of three.

For Anne, living in the cabin was already a crash course in navigating the north woods, and she was in the midst of her PhD work, which gave her a lens to understand the ecological web of the region, but that guide pin gave external proof of her expertise. It gave her another way to work outside. It was part of the puzzle of making her life valuable, stringing together different jobs and different sectors, combining the things she cared about. "The environmental movement and the feminist movement began about 1970, making my profession even more legitimate and justifying my long quest for women's equality," she wrote.

Yet despite cultural shifts, she still faced roadblocks. Many of the other male guides didn't take her seriously, especially because she focused her business on teaching ecology to women, instead of the hunting and fishing that had long been the core practices of the guides' association.

She led all-women retreats like the one I'm on at Sagamore, but she also felt trapped by the way women were sidelined or siphoned off to smaller venues. For her, both not guiding women and only guiding women were frustrating. I can relate to that tension. I inadvertently cringe at anything labeled *just for women.* I even feel a little embarrassed about being at this retreat, even though it's getting me closer to Anne.

One afternoon, Leslie and another woman, a local poet, lead us on a guided paddle around Sagamore Lake. Leslie lets me borrow Anne's solo canoe, an Old Town Royalex that

Leslie unearthed from under a tarp on Anne's property and refinished. The boat is light and nimble, and while a canoe is not my craft of choice, with my wonky J-stroke I can almost keep up with the others, who are paired up in their standard canoes. We curve around the rocky edge of shore, stopping in small coves to circle up and talk about the tenor of this place and about Anne. The lake is still under a scrim of clouds. It feels good knowing Anne spent time here, paddling this particular canoe. I like that in some small way I'm layering my story on top of hers.

Starting in the 1860s, a curious lawyer from Albany, Verplanck Colvin, began surveying the natural resources in the Adirondacks. Tourism, the timber industry, and canal construction had taken a toll. Whole hillsides were eroding, and streams were choked with debris. Colvin was a mountaineer who had made first ascents of some of the Adirondack High Peaks. He spent the next 30 years conducting a wide-ranging geological survey of the area and linked deforestation and logging with erosion and reduced stream flows. In 1873, he published an excoriating report, concluding that the deterioration of the Adirondack watershed would threaten the economy of the whole state.

His work inspired conservation efforts. It took nearly a decade, but on May 15, 1885, Governor David B. Hill signed the Adirondack and Catskill Forest Preserves into law, with the requirement that state lands in 14 counties "be forever kept as wild forest lands."

It was a start, but people like Colvin pushed for more protection. The Adirondack Park was established in 1892 by New York governor Roswell P. Flower. And in 1894, in part because the

Board of Trade and Transportation wanted to protect its commercial waterways, New York ratified the state constitution to include Article 14, which is commonly known as the Forever Wild clause. It reads: "The lands of the state, now owned or hereafter acquired, constituting the forest preserve as fixed by law, shall be forever kept as wild forest lands. They shall not be leased, sold or exchanged, or be taken by any corporation, public or private, nor shall the timber thereon be sold or removed or destroyed."

The Forever Wild clause halted industrial growth within its boundaries and gave Anne a personal stake in a large, untouched wilderness. "This far-sighted, totally unprecedented, wise conservation act is actually what made my dream of building a cabin in the wilderness—in the second-most-populated state of the Union—possible," she wrote in *Woodswoman.* "Because of it, I have almost three million acres of untouched forest as my backyard. Without it, I shudder to think what scruffy piece of cutover land I might have purchased in my search for a home in the woods."

The 6-million-acre Adirondack Park holds 2,759 lakes, 30,000 miles of waterways, and 46 high peaks. No other state has their forest parks protected under their constitution. But the protection is complicated. Forty-five percent of Adirondack Park is the state-owned Forever Wild forest preserve, and a million acres of that is true, designated Wilderness, but there is still logging, development, and building within the park. The state land can't be touched, but, because of the history of selling sections off to lumber companies and the way the robber barons bought large wilderness tracts, more than half of the land within the park boundaries is private. It's a patchwork of industrialization, tourism, and personal use, tied to the history of extraction and recreation, and how that use follows the curve of capital.

It's a poignant example of how, in the US, we theoretically love the idea of wide open places, but in practice we carve those places up wherever we can.

Right now, I can feel the impact of those land-use choices. There are fires over the border in Canada while I'm staying at Sagamore. What will end up being a record-breaking wildfire season is stretching its legs across all the provinces. The fires started in May and didn't stop, and some of them would burn through the winter. And by June the smoke had sunk south.

At Sagamore, the wind shifts and a heavy purple haze settles in over the lake, diffusing the daylight. Even with the windows closed, the smoke seeps into the old buildings; everywhere is ashy.

I can feel the smoke in my throat. I don't sleep well. My heart races, the same feeling I get when I'm anxious. And really, I *am* anxious. Those fires feel like a clear example of the danger of our changed climate. The worry compounds itself in my body. I wake up gritty-eyed and mealy-mouthed, mildly panicked, trying not to extrapolate the fires too far into the future.

But in spite of the air quality warnings and my racing heart, I decide I want to paddle on the last morning. As the sun tries to break through the smoke, I slip out of the lodge, slide a kayak into the glassy water, and paddle out to the point, trying not to breathe too deeply.

I can feel the history of deforestation when I breathe, how we've changed the way the forests cycle their carbon and their growth. It comes from logging, from tamping down good fires, and from the well-intentioned but poorly planned protection of places like this. Those stresses seem condensed here on these landscapes we say we love. That noticeable change is what radicalized Anne and made her care.

From the time the Durants built the camp on the lake to when I paddled around it, interest in the region drastically changed. First the rail brought people in, and then cars did. There were 8 million automobiles on the road in the 1920s; by the end of the decade the numbers had nearly tripled to 23 million. Car traffic was also foot traffic: It brought people to the edges of the woods, where they could then trample in. When I-87, the Adirondack Northway, was built into the eastern edge of the Adirondacks, it brought more people, more cars.

Emilio Meinecke, the US Forest Service plant pathologist who invented the now-pervasive loop campground as a way to mitigate car-tire damage on fragile ecosystems, called camping "peculiarly American." He said it highlighted the tension between freedom to roam and explore and the long-term damage that personal actions can create. In the late 1920s, Meinecke worried that nature was being loved to death.

The post–World War II era saw another uptick in recreation, similar to the one after the Civil War. Recreational visits to forest lands increased from 18 million in 1946 to nearly 102 million by 1961. People had money and mobility, and they wanted to explore. A surplus of military outdoor gear came back to the States, flooding the market—that's how Georgie got her raft—and veterans went to the woods seeking solace in the come-down after traumatic combat. In the Adirondacks, the veterans created ski resorts, like Whiteface, and outdoor schools, like the Winter Mountaineering School.

The new wave of outdoorspeople wanted to travel deeper into wilderness, alone, under their own power. By the middle of the twentieth century, backpacking became a popular pastime. In the '60s and '70s, nearly 1 million people moved out of urban areas to rural places, many of them homesteading, as part of the back-to-the-land movement, which rejected technology and globalization in favor of self-sufficiency and connection to nature.

But as environmental disasters, like the Santa Barbara oil spill and the Cuyahoga River fire that led to federal environmental regulations, started to happen more frequently in the '60s, the growing outdoor-recreation culture began to align with a burgeoning ecological awareness. It became clear that the idea of unlimited, untouched nature was a fallacy, and recreationists became some of the loudest voices for conservation and regulation.

America has more public land than any country in the world, but in the first half of the twentieth century, land managers were trying to thread the needle between protecting landscapes and promoting recreation or industrial use on those lands. There was no one-size-fits-all definition of what public land meant, what kind of value or use was appropriate, or who got to decide.

To try to make that clear, in the 1930s ecologist Aldo Leopold, US Forest Service chief Bob Marshall, and Benton MacKaye—the guy behind the Appalachian Trail—formed the Wilderness Society. They wanted to permanently protect fragile, valuable landscapes.

In 1956, they started drafting the Wilderness Act, a bill to protect wilderness areas across the country in perpetuity. They submitted the bill 66 times, tweaking it along the way. At the time, taking land out of commercial use or production was a fundamental framework shift. It went against ideas of productivity that were considered deeply American.

In 1964, the same year Anne moved to the cabin, Congress finally passed the Wilderness Act. President Lyndon B. Johnson signed it into law in September and immediately put 9.1 million acres of land into the National Wilderness Preservation System. It was unprecedented: No other country had a policy anything like it.

The act, notably poetic and lofty for a piece of legislation, defines wilderness "as an area where the earth and its community of life are untrammeled by man, where man himself is a visitor who does not remain." In addition to being free from human impairment, wilderness had to be at least 5000 acres and contain "outstanding opportunities for solitude or a primitive and unconfined type of recreation."

The act was radical in stating that wild places have intrinsic value, but it was also inherently flawed. The act's definition of wilderness separates humans from nature in an unnatural way by placing boundaries around protected land. In doing so, it ignores Indigenous history. Much of the land that was considered public or wild had been taken, often violently, from its original inhabitants. The idea of untouched nature is a myth, one we continue to perpetuate. Even the Wilderness Society founders were obsessed with the false idea that their grandparents had enjoyed a more pure experience. But they were also onto something. The way we started to use landscapes after industrialization was different: faster, more punishing, more resource-intensive. Cars and chainsaws changed the game. In the face of rising human encroachment, the Wilderness Society proposed an ethic of stewardship and preservation. "Better a wounded wilderness than none at all," Wallace Stegner wrote.

That ethic wasn't isolated. In the 1960s, organizations like the National Outdoor Leadership School and Outward Bound started programs that connected moral character with outdoor activity. They took young people into the backcountry for long stretches of time to teach them self-reliance and the importance of wild places. Both NOLS founder Paul Petzoldt and Outward Bound cofounder Lawrence Holt had served in the military and brought ideas about navigation and precision to their organizations, alongside lessons in environmental impact and self-discovery.

I know the impact of those ideas firsthand. The summer after I graduated high school, I set off on a monthlong Outward Bound course. It was my graduation present. I'd come up with the idea of going, but it proved to be more complicated than the starry-eyed vision of nature submersion I'd conceived. We'd watch the sun sink down over Colorado's Collegiate Peaks after satisfyingly exhausting days, but we'd also eat lumpy powdered eggs under a patchy tarp in a downpour. I'd hope my squelchy boots would dry and that the blisters on my hip bones would callus up.

As hard as it was, that trip was pivotal for me. It was my first glimpse of how important extended time in the wilderness can be. At the end, they sent us off alone for 3 solo days. I spent the time journaling about the ways I would spin my new skills out into the future, rationing the packet of nuts and raisins they gave us, feeling the newly hardened muscles in my legs. I still crave that feeling of satisfaction.

By 1971, right around the time when Anne was getting certified as an Adirondack guide, women made up a third of NOLS participants. It was a positive spike, attributable perhaps to a coalescence of '60s feminism and the way it dovetailed with the environmental movement.

But while other parts of the outdoor world were evolving,

in Anne's time the outdoor scene in the Adirondacks was still male dominated and oriented around hook-and-bullet culture. That wasn't what Anne cared about. "I don't guide to hunt and fish; I guide to show people about the ecology," she wrote.

She wanted to give people the language and skills to understand both ecosystem connectivity and the fragility of the Adirondacks. "I want to show, with local, concrete examples, how the destruction of our environment has speeded up, and how fast we are losing natural resources, clean air and water, even silence," she wrote.

As she became more established, she said she had two goals for guiding: One was that ecological bent, and the second was to inspire women to get out. She wanted women, "particularly older women—those of my generation who did not grow up with women's liberation—to act with more independence and self-reliance." She was sure that the wilderness could be a wellspring for them, as it had been for her.

Anne said that when she was guiding women, who became her main clientele, even just setting up camp could feel groundbreaking. She would show the women how to dig catholes and stake tents and take them swimming with loons. She tried to make the campouts comfortable, safe, and, above all, joyful. They would paddle through the lake and then be quiet, to see what they could hear. During the day, she'd show her clients how to live lightly on the land. She'd teach them the names of plants and animals and how to travel efficiently. Around the campfire, she'd read Leopold and Thoreau.

Yet even in her expressed empowerment, Anne could be dismissive of other women. Like Georgie, she clung to her singular status. On her all-women trips she relished her role as the expert. When she wrote about the women she guided, she flattened and minimized them, calling them *fleshy* and *unconfident*, noting their lack of skills. It felt like she didn't quite take them seriously, like they weren't as good as she was. She didn't like being lumped in with other women; she wanted to be special.

I'm uncomfortable with this dimension of Anne, maybe because I recognize the same judgmental streak in myself. I feel it bubbling up at Sagamore. I think less of other women in the canoe circle when they fumble from lack of experience. I try to distance myself from the group, even though I chose to be here. I don't want to be minimized because I'm female: I want to be considered just as capable as anyone, and it shows up in ugly ways. So to untangle my feelings, I head out on a solo night of backpacking after the Sagamore trip. I hope to get to the heart of what I really want.

Hiking in, I had an idea of where I could camp, but once I get there, the lakeshore is boggy and buggy, with nowhere perfectly flat and dry. I berate myself a little for picking a bad place. There is no one else to blame.

I set up my small red tent in a wedge of a meadow and unstuff my sleeping bag and the rest of my gear, setting it up the way I want, taking my time. After a sandwich for dinner, I sit by the edge of the water to watch the light change. A sliver of sundown, no bold sunset, just gradual darkening until it's too dim to read without a light, and my circle of awareness shrinks. I settle into my sleeping bag, and once the ruffling of polypropylene stops I can hear the night around me breathing in.

I go out camping as often as I can. I love the physicality and the plain directive: move forward, eat, sleep, see things. I love being tired, I love going to bed as soon as the stars come out and waking up in the sunny morning dust.

But often I feel like I'm performing a false austerity, a preprogrammed pattern of slight suffering so I can pat myself on the back. In this way, I'm not much different from the robber barons or the guys who started NOLS.

But I also know that camping brings me back to myself. I spend nights on the ground because it reminds me that the planet supports us, that I'm just a tiny piece of an enormous interconnected system. I think Anne, even when she fumbled, was trying to give other women that feeling of connection because she felt it so strongly in herself. It was what she felt on her first solo backpacking trip, venturing out from Covewood alone with just a cache of dried soup, learning the simplicity of days outside. "In my opinion camping can be the greatest expression of free will, personal independence, innate ability, and resourcefulness possible today in our industrialized urbanized existence," she wrote in *Woodswoman*. "Regardless of how miserable or how splendid the circumstances, the sheer experience of camping seems a total justification for doing it."

IN THE FIELD

Despite my complicated feelings about Thoreau, I'll always be drawn to the lake I knew first and best. Every time I go home, I go back to Walden Pond with my father, who gave me the maybe-misguided moral baseline that being physically tough was a part of being good. We've been swimming here most of my life by now. These days I swim alone in other, bigger lakes. My strokes are longer than his, and I've gotten better at letting the water carry me, but as a kid I would follow the white ghost fish of his feet and tell myself that nothing bad could happen as long as I kept them in sight.

On a trip to the Adirondacks, I squeeze in a visit to my parents, and on the morning my dad and I can find time to swim together, we dump our towels and sandals on the concrete wall at the back of the Walden beach. I stretch on a cap and goggles as I walk to the water. Usually we swim along the north shore, tracing the underwater ledge where the depths drop off. My father likes to watch the scrim of the bottom glide by. I find the dark void less scary somehow.

I stop short at the lake's edge. There are hundreds of tiny, silver fish, finger-sized, shiny, dead. Their bodies are tangled in algae scum and sloughed-off Band-Aids. I recoil, unnerved.

"What do you think," I ask my dad, who so often has a reason. "Something in the water?"

"Maybe too hot?" he says, guessing.

Later I would learn that the fish kills were happening in other ponds and in other places that summer, too. Too little dissolved oxygen, too much heat. The biogeochemistry pushed beyond sustainable for the fragile fry. Their bodies evidence of bigger changes in the ecosystem.

Past the mica-flecked flash of fish bodies ringing the flat belly of the lake, the water level is lower than I ever remember. Standing there in my Speedo, I feel unhinged by the change. But the lake is supposedly still swimmable. So we do what we've always done—we dive in.

I open my eyes underwater as I started gliding, like I usually do, until I realize there are more dead fish. I screw my eyes shut inside my goggles and swim. Later I will struggle to get the smell off my skin. But there in the shallows it feels like the only thing to do is to keep going.

It's not just the fish that are impacted by climate change. In 2003, when scientists from Boston University looked back at Thoreau's writing—which tracked the dates around seasonal shifts and flower blooms—they found that spring plants were budding out 18 days earlier than they had when he was writing. It's sped up even more since then, and the acceleration impacts birds and bugs and more.

Anne kept similar notes, and observational data like theirs shows that subtle, variable changes are slanting our planet toward ecosystem erosion. We see the impact of acid rain from accrued industrial pollution or the curve of rising lake temperatures. Maybe, like me, you've felt the filament of dead fish against your skin or sensed that every spring seems to come sooner and hotter. Putting facts behind those feelings is core to our ecological understanding—and our ability to do anything about it.

Anne went to the lake, in part, to understand those changes. You need the power of observation to be a good writer and a good scientist, and her time at the cabin sharpened those senses. "Becoming a woodswoman was merely an extension of being an ecologist and nature writer," she wrote.

Anne checked the lake temperature every day. She noted the dates and direction of bird migration. Over the years, she saw major changes in biodiversity, soundscape, chemistry, and heat. She noticed the lake was warmer earlier, and she saw fewer otters and bullfrogs. And in time that attention led from casual observation to quantifiable research. She bought instruments to track the pH of the lake and conducted animal surveys. "She was pretty early on the side of climate change recorded in literature, that's landmark," says Middlebury professor Megan Mayhew Bergman. But sometimes, when Anne's story gets told, that landmark research gets sidelined.

While Anne got attention for the independence she wrote about in *Woodswoman*, she really wanted to be known for her research. She wrote that goal in her teenage diary that Leslie found. She vowed to break ground in science, so other women could, too. She worked hard to be respected as a researcher and she lamented that her work was overshadowed by the story of being the lady alone in the woods.

Anne said her spiritual home was the Adirondacks, but some of her most notable conservation work happened half a world away, at a remote lake in Guatemala.

She'd had ties to South and Central America since she'd

traveled there as a child while her mother chased down artifacts and her father worked. With Major, she'd frequently led expeditions to the Caribbean and Central America. She'd been with Major when she first went to Lake Atitlán in 1960 and spotted a short-billed water bird she couldn't identify in any field guide. Locals said it was a sneaky, flightless bird that could stay underwater for 30 minutes. She was gripped by the lack of information and by the bird's quirky habits. As a naturalist, it was her job to identify species, and later that week, at the museum of natural history in Guatemala City, she learned the bird was the giant pied-billed grebe, an endemic species of Atitlán. Two scientists had conducted partial census studies before. Each saw about 200 birds, so there was a tiny bit of scientific data, but otherwise the research was scant. Anne, who loved lake birds, and who must have been looking for a research challenge, was fascinated by the mystery.

After they left, the birds and the clear blue volcanic lake in the Sierra Madre highlands stuck in her mind. She decided she wanted to go back to the lake as a researcher instead of a guide to spend more time with the little-known bird.

But she didn't get a chance to go back until after her divorce, 4 years later, when she no longer had to work as a guide alongside Major. That winter, she bought a ticket to Guatemala with plans to stay for a month in Panajachel, the only lakeside town with a paved road. She rented a room from Dona Rosa, a woman she'd met on her last visit. Major was sending her $100 a month in alimony, which she used to pay for the room and rent a boat. In addition to field gear, she purchased a dress in hopes of assimilating with the locals.

Poc is the Tz'utujil name for the bird because it makes a *poc-poc-poc* sound when calling its chicks. The grebes were mythic.

Locals spun folktales about how they committed suicide by diving down and biting onto reeds at the bottom. Anne decided she would take a survey of the grebes and track their population.

Lake Atitlán is a mile high and 1,200 feet deep, surrounded by volcanic cones and lush cloud forests. In the '60s, approximately 38,000 people lived in the 12 villages along its rim, mainly connected by boat. It was beautiful, but it could be dangerous. Windstorms, called *chocomil*, would kick up in the afternoon as the temperatures climbed, sending angry, mixed-up waves across the lake. Anne's first day out, the motor on her ancient rental boat died in the middle of the lake, just as the storm started up. It took her nearly an hour to get to shore, and she said she came close to sinking twice.

A neighbor found a safer boat for her and helped her navigate into the reeds, where the birds nested. She put herself to work, trying to count every giant grebe on the lake. Mated pairs of birds built 100-pound floating nests deep in the reed banks along the shore. Anne had to crawl through the reeds to find them, sometimes in snorkel gear, sometimes floating in an inner tube.

She started to record their calls and identify their patterns and mating rituals. She was thrilled by her new discoveries, even when she was pummeled with sunstroke and mystery rashes from the water. She found 22 nests, and estimated there were 88 grebes on the lake, less than half the number that had been reported before.

Anne saw some of the locals cutting reeds and thought that might be the cause of the die-off. But Dona Rosa corrected her: They'd been cutting reeds for generations, so that was unlikely to be the reason for the decline. Anne kept wading through the reeds, looking for clues. One day she saw divers spearfishing for non-native black bass and figured there might be another cause.

It turned out that Pan American Airways and the local Panajachel hotel association had teamed up to introduce the bass for sportfishing—a draw for foreign tourists. "This was done without any experimentation or research, and against the recommendations of a US Fish and Wildlife Service technician. The first release was several dozen fingerlings; the second, 2,000," Anne found.

She was determined to do something about the invasive fish, which she was sure were eating the grebe's food source. But tracking the cause of an issue and translating it into action is one of the trickiest parts of conservation. Once the invasive fish were introduced, the impacts were diffuse and hard to control. At the time, Guatemala's natural resource department was just 4 people. They didn't have the bandwidth to focus on Atitlán's grebe population. Anne decided to stay for another month and reached out to the World Wildlife Fund, who gave her a little bit of grant funding, and to *National Geographic*, who commissioned her to write about the birds.

Anne went back to the US motivated to help the birds and applied to the wildlife ecology PhD program at Cornell. She figured the work in Guatemala could be the basis for her dissertation, and she loved being back out in the field, running research and solving problems on the ground.

She went back to Guatemala the next winter with funding for a conservation campaign from the World Wildlife Fund International. More grants followed from the Smithsonian Institution, the International Council for Bird Preservation (now called BirdLife International), and the National Geographic

Society, among others. She'd also identified potential legal pathways to protect the birds. "There were two Guatemalan laws that might help, but few people knew of them, and there were no game wardens to enforce them in Guatemala. One law protected all water birds at Lake Atitlán, and the other declared the lake's surface and watershed a national park," she wrote.

A local friend encouraged her to lean into the laws. He helped set up a meeting with the Guatemalan minister of agriculture, who appointed a game warden to enforce the laws as best as possible. Anne was also given an honorary warden title, which she loved.

"All my life I'd wanted to be a game warden. Perhaps it was the pride of wearing a uniform and having the authority to protect wildlife. Perhaps it was the challenge of an all-male profession where women were the exception. Perhaps it was the romance associated with working in the field and under rugged conditions," she wrote. "I was probably the only female conservation officer in the Western Hemisphere, albeit an honorary one. It was not usual for women to work professionally outdoors and shoulder to shoulder with men in law enforcement. My head was high, pigtails flying in the wind."

Her time in Guatemala felt great, but back in New York, where she was trying to adjust to life at Cornell, things weren't as easy. She was shuttling back and forth to the cabin at Twitchell because she didn't want to be constrained on campus. She felt like a cooped-up teenager instead of an adult who had been running a business for nearly a decade. Her grades were poor, her dorm room was depressing, and she was mired in busywork and misogyny.

She found solace in the ornithology lab with professors

like Bill Dilger, who helped talk her out of quitting many times. She took an international conservation class, which gave her ideas about winning public support and sympathy for the *poc* through cultural programs. Together with people on the ground in Guatemala, she drew up plans to build a bird refuge and to mitigate the impact of invasive fish. They talked to the villagers about how to sustainably cut reeds—a plan that became a presidential decree in 1968.

"By June 1968, we had completed a three-acre refuge with a visitor's center and dock near Santiago Atitlán. At the inauguration, our small sanctuary was officially declared Guatemala's first national wildlife refuge," she wrote. "And best of all, the grebes had reversed their downward trend. They continued to increase until 1975, reaching a high of 232."

But the next year, when she went back to Lake Atitlán with two of her Cornell professors, she found the lake changed. The villages were busy with tourists, and vacation homes were cropping up. Multiple hotels and a 16-story condo tower were being constructed on the lakeshore. There were fewer reeds along the banks because developers weren't constrained by the same reed-cutting laws that the locals were, and effluent from the building was piped straight into the lake without regulation. The lake, which she'd seen as pristine, was changing.

On her visit, Anne learned about a proposed hydroelectric project, which would have dropped the lake's water level by 40 feet, killing the reedbeds and diverting polluted rivers into the lake. Ecologically it was a nightmare, but the developing country needed power, and the project would have created local jobs. Anne wrote stories and told her international network of environmental advocates about the damages it would cause, and because of her exposure the dam was never built.

She kept working, pulling in international grants to fund the conservation work, publicizing the *poc*'s plight. After finishing her thesis, she returned to Guatemala in 1972. The game warden told her things were good, the bird population was steady, and that she shouldn't worry.

In 1974, she was awarded the World Wildlife Fund Gold Medal for Conservation for her work with the *pocs*, an accolade Leslie said meant a lot to her, because she felt like it legitimized her work connecting the dots on conservation, development, and invasive species.

Everything was stable for a few years. But there were bigger geopolitical and ecological forces at play.

In 1976, a 7.5 magnitude earthquake hit Guatemala and ran 240 kilometers along the Motagua Fault. Across the country 23,000 people died, and 3 times that many were injured. At first, Anne's community at Lake Atitlán seemed like they had been spared much damage because they were far enough away from the epicenter of the earthquake. No one was harmed. But then the lake started dropping, and it didn't come back up. The quake fissured the lake's lava-rock base, and water was seeping through. Over the next 2 years, the lake dropped 4 feet. The sanctuary they had worked so hard to build dried up, and most of the historic reedbeds sat above the new high waterline. The grebes didn't have anywhere to nest. Their population plummeted. By 1980, their numbers were down to 100, and they were considered endangered.

Then the political situation exploded. Civil war between guerrilla forces and the government had been raging in Guatemala since 1960. In the late '70s, military rule and violence ramped up, and in 1982, General Efraín Ríos Montt seized power in a military coup. He annulled the constitution, leading to the most violent period of the 30-plus-year war, especially against Indigenous Maya.

In 1982, Edgar Bauer, the man who had become the game warden and Anne's closest friend there, was killed, likely by guerrillas. The Guatemalan military took over the site of the former grebe sanctuary and turned it into a prison and an armed stronghold. Any kind of work to protect the birds collapsed.

Anne didn't go back to Guatemala until 1984, when the US Fish and Wildlife Service and the Guatemalan government set up a survey to check on the birds. The reed habitat had diminished by 80 percent, and they only found 50 birds, barely enough to sustain a population. They tried to undertake a captive-breeding program, but they didn't have enough *poc*s to make it work. By the summer of 1986, when the population was down to 20 birds, not enough to adequately reproduce, the giant pied-billed grebe was declared extinct.

Anne was outwardly resigned—she wanted to seem like an objective scientist—but on the inside she was crushed. She'd tried to get everything right. She'd wheedled locals to change their ways and lobbied international organizations. She'd worked herself sick in the reeds. But in the end the struggle didn't matter, and the quirky flightless bird was lost to a jumble of development choices, deregulation, violence, and overwhelm. She'd brought the *poc* population back from the brink, only to lose them to factors out of her control. She decided she had to do more. She couldn't just be an impartial researcher.

"Always I'd considered myself nonpolitical; my concern had always been more for the natural world than the sociopolitical arena. But now I saw that ethics and politics are critical to the safekeeping of the environment, as much so as the natural activity of soils and precipitation."

After her time in Central America, she had more experience, more tools, more international recognition. She'd learned how to organize and how to work with governments. Back in New York she was seeing similar factors play out across her home landscape. Even in the protected Adirondack Park, inholdings like the area around Twitchell could still be developed. She'd seen effluent pumping into the lakes, just like at Atitlán. And she'd seen how tourism could erode wild places, bit by bit. The ecosystem was impacted by pollution, ineffective policy, and overuse. She threw her energy into researching and protecting the Adirondacks, using the lessons she'd learned in South America.

But her work in Guatemala confused a lot of people. It didn't align with the idea of the Adirondack woodswoman. When *Mama Poc*, her book about the grebes, came out in 1990, it didn't sell well, and Penny Harr says Anne was frustrated by the lack of interest. She wanted to be taken seriously for the science she was conducting outside the Adirondacks. She knew she could be both a hermit at the cabin and an international conservationist. But by then her image had calcified, and it was hard for people to see her as both. "People criticize her for not paying more attention to issues of this country, and for pouring her resources into Central America and Latin America, but she was passionate about conservation in underfunded and underdeveloped countries," Leslie said. "She thought her work at Atitlán was the groundbreaking work in her life."

Anne was constantly frustrated by how she was perceived. After fighting through her master's program, and then largely sidelining her ambitions for Major's ideas, she craved legitimacy and recognition. She applied to the Cornell PhD program to try to achieve that. She thought her unprecedented grebe research would get her there.

In 1948, a few professors had broken out of Cornell's former Department of Forestry and joined with ornithologists and ichthyologists to form the Department of Conservation. By 1970, it would become the Department of Natural Resources, to reflect the rapidly changing ways researchers studied the natural world. Resource management was by then expanding to incorporate new fields like conservation biology and environmental science. Anne waded into that changing ecosystem in 1965, ready to get her PhD. The Wilderness Act had just passed, and Rachel Carson's *Silent Spring* had recently been published. Broader culture was slowly connecting the dots between people and environmental changes. The word *ecosystem* had only been coined in 1935. The idea of human-driven climate change had been studied in some form since the 1890s, but the term *global warming* wouldn't be coined until the 1970s, and *climate change* would show up for the first time in a 1979 National Academy of Sciences study on carbon dioxide.

Research was skating around those connections between human impact and broadscale environmental change. Anne had seen those changes firsthand in Guatemala, and she came back to the States eager to share what she'd learned. But once she was back in Ithaca, she grew frustrated.

The field was starting to tilt toward the kind of interdisciplinary work she was doing, which braided ornithology, ecology, and more, but at the university she wasn't taken very seriously because of how she conducted research and how she shared it. She was connecting the dots between global choices and point source impact and writing for a broad audience instead of just academic journals. She'd published an academic paper about her research in Guatemala, but she'd also published articles in *National Geographic* and other popular magazines. The grebe research was powerful because she'd translated it into conservation and species preservation, but Jim Lassoie, a friend and fellow Cornell professor, said that the kind of science she was doing—widely focused and intended for a broad audience, with an explicit call to action—wasn't respected in the ivory tower of academia, where journal-paper numbers were the ultimate sign of impact. "I had wildlife ecology friends of mine into the '80s who called her work *fluff* and would completely discount it," he told me.

Anne felt alienated from the other, younger, male students who didn't feel like her peers. She said some of her professors were her age or younger and had less experience than she did. They were all men. She found it hard to connect or to be taken seriously.

I asked Jim, who joined the Cornell faculty in 1976, how much of that was because of her nontraditional methods and communication style and how much of it was because she was a woman. He said that some of it was just flat-out gender discrimination and that there was heavy gender bias. "In a forestry school in the '60s, women were by today's standards harassed," he said. It wasn't just Cornell. Other female scientists and wildlife biologists, like Anne Innis Dagg, who was one of the first people to study giraffes in the wild, faced similar barriers and disrespect.

Despite that lack of equity—or perhaps because of it—in 1969 Anne was hired by Cornell as the first female professor in the department. But she only lasted 2 years in the role. By 1971, she had resigned from teaching and become a consultant.

Anne was outwardly diplomatic about her choice to leave.

She never spoke badly about the school, but both Leslie and Jim Lassoie told me that she felt frustrated and pushed out. She liked teaching and having students, but she felt boxed in by the strictures and schedule of academia and by the scrim of misogyny that sat just under the surface. Leslie said some of her all-male coworkers were jealous or mad about the international attention she gained, like the 1974 WWF conservationist award. Even that was a symbol of how she was doing things differently.

I'm sure it wasn't just the others who made things hard for her. She was also stubborn and independent. Bullheaded to a fault, she didn't want to conform or change her lifestyle or her way of doing research. So when she ran up against roadblocks at Cornell, she decided not to fight the culture. She quit and became a consultant, back at the lake.

It's a little over 3 hours from Cornell to Twitchell Lake. You drive up through Rome and Remsen, cutting through the Black River Wild Forest and the Ha-De-Ron-Dah Wilderness, getting deeper into the woods. "There is a clarity to the web of life here, a clear sense of the vital force at work in our ecosystems, even though it is the warp and woof of only 12,000 years of evolution since the last ice age," Anne wrote, when she came back. She loved the dense ecotone where the boreal forest meshed into the woodlands and marshes, and the range between the harsh, rocky high peaks and the myriad lakes. But even the Adirondacks weren't immune to environmental change.

In 1971, in part because of her work with the grebes, Anne was hired by the newly formed Environmental Protection Agency as part of the Documerica Project. One hundred photographers were commissioned to shoot photos of urban blights and eroding forests, strip mines, and leaching sewage to show the impacts of pollution and unchecked industrial growth, and to underscore what needed to be done about it. They captured kids playing by billowing smokestacks and chemically mutated fish. Anne documented change in the Adirondacks, where increasing levels of industrial pollutants and the fallout of fading industry was coming to bear. She shot black bears breaking into trash heaps and paper mills leaching effluent; she shot tourist traffic and clear-cut tree stands. "The color images from the 1970s show us that Americans must keep lenses sharply focused until environmental solutions are realized," C. Jerry Simmons, from the National Archives, said about the project. Now we're more aware of the rising heat and rising storms, in part because of the point-source storytelling that comes through in things like those pictures. And after that project, Anne's focus followed the trail of those environmental pollutants and how they were seeping into the Adirondacks.

Anne felt the difference when she swam. The lake seemed changed. It was too clear, too quiet. She noticed fewer ospreys and kingfishers around the banks. Fishermen said trout numbers were down. The bullfrogs, which had once been loud around the lake, had gone quiet. She counted only five where there had once been hundreds. Sphagnum algae and blackflies thrived, but the ambient sounds, the mix of species, the markers of seasons all seemed different.

In the late '60s, scientists in Europe had started to track the way that acidic rain—which happens when nitrogen oxide and sulfur dioxide, pumped out of factory smokestacks, tailpipes, and power plants, react with water molecules—was turning lakes sour and then seeping into the soil. By the '70s, awareness reached the US, and in 1978, *Outdoor Life* magazine asked Anne to do a story on the topic.

Anne became obsessed with monitoring the impacts of acid rain. She bought a portable pH meter to measure lake acidity and found the water was as sour as vinegar. In the otter droppings she collected in leftover Cool Whip containers, she found no traces of fish bones. The food chain was failing, and it seemed like acidity was the cause.

She broke out her snorkeling gear to see what was going on underwater. In nearby Brooktrout Lake, she found no fish or birds or frogs. "Brooktrout had the eerie feeling of a cemetery," she wrote. It was an unnaturally clear blue. No zooplankton, no freshwater mussels. Just a layer of limp gray slime along the bottom.

Acid rain was hard to track because it had no color, taste, or smell. It was hard to see the impacts until after they were significant, but more than 600 lakes in the Adirondacks were made acidic by what Anne called the "invisible death from the sky."

The next year, *National Geographic* commissioned her to write about acid rain, because she had longitudinal knowledge and because the Adirondacks had become a hot spot for acid rain pollution thanks to the area's prevailing winds, high elevations, thin rocky soils, and heavy precipitation.

She went to other countries for her reporting. In Sweden, where the most progressive research on acid rain was happening, she saw dead lakes, devoid of vegetation and animal noise. They had the same pH as Twitchell Lake. Sweden had effectively reduced its national pollution levels by 80 percent in recent years, but these efforts seemed to have had no impact.

The Swedish researchers were trying to track the source of

the acid. They were pretty sure pollution was blowing in from factories in the Midwestern US as well as from industrialized upwind countries. Anne went to a UN conference and watched emissaries from the UK and Germany deny their emissions impact, saying they couldn't trace it. Just like now, when we're wrestling with the international disparity of carbon emissions and their impacts, it was hard to make the biggest polluters accountable.

Incensed by the lack of accountability and government response, Anne fought back with the same tools she'd used to protect the grebes: writing stories, conducting her own research, and lobbying local and national governments.

"Bringing this about has become my burning ambition and goal. After living in my cabin for 20 years, concerned primarily about bears breaking into my kitchen and trees falling on my roof, I have been suddenly catapulted into space age worries. How could this happen to a simple woodswoman?" she wrote.

The Northeast—and the Adirondacks in particular—was particularly vulnerable to the impacts of acid rain due to weather patterns that carried smog from massive Midwest power plants. Aluminum, mercury, copper, and lead were turning up in drinking-water sources, and that corrosive, acidic water was eating through pipes. As it seeped into the soil, native spruce trees went into decline, turning greenish yellow, then desiccating and splintering.

Anne found that utility companies could reduce acid rain impacts by up to 80 percent by controlling their emissions. She knew what needed to happen. "Power companies have the technology to eliminate most acid rain but are not doing anything about it," she told a conference in 1982. She lobbied for them to be held accountable. She started writing about it more. She got the New York State Department of Health up to the Adirondacks to test groundwater and show the prevalence of acid rain. But progress on big, diffuse environmental issues is categorically slow, and even into the late '80s, the Reagan administration said there wasn't enough evidence about the threats of acid rain to support stricter pollution regulations, despite widespread ecosystem die-off. There was no federal legislation to address the national threat until 1990, when Title IV of the Clean Air Act Amendments was passed, which limited the amount of sulfur dioxide power plants could emit, greatly reducing the spread of acid rain. It passed thanks to collaboration, across-the-aisle politics, and international agreements.

It took decades of national and international work to regulate the causes, but all things considered, acid rain proved to be relatively easy to deal with. Once those Clean Air Act Amendments were in place, emissions dropped by up to 85 percent. The program worked well enough that acid rain feels like a vestige of the past.

Acid rain is one of the best examples of how to successfully address a diffuse environmental problem. Clear international standards that target the sources of the issue—sulfur dioxide and nitrogen oxide from power plants—were imposed, and federal regulations held the biggest contributors responsible. Anne had a hand in it, but as she would learn, history would prove hard to replicate.

In 1988, NASA scientist James Hansen testified in front of Congress about the coming threat he called *global warming.* He predicted that year would be the world's hottest on record, thanks to the burning of fossil fuels, and that the heat would keep increasing if emissions weren't immediately addressed. He said there was only a 1 percent chance he was wrong. His testimony was seen as the beginning of the national dialogue about climate change, even though it would take decades for those facts to be widely recognized.

By the time Hansen was in front of Congress, Anne already felt the changes he was talking about. The skin of ice that had once frozen fast across Twitchell every winter was her clearest marker. By the end of the '70s, it wasn't freezing consistently, making it unsafe to get to the cabin over the lake in the winter.

The Adirondacks were broadly protected by Forever Wild legislation, but by the 1990s, Anne could sense the accrual of human impact. Over the decades, neighbors around Twitchell built and renovated weekend cottages. Power came in through a line that ran under the lake, alongside phone cables and TV antennas. As traffic to the area increased even in that protected parcel, people were collectively living heavier on the land.

Diffusion has long been part of the backcountry fantasy. It's the idea that your impact doesn't matter because the landscape is so vast. *Dilution is the solution to pollution* was long the ruling philosophy for managing environmental toxins, particularly wastewater. In the Grand Canyon, that's what they tell you when you pee in the river. It'll all get washed away.

But there's a tipping point past which diffusion doesn't work.

This was what Anne was learning at the lake, as trash piled up and the water quality changed. "Living in backcountry has taught me not to meddle, except under crisis conditions. Nature is running its own show," Anne wrote, but she felt the Adirondacks had reached that inflection point.

From the moment she got to Twitchell—before she'd even made an offer on the property—Anne delighted in drinking straight from the lake, sucking up what she called *wild water.* But as the lake soured, she worried the off-grid hodgepodge of unregulated plumbing, leach fields, and pit toilets was failing and effluent was running into the lake. When she brought it up at a property-owners meeting, they decided to have volunteers run dye through their faucets and toilets to see if anything leached. They hired a pollution-control officer to run the tests, and Anne shuttled him around in her motorboat. Three places had leaky water, and the homeowners had to address the issues at their own cost.

It seemed a relatively inoffensive ask, but it stirred up animosity. One night Anne came back to her dock at Twitchell and tried to start her boat. When the engine wouldn't turn over, she opened it up and found that her gas lines had been cut. It was the beginning of a barrage of threats. Anne was already unpopular for a range of reasons. She could be difficult, stubborn, emotional. She'd been accused of trying to use her looks or femininity to her advantage. But she started getting explicit threats when she became an advocate for Twitchell's water quality. And then tensions flared even further when she tried to limit motorboat use on the lake.

There had been motorboats on the lake as long as she'd been there. She had a 15-horsepower skiff, which made her life there tenable because she could chug in gear and supplies. The mail boat made laps in the busy season, and on summer evenings neighbors would raft up their motorboats in the middle of the lake for happy hour.

Neighbors started bringing in powerful water-ski boats with 100-horsepower motors. Quicksilver oil slicks mired the surface and drenched the loons. Wake slop washed out shorebird nests, and the cranky hum of motors started early, when the lake was glass. Anne wanted the powerful boats out. She wanted quiet and calm water and was worried about added pollution. Mostly, she wanted things the way they were when she'd first come to the lake. She could lean into science to show the proof of impact. But one of the tenets of recreation is freedom, and this was the freedom those particular people wanted.

Nostalgia is a tricky ideal that underlies a lot of environmental work, from the Wilderness Act, with its mandates to "preserve the wilderness character" of designated places, to the way forests are reseeded after fires. It can be reductive and unrealistic—and occasionally dangerous—to try to freeze environments in time. But nostalgia can also be a necessary piece of idealism, to hold on to the integrity of places that are big and wild, and to fight the inertia of capitalism and industrialization.

Most people around the lake were also in favor of smaller boats, so they collectively put up a petition and then voted on a community-enforced set of regulations. They settled on times of day when fast motors could run and set up future constraints for boat and motor sizes. Existing boats could be grandfathered in, but when they died, they'd have to be replaced by smaller ones that fit the code. It was policy by peer pressure. It worked, and it still stands now.

But Penny Harr, who grew up in a long-standing Adirondack family, says many longtime locals thought Anne was overstepping. It didn't help that she was loud and stubborn and a woman. She was still considered a transplant, even after two decades. It inflamed the locals who had long felt that outsiders with money and power were coming in to change the landscape they loved.

Anne became a lightning rod for that change. Even the way she operated as an Adirondack guide, giving botany tours instead of hunting and fishing instruction, was seen as suspect. In the '70s and '80s when environmental protection and policy ramped up, she became a poster child for government overreach. She wasn't shy about saying she wanted to reinforce the initial legislation that protected the park, a move in line with the sweeping federal environmental protections of the 1970s. But there was tension in speaking up. By the early '80s, Anne sometimes felt her life had become a contradiction. "The gratifying struggle for Anne LaBastille was how to balance her yearning for the serenity of solitude in the wilderness with her mission to let the world know, as best she could, that it must preserve wilderness," *The New York Times* wrote about her.

She said her best tactic for ecological advocacy was to fight short battles against overuse and abuse. "Then you retreat, rest, and restore yourself in quiet, beautiful places," she wrote in *Woodswoman III*. "Thus you can gain strength and inspiration for the next battle. Perhaps that's why Thoreau wrote 'In wildness is the preservation of the World.'"

In wilderness is, at least, the preservation of some sanity. I know that when anxiety tightens my chest, the answer is almost always to go outside. I walk the trail behind my house until it links up with a wider one and then weaves up into the tract of public land that stretches north and west.

Sometimes it's just knowing that the mountains go on beyond me. Sometimes it's the meditation of repetitive motion, coming back to the same trail and noticing how native grass has gone to seed, or that there is a set of animal tracks in the rain-softened dirt, or the way my breathing changes after I hike uphill for a while. Anne needed that, too.

Leslie says that in the days after she hosted retreats or went to public meetings, Anne would disappear with her canoe and slide it into some big, lonesome lake to get back to herself. That lesson comes through in her writing: both the fight and the release. Caitlin Kelly, who has held a wide range of outdoor jobs in the Adirondacks, says that one of the things she loves about Anne is the way she puts physical knowing into words. Anne's pieces about hiking to the high peaks made Caitlin feel connected to her. She could explain the feeling of being up high in those rugged mountains and then show how the experience was linked to a broader understanding of how humans were changing the places around them.

Anne often felt like she was yelling into the void, but she was ahead of her time in connecting the dots. The broad fields of ecology and environmental science have evolved to become more international, more interdisciplinary, and more concerned with climate change. We now know that ecology is how we live in the world, woven in with the birds and the algae and the trash on the shore, unwittingly sucking in tainted water, wishing the ice would still freeze.

GETTING BURNED

One afternoon, driving back from Twitchell in the gathering gray of a storm, I stop for a sandwich in Inlet, a hamlet along Highway 28, one of the few roads across the park, which all seem to wind along waterways and then pool up in the knotty little towns. I pull over in what seems like a summer town, even though it's not quite summer vacation yet and the sky feels threatening. I wonder what it looks like in November.

I eat my lunch and wander along at vacation pace. I get a coffee for the road at the Blue Line Coffee House and poke my head into the hardware store, which is stocked with balsam incense, beach towels, and pillows shaped like loons.

The Adirondacks have 123,000 full-time residents, and, like Penny, many of them have generational ties. They hold down the businesses in towns like Inlet, working in construction or manufacturing or agriculture or tourism, which is one of the area's biggest economies. Somewhere between 7 and 10 million people visit the Adirondacks each year, stopping through towns like this on their way to hike or hang around the lakes or climb high peaks.

In his 1960 wilderness letter, which was a part of the argument for the Wilderness Act, Wallace Stegner wrote of the need for spaces like this. "We simply need that wild country available to us, even if we never do more than drive to its edge and look in. For it can be a means of reassuring ourselves of our sanity as creatures, a part of the geography of hope."

Anne could be a woodswoman because of that edge; she could easily disappear into the wilderness, but over her years at the cabin, it was changing. After the Northway interstate was finished in 1967, developers started building up resorts and condos on chunks of private land. Motels and mini-malls cropped up. Adirondackers were divided about the best ways to keep a balance between nature and the built world.

The state government stepped in. In June of 1971, New York governor Nelson Rockefeller signed legislation creating the Adirondack Park Agency, which would prepare master plans for the public land in the face of increased use and manage growth and development on those private inholdings within the park.

In 1973, Governor Rockefeller signed the Adirondack Park Land Use and Development Plan, which further delineated use in the private sector, limiting what could be built. The bill was controversial, and many property owners were incensed. Statewide, about a third of the comments about the plan were in support, and some environmental groups worried that the new plan didn't do *enough* to preserve the wilderness. But the vast majority of park residents opposed the plan. They argued that the rules were being imposed by outsiders who didn't understand their values or desires. They felt like the agency was stealing their property and limiting their rights. They said the plan was unconstitutional, and that it was crushing the local economy, which was already fragile. The whole country fell into an economic slump in the mid '70s, driven by stagflation, but within the park it was easy to blame the agency for the lack of opportunity. It didn't help that the agency was bureaucratic, disorganized, and overwhelmed with a small staff and a big mission.

"One man told me, 'I'd rather burn the woods to the ground than let the Adirondack Park Agency tell me what to do!'" Anne told Henry L. Diamond, who was then commissioner of the Department of Environmental Conservation. "Another guy I know calls it 'the biggest land grab since the Bolshevik Revolution.'"

The angry locals formed lobbying groups like League for Adirondack Citizens' Rights, which hosted rallies and protests, and the Adirondack Defense League, a spin-off group organized by vocal residents Tony D'Elia and Frank Casier, who would later admit to petty violence against the APA.

Other groups sprang up to lead counterprotests in favor of increased conservation, and over the next few decades the divergent groups factionalized over wildlife, economics, community, politics, and the way land was used.

"They say we want to erase the hands of man from the Adirondacks by the year 2000. We say keep man in the center of his natural environment as the protector and steward of the great Adirondack wilderness," the League wrote in their Adirondackers' Survival Kit in the mid-1970s, a clever piece of anti-APA propaganda.

It opened up hard questions about values, ones that are still relevant. Where do people fit within a highly valued and regulated landscape? Is Adirondack Park a place to visit or a place to make a living? And if you divide the small number of locals from the big number of visitors, which group should have more of a say?

Anne became an APA commissioner in 1975, at a moment when journalist David Helvarg noted "one of the most militant property rights movements in the United States . . . escalated from protests to punches to vandalism and an organized campaign of terror involving death threats, arson, and gunfire . . ." She became a target for the vocal, and sometimes violent, opposition to regulation.

Anne was the first commissioner with a science background (the others were foresters, and business- and landowners) and the second woman. Leslie said Anne lobbied for herself to get the position. "She liked the recognition and liked to be in an important position and have influence," she told me. She saw it as a continuation of her work blending conservation biology, land management, wildlife protection, and pollution monitoring.

She was the most conservation-minded person on the commission, against development and for regulation because of the concrete harms she saw happening to the park. She was frustrated that others weren't taking protection seriously, and that she had to fight for things she saw as obvious, like regulating water pollution. "She once slammed her hand down three times at a meeting. 'It's a park it's a park it's a park,' she said," her friend Marty Hogan told me.

Elizabeth Thorndike, who served on the APA with Anne, said she wasn't great at compromise or listening to other views, which made her an easy target. "Much of the work of an APA commissioner is political in nature, and that was not her strong suit."

By 1990, tempers boiled over about plans for the park. In May, a group of anti-APA protesters shut down the Northway. The group, led by state senator Ronald Stafford, was protesting a recent building moratorium and a plan for the state to purchase an additional 650,000 acres. They were worried that if the state bought large tracts of land for preservation, the local economy would suffer, so they started staging protests. "The Adirondacks had their own version of a Sagebrush Rebellion," Leslie said.

Similar conflicts had been bubbling up across the country, most notably in Nevada, where large chunks of the landscape were federally owned. In the 1970s, when the Federal Land Policy and Management Act ended homesteading and made the remaining unclaimed land the property of the government, a number of people, particularly those in Western states, objected. They started calling themselves Sagebrush Rebels. They wanted local control, less regulation, and minimal government interference. They saw the regulations as a cultural attack from out-of-touch Washington politicians, particularly President Carter. In a time when industry and extraction were slumping and the economy was down, the federal government seemed like the right place to place blame. They staged protests, got into altercations with officials, and put forward political candidates, often bankrolled by extractive industries. They violently raised a perpetual factionalization in land-management philosophy about whether decisions should be made on a broad, landscape-level scale or a local one.

The first wave of the Sagebrush Rebellion quieted in the Reagan years, but we still see its specter, including famously in 2016 when armed members of the Nevada-based Bundy family of ranchers, who had clashed with the Bureau of Land Management over grazing fees, took over the Malheur National Wildlife Refuge in Oregon in a standoff. The anti-government militants were fighting for a misplaced belief that the public lands should be returned to them by the federal government. Forty-one days later, one of the militants was dead, and their argument did not hold up in court.

Anne valued individual freedom as much as anyone. She didn't want to be constrained by rules, but she'd also seen the impact of human incursion, from leaky septic tanks to industrial pollution. She believed in the power of government regulation, and she was loud about it, which made her enemies.

"The people who didn't like her didn't like her because she was stubborn," Penny said. "If it was a man, it wouldn't be as much of an issue. Women get trashed for being who they are."

Anne was frustrated that developers were putting corporate profits before the sanctity of the natural world. She was angry that she couldn't just regulate emissions. Pissed that she wasn't being listened to or taken seriously. And that rage further heightened tensions with the people who had been threatening her.

In 1993, psychologist Sandra Thomas conducted what's commonly called the Women's Anger study and found that women's anger had three main roots: powerlessness, injustice, and the irresponsibility of other people. While men and women tend to experience anger with the same frequency, women's anger, and negative emotions in general, are less culturally normalized. As girls we're often told to be agreeable and likable. We're shamed for outbursts of emotion. Additional studies have found that men gain power when they express anger, while women lose credibility if they do. They found that both men and women judge angry women. It's no wonder Anne became a target.

Nature didn't scare or disappoint Anne, but people did. Harassment had been part of her world since she first published *Woodswoman*, and arguably before that. "Developers would hire guys to threaten her. She had her cabin broken into. Every misogynist in the world was after her," her friend Marty told me.

In 1988, she bought a farmhouse in Wadhams, New York, on the east side of the park, with money she inherited from her mother. It was no longer safe to get to the cabin in the winter. Anne was nearly 60 and sick of fighting off visitors. As the lake got busier, the farm was supposed to be a new kind of hideout.

The farmhouse was in rough shape. She cleaned out the inside and moved her mom's furniture in, chopping the legs off tables with her chainsaw to fit them through the front door. She started working on the outbuildings and the grounds, growing the garden she'd never had at the lake. By the summer of 1992, she'd started restoring the 85-year-old barn where she'd keep a truck and a small sailboat.

One evening that August, in the heat of the controversy over the park commission's rules, she thought she heard noises in the woods, but her dogs didn't seem spooked, so she figured it was nothing. She puttered in the garden and then took off for the cabin.

The next morning her handyman called. In the middle of the night, a plane bound for Burlington, Vermont, had spotted something burning and alerted the local fire department. By the time they showed up, her barn was engulfed. They spent the rest of the night fighting the fire, but by the morning it was a scorched husk of century-old timbers. The truck inside was reduced to twisted metal and ash. Sleeping bags had melted into puddles.

In 2004, Frank Casier, who was a founder of the anti-APA Adirondack Defense League, made a passing comment to a journalist that indicated he'd had something to do with it. "Now, there was a woman named Anne LaBastille who was a lady commissioner on the APA had a barn burned, where she had a play farm. That was probably the most aggressive thing. I think if I had to do it over again, I would do more aggressive things than we did," he told writer Brad Edmondson. That confession seems suspicious to me, but at the time, the Bureau of Criminal Investigation inspector couldn't track the cause, and no one was ever charged.

Anne was devastated, her sense of safety irreparably shaken. Later she learned that the same morning a prominent local environmental lawyer woke up to graffiti scrawled across his office building. There was an attempted arson at the APA's main office. APA staff had been shot at. Anne was scared that whoever burned the barn might go further and harm her or her dogs.

"I'm a woman alone, so I'm a great target," she said.

She said it felt like a nightmare. "I never went out at night around the farm. I never drove anywhere or went to bed without a firearm. I never slept more than four hours a night at a stretch. I never stopped jumping at loud noises. I never stopped thinking about this assault to my professional life and the mockery it made of my environmental convictions," she wrote.

In 1993, after 17 years as a park commissioner, she stopped attending meetings and eventually resigned. She said she felt ineffective. She was afraid to be outspoken and to vote for the environment. The fire took her courage and her voice.

Scared out of public environmental-advocacy work, Anne focused her energy on another issue: getting more women outside. "We need to feminize ecology and bring on more grassroots activism. We should use our female powers of keen observation, extrasensory perception, diplomacy, and persuasion," she wrote in *Woodswoman II*, tying together women's liberation with environmental advocacy.

Her words are strident and bossy. I want to roll my eyes a little. But I also believe in that connection. And I know that she was trying to live up to those words.

In addition to the workshops and guiding, in 1980 she published *Women and Wilderness* with the Sierra Club, where she profiled 15 other women who were working in the outdoors, including Becca Lawton, the Grand Canyon guide. She set up a scholarship at Cornell for female PhD candidates and remained a symbolic mentor to many more, but she prioritized one-on-one relationships, too, like the one she had with Leslie, which evolved from the first time they met, when Leslie was a kid and Anne rescued her after she flipped a snowmobile, into an adult mentorship.

Leslie says Anne was often frustrated that her ideas weren't seeping into broader culture, especially as environmental regulation stalled. She had enough ego that she wanted to be seen. But her impact was diffuse, and it persists today. Penny Harr notes that women will sometimes visit the Adirondack Experience Museum, put their hands on Anne's cabin, and cry. She's seen people bring their daughters and granddaughters. She recommends Anne's books, and patrons will sometimes come back, having read them, eager to chat. "She basically bucked the system at every turn. I think that's why she resonates. She had the guts to do what she wanted to do," Penny says.

It's hard to be a hermit as you age. For Anne, tendrils of dementia rooted into her brain, and she grew increasingly disoriented. She didn't have any close family, and many of her friends were scattered or distant. At one point, worried about her during a huge blizzard that shut down the Northway, her friend Marty called the state troopers and asked them to visit the farm for a welfare check. "She's fine," they reported back, "but she has no idea who you are."

By the early 2000s, her ability to process and make decisions started to slip. Penny Harr thinks her habit of drinking straight from the lake might have played a role, especially after traces of aluminum and other minerals started showing up in the water. Megan Mayhew Bergman wonders if her isolation was a factor. The Center for Disease Control says that being alone can break down your neuroplasticity, and that social isolation increases your risk of dementia by 50 percent.

In 2008, Anne checked herself into long-term memory care and gave away her pets. It was the first summer since 1964 that she hadn't spent at the lake.

Inside, under the fluorescent lights, she withered. Like Georgie, she didn't do well away from her home landscape. Anne died in 2011, in long-term care, away from her home on the lake.

That next Monday, Leslie came home to a message from a lawyer. "It said, 'I'm an attorney and you're Anne's successor,'" she told me, shaking her head. "I had no idea that she'd even put me in that role. Five years before, she'd called me and said, 'You know I think the world of you. I'm setting things up for when I'm no longer here. Will you help see that things are done?' Five years go by and here I find out I'm the executor!"

Leslie is a scientist who likes to do things right; she's both hyperlogical and loyally tender. Anne was 25 years her elder, but the two became adventure partners and close friends. And now she had the complicated task of wrangling with her legacy.

Anne laid out grand plans in her will, including long-term funding for the scholarship at Cornell and a writing retreat at the cabin supported by a nonprofit. But as Leslie quickly found, the details of her final wishes weren't always logistically or economically feasible. She met with lawyers, judges, and Anne's distant relatives to come up with a plan that retained the spirit of what she wanted. Leslie set up the scholarship, sponsored a writing retreat on Twitchell, and turned the cabin site over to the forest preserve.

She also handled Anne's papers and effects. All the storage at the cabin, under the deck and in all the outbuildings, was stuffed with drafts and slide film and tchotchkes. Leslie spent 4 years of vacation time cleaning the cabin and making plans with the state and the museum to take over the land and the buildings.

Anne didn't feel like she got the attention she wanted, but she had rabid fans, even after her death. "I had one guy who took it upon himself to go on her land and take pictures of the things piled up and post it on Facebook," Leslie told me. "This guy picked a big fight, and he thought he had every right to do it because he was a fan."

He was angry because he was holding on to a specific vision of Anne as the capable, sparse woodswoman, holed up in her simple cabin.

"Anne was very hard to put in any kind of particular box," Jim Lassoie told me. "She was constant confliction." He thinks of her muddy feet and painted toenails as a perfect reflection of the dichotomy.

Once I knew the way to West of the Wind, I went back a bunch, and each time I noticed more. At first, I'd just seen the bones of the cabin site and the plaque, the dock. I could still imagine the simplicity. But after visiting with Leslie, I learned of a series of decomposing outbuildings, including the one for

Anne's phone and a fax machine. I'd been fascinated by Anne's asceticism and devotion to nature, but I now know that in later years Anne had had to add layers—the second cabin and the technology—to realistically protect her core value of living close to the land. I came in looking for clues about how to live independently in the woods, and about what might make that kind of devotion to nature work, and I learned that it's not that simple and that if you think it is, you're ignoring the changes, neglecting to notice your own lake getting hot.

One evening I stay late on the edge of Twitchell, watching the shadows go long, wrapping a layer around me in the faint summer chill, sitting with the ghosts of Anne's desires. Dusk was when Anne felt her most victorious and her most lonely, and she wrote about the whole range: how good it felt to canoe out into the lake in the dark and stare up at the stars, as well as how she felt flattened by harassment and isolation, both in her body and in her mind. Penny says Anne is a beacon of independence, defiance, and physical competency. She represents the importance of science, observation, and being outside. She had the guts to keep doing what she felt was right.

As the lake grows dark, I get up from the dock and head back to town. Before I go, I dip my hands in the water and thank Anne for the chance to see the whole story.

Our last night at the Camp Sagamore retreat, circled up inside to escape the smoke, Leslie breaks out a bottle of Jack Daniel's and a case of Coke cans so we can make Anne's favorite cocktail. It was the first week of July, the same time of year, nearly 60 years ago, that Anne moved into the cabin. We toast to her and to the enduring pull of her stories, and then Leslie reads a bit from *Woodswoman III*. In the passage, Anne comes back to the cabin to see that one of her favorite spruce trees has died and fallen down. She'd been at the cabin for more than 40 years, and the tree had been there for far longer. She mourned the loss. But she also saw something in its downfall. "Its very decomposition can teach me another lesson about life," she wrote. "As the spruce merges with the earth, I'll witness another phase in its energy cycle, one common to all living things. If I can see this botanical reincarnation take place, I can find courage. I can then truly believe that life leads to death leads to life."

DOLORES LaCHAPELLE

TUNING IN

It's Wednesday morning, the day after the equinox, when the light begins to shift and change. Long spring shadows are already starting to slide through the trees, and although it's 25 degrees in the parking lot when I pull in, I'm guessing it will be T-shirt weather by the time I get moving.

This is the rhythm of backcountry skiing. Cold at the car in the blue early light, stomping feet and rushing to switch layers and boots, swilling coffee to stay warm. I throw my puffy jacket into my backpack and take my gloves off quickly to buckle everything down. I switch my avalanche beacon to Transmit. I click my boots into my binding and start skinning uphill, getting into the pattern of the slap and glide and pull. I pump my arms and wait for my body to warm to the climb.

I'm alone on the McMillan Peak ski track, one of the most popular places to backcountry ski here in the thin air of the San Juan Mountains, just north of Silverton, Colorado. McMillan is popular among skiers because it's easy to access and because it's too shallow to be avalanche-prone. It's a safe zone to ski when avalanche danger is high, or if you're alone, like I am. McMillan was also, I've heard, one of Dolores LaChapelle's favorite places to ski.

The mountain, deceivingly, gets flatter as you climb. Above

tree line, McMillan becomes a moonscape, a wide stretch of bowls and peaks marred by ski tracks and roughened by wind. In a thin skiff of snow, I see signs of one skier ahead of me, but otherwise the terrain is covered in a feathery glitter of surface hoar, the snow crystals that form on cold, windless nights when the air sucks moisture out of the snowpack. It makes the mountain gleam as the sun climbs higher.

I strip down to a base layer in the rising heat and push up the last pitch to the peak, which drops off steeply on the other side. I am conscious of the hollow pockets in the snowpack, which have a Styrofoam echo underfoot, and of the concavities that could cause an avalanche. I picked this place because it's relatively safe, but because I'm alone, I'm still on alert.

You can feel the San Juans in your body. The sky is so big and the air so thin. Every little high point reveals a new horizon. I can see cloud shadows on the peaks to the west. I watch a bird track a lazy thermal on the ridge of Trico Peak. There is texture all the way to Telluride, and up here where it's strangely windless I can hear an airplane going by.

Up here I can think better. I'm trying to do what Dolores called *tuning*: paying attention to the terrain and what the mountain might be trying to tell me. Listening to my body. I am trying to quiet my mind in the way she might have.

Dolores was an independent environmental philosopher, enmeshed in the nascent idea of deep ecology, which took a holistic view of ecosystem connectivity starting in the '70s. She was a thought leader in the radical environmental movement, where her ideas about ecology impacted activist groups like Earth First! That came, in a lot of ways, from these particular mountains.

She's the next link in the genealogy of Georgie and Anne. In my mind, she's the *why* to their *what* and *how*. Like Georgie and Anne, she didn't compromise on her commitment to a specific landscape, even when it cost her credibility, comfort, companionship.

That's because she was a skier first. Dolores was an early pioneer of what we might now call big mountain skiing. She shaped the way I'm currently moving in these mountains and the way I think about them. Skiing is what led her to philosophy and shaped her desire to understand the natural world and her place within it.

Like Georgie, she had a spiky, uncompromising desire to go hard in wild places. Like Anne, she fought for the health of the landscape as an observer and an advocate. She was knotty and complicated. I'm up here because I'm hoping that I can learn something from the way she tried to understand *why* we want to be outside.

Dolores is an important link for me because skiing is a big part of the reason why I've focused my life on being outside. It was the catalyst. I moved West to work at ski mountains, and then, when my body and brain wouldn't take it anymore, I became an editor at skiing magazines. While I cover a wider purview today, skiing often still governs how I spend time and who I spend it with. It's a visceral obsession I can't shake, the most clear distillation of myself in motion, and the most tangible way for me to feel connected to nature and the way it's changing. Dolores worked to explain that precise feeling.

Though the San Juan Mountains shaped her philosophy, she ended up here by accident, following her then-husband, famed snow scientist Ed LaChapelle. Like Georgie, who went to the canyon after the death of her daughter, and Anne, who sought solitude in the wake of divorce, it would take a life-altering event to radicalize Dolores.

It would take an avalanche.

In 1963, Dolores was living at Alta, Utah, where her husband, Ed, was working to develop avalanche-control protocols for the ski area and the Forest Service.

When they got there, Alta, one of the first American ski resorts, was under the radar. Snowbird Ski Area, which would become a behemoth on the other side of the Mount Baldy ridgeline, wouldn't exist for nearly a decade, and the LaChapelles were part of a small group living and working at the end of the canyon, tied together by their singular focus on snow. It was the kind of tight-knit community her friends said she chased for the rest of her life.

At the end of the ski day, after the tourists cleared out and the light got glittery and low, Dolores would join some of those friends—including people like Jim Shane, who built the Goldminer's Daughter Lodge, and Junior Bounous, who laid out and ran Snowbird—for one last run. They'd ski trails like Gunsight or High Nowhere or slide out to the end of the High Traverse, Dolores often leading the charge, known for her witchy ability to predict when the clouds would clear.

Dolores, who had always been introspective and hyperanalytical, was already thinking about the point of skiing and what it meant to her to be in sync with her environment. She said that when they skied big, uncontrolled lines, like they did on those last runs, they'd pause at the top of the slope and ask the snow if it was ready for them.

The LaChapelles had come to Alta in 1952 for Ed's job, and

while the couple had initially connected over their love for the mountains, by the spring of 1963 the relationship had grown stagnant. Dolores felt constrained by the strictures of gender and motherhood. That spring she was in an excruciating flirtation with another man at Alta, even though she was married and he had a girlfriend. She felt tortured by the guilt of her Catholic upbringing, which made her feel like she was sinning. Stressed, angry, and frustrated, she tried to work through her feelings by skiing.

In the first week of March, friends were visiting, and after a skimpy winter, a big storm finally came in, blanketing the mountain. Their group skied bell to bell, tracking out every part of the ski hill, and then, for that last run, they decided to ski a steep section of terrain called Gun Tower Bowl, in what's now Snowbird terrain. It's a rarely skied rocky ridgeline pinched by gullies and framed by what's called the Menopause Cliffs, which she said were named because they were so steep and dramatic that they could change your life.

Dolores was comfortable in high-consequence terrain. She'd already claimed first descents in the Wasatch, including down the famed Baldy Chute. She had some ego. She was cocky and impatient.

That afternoon she was out of sorts, distracted by her torturous crush, by leading visitors, by the rush of storm skiing. When they went to ski the last line, she was behind the group. Her binding had come off, and she stopped to fix it. By the time she got to the top of the run, her four male ski partners were waiting for her partway down the trail, right before the pinch point. Usually you wouldn't ski steep, avalanche-prone lines the day after a storm, but Dolores said the snow had felt solid all day. She felt confident and hungry for a rush. Clare

Menzel, a historian who studies Dolores, says she wonders if she stopped to ask the mountain if it was ready for them on that run.

She skied past the group. Maybe words or warnings were missed as she pitched over the slope. At the top of the chute, she skied out into an opening and felt the world evaporate. The surface dissolved as a weak layer collapsed, and cracks shot 100 feet across the slope. The snow beneath her started to accelerate.

She yelled for her partners as the slide took her down the mountain, raking her over cliff bands and pushing her through the trees. The snow pummeled her as it pinched into the gullies below, picking up steam as it did. Her first thought when she was tumbling was that if her husband or his colleagues had to dig her out she'd never be allowed to ski powder again.

Snow swiftly hardens when its crystals are rearranged by force, and as it slowed down, Dolores knew her best chance at survival was giving her friends a clue to her whereabouts. She punched her hand toward the surface as it solidified. Luckily, she was close to the surface. Her friends dug her out fast, but she'd broken multiple bones, and her recovery was brutal and long. While she was trapped, she wondered if the slide was punishment for her unchaste thoughts, and then her thinking flipped: If the gods were that vengeful, why would she want to believe in them? The slide must have been because of her ego. She hadn't been listening to the mountain.

As she lay in a hospital bed in Salt Lake City, in a cast from her chest to her toes, she started writing. She wrote a spoof about avalanches as romantic interests and why she felt so transfixed by snow, and then she kept going, digging into bigger questions: Why was she this obsessed? Why was she spared? What was she supposed to learn?

In the slide, she dislocated her right hip and broke bones in her left leg, but she also fractured her sense of control over the environment. An avalanche is an apt metaphor for releasing trapped tension. She knew that she'd been lucky and that she probably wouldn't get another chance to be so cocky. To ski in deep powder you had to give yourself over to the mountain, listen to the slope and the snow, let it move you. She started to call that listening *tuning*.

From there her ideas expanded into what became her core philosophy: that skiing was a way to fully integrate yourself within a larger ecosystem. The avalanche also led to epiphanies in her personal life. She vowed to leave her fraught marriage and abandon the Catholic teachings she'd grown up with, which now seemed at odds with her newfound feelings around openness and ecological consciousness.

It was a slow burn. She wouldn't leave Ed for another decade, once they'd already moved to another mountain range, and she would struggle with the framework of religion for years, but in the hospital she started writing and gathering the threads.

I can't remember when I first heard Dolores's name, but I know that when I was deep in researching a book about the idea of being a ski bum, her book *Deep Powder Snow* became a kind of totem. I'd heard that the slim palm-sized book was a sacred text for skiers, out of print and coveted. Copies sold online for hundreds of dollars.

It came to me when it was supposed to, I think. I was in Silverton, stuck there in a storm cycle, with the passes on both sides closed. I was at the brewery with Jen Brill, a Silverton transplant who started a ski mountain in town and who had become friends with Dolores. Both of them were seekers, strong in their convictions, trying to find ritual and connection. Jen had inherited some *Deep Powder Snow* copies after Dolores died. She had a box of them in storage, she told me. She wanted me to have one.

I read the book that evening—ripped through it, really—by the fire in my friend's cabin in Silverton, as he was out avalanche forecasting, part of Ed's legacy. Even though I had been searching for the book, I'd been a bit skeptical about Dolores. Before then I'd only heard quotes out of context. I'd thought of her as New Agey, maybe a bit out to lunch and unserious, just obsessed with skiing.

Feeding logs into the fire, a black dog by my feet, I found the book, which shows how skiing shaped her philosophy, to be something very different. Parts of *Deep Powder Snow* are difficult to read—Dolores skips around; sometimes the language is heavy-handed, dull, and self-reverential—but the pages articulated something that I'd been trying and failing to say about why being outside, pushing my body, felt important and about how it connected me to something much bigger.

Dolores writes about why physical motion is worth chasing, and how seeing ourselves as small pieces of an ecosystem soothes something neural and deep. *Deep Powder Snow* outlined a philosophy of place, and our place within it. That feels like the heart of the question I've been asking about these outdoor heroes, and why they feel important to me.

Dolores published 5 books over 25 years, some of which are dense and complicated. *Deep Powder Snow* is her most condensed, cogent work. The book established her as a guru in specific snowy circles. Parts of it are highly quotable ("Powder snow skiing is not fun. It's life, fully lived" gets tossed around a lot), and it often gets distilled to make Dolores seem like a thrill-seeking ambassador of pleasure. But that simplification frustrated her. Skiing was important because it gave her a sense of ecological connectivity, but it also showed how industrialization and growth were wrecking the fragile ecological balance. She didn't like the way skiing had become selfish and commercialized, and like Anne, she considered herself much deeper than the one cultish piece of writing that placed her into a bit of a spotlight. She thought people were missing the point. She was worried about change.

On my climb up McMillan I move through the ruins of multiple former mines. The Weminuche, the largest wilderness in Colorado, stretches to the southeast of here, but the peaks are stippled with centuries of mining and industrial use, tunnels and ghost towns. It looks pristine until you notice the wildflowers growing around the tailing piles, and the streams that run coppery with minerals. Scars of what Dolores called the *industrial growth society* are everywhere.

I can feel the change she was afraid of. This year will be the hottest in history, as has been almost every year this century, and I can see it here in the alpine, where the snow turns thick and leaded with heat. It's so present it feels painful, and I'm hoping her ideas about tuning in can teach me what to do about it. It feels good to be thinking about it here, in a landscape I want to settle in, where I'm honing my own sense of place.

I sit on the top of McMillan long enough to follow the

light on the peaks. I can trace the summit of Golden Horn down the ridge to Ice Lakes. I know the angles of the Battleship mountain, which looks bigger and steeper and more striated from different directions.

I rip off my climbing skins, put my skis back on, and look down into the bowl, planning my line. So many ski decisions around here are made by wind or light or heat. You can use the mountain like a compass, feeling the south side warm up first. Picking your aspects based on the breeze.

I ask the slope if it's ready, like Dolores did. Then I tip over. The snow feels like smooth ball bearings, a texture that comes from the warm granularity of spring, frozen and rewarmed. The feel is familiar, but today the surface formed hollow and bright and something in the snow crystals sparkles like a dense carpet of sparks. I'm dropping through a meadow of sequins, every crystal catching the light. My turns swish with a metallic crispiness, and everything feels smooth.

I finally stop at the edge of the meadow, unbelieving. I catch my breath and look back up at my tracks, tracing the sparks, tuned in.

THE BEST WOMAN POWDER SKIER IN THE WORLD

Six months before my spring ski, on the eve of the fall equinox—after I'd come back from the Adirondacks—I am outside the Silverton Powerhouse, in the clear autumn air, listening to Katrina Blair, one of Dolores's disciples, talk about plant medicine. I am here for a gathering of people who are trying to hold on to her legacy. I feel like a bit of an interloper. I never met Dolores, and I'm still new to this particular pocket of the San Juan Mountains.

The season is starting to slide, the hills are golden around us, and the wind swirls the grass in the field. Katrina is a biologist who runs a community farm and restaurant. She teaches classes about foraging and permaculture, but her biggest focus is wild edible plants, the neglected and underloved weeds we often remove but which are part of the local ecosystem. She's also a hardened adventurer who has spent months at a time in the woods, living on foods she's foraged from these harsh, dry mountains. Katrina calls Silverton the only place in San Juan County flat enough to hold a community—everything else is vertical mountains.

Every year Katrina walks from her home in Durango to Telluride, surviving on what she finds. She tells us about some of her favorite plants to forage, but she keeps backing up to the personal history that had brought her there. It turns out, the hook came when she was a kid, alone on a lakeshore, separated from her family, slightly freaked out, and she says that the plants there told her to sit still, to be among them, that they'd be with her forever.

She says that when she first met Dolores, she mentioned that story, even though it sounded hokey, and Dolores kept nodding. She knew what Katrina was talking about because she'd had a similar experience. As a kid, wandering home from a friend's house in the north Denver neighborhood where she grew up, Dolores felt compelled to sit down under the cottonwoods that lined the local irrigation ditch. She lay in the grass watching the clouds move across the sky and listening to the seedpods rustle. "I was suddenly enveloped in a feeling of complete happiness. I felt totally at one with everything yet totally myself—and infinitely important," she wrote in her book *Earth Wisdom*. She'd chase that feeling of connection for the rest of her life, but it was a desire she hid for decades because it didn't align with the religious doctrine she grew up with or the scientific world she grew into.

I had early moments like that, too. I remember being in the ocean, past the dunes from my grandparents' house, one summer when I was small. I was floating past the break when I realized I could predict the pattern and pulse of the water if I paid attention, and that I could let it carry me. I felt a similar sensation the first time I learned the swirl and flush of a river. Maybe you've felt that, too.

Dolores was born in Kentucky, but soon after she and her sisters, Pat and Tiny, were born, her family moved to Denver, right on the edge of the city limits. Her father, Adrian, had been diagnosed with tuberculosis during his service in World War I, and Denver's climate was considered good for lung health. The three girls roamed the neighborhood, sledding the ditches, finding animals to bring home, exploring the meadows that stretched out past the edge of the houses. They had free rein physically, but they were constrained by the strictures of their Catholic faith, which Mary Dolores—her given name—took very seriously. As a kid she loved the ceremony and sense of community that came through the church.

Right after her seventeenth birthday, her father, who was working at Lowry Field, a US Army Air Force training facility that was built in a former sanatorium for tuberculosis patients, found a flyer for a Colorado Mountain Club climbing trip to Pikes Peak. Dolores begged to go, Adrian called to see if high-school kids were welcome, and in July her parents dropped her at the bus stop for the trip to Colorado Springs. Along with 40 others, Dolores spent the night at the base of the mountain and woke up at two in the morning to attempt the summit. She was ill-prepared and inexperienced. She'd left all her layers at the base camp and didn't know how to pace herself at altitude. Her flimsy tennis shoes wore through, so she reportedly hiked down barefoot.

She was in love. From then on she spent most weekends on club trips and spent all the money she made in her part-time job at a bakery on boots and gear.

Like the church her family was devoted to, the CMC was a community that could sweep her up, bring her along, make her feel like part of something. Similar outdoor groups were growing across the country as part of that widespread push toward outdoor recreation that emerged in the post–World

War II era. It was democratic—groups were broken up by skill level—and collaborative. To Dolores, it made the mountains seem open; she was only limited by what her body could do.

That next winter was a stormy one, and Dolores was committed to keeping up with the club. The week after Christmas, she and her sister Pat signed up for a trip to the Zipfelberger Cabin on Loveland Pass, which crosses the Continental Divide an hour west of Denver. A flood of outdoor gear was coming back from the war, and she'd been bilked into buying 7-foot-long hickory army surplus skis by a clerk at a Denver ski and tennis shop who had no idea what he was talking about. They got into the club truck with a group of strangers and were dropped off beside a snowfield halfway up the pass. She and Pat slid down the hill on their new, clunky gear, snowplowing under a full moon, fumbling and falling, losing the rest of the group. Dolores said despite the heavy skis and general disorientation, that was the day she decided skiing was what she wanted to do for the rest of her life.

In the spring, she went on another trip with the CMC that sealed the deal. They spent multiple nights at the cabin, skinning and skiing in the belly of a big storm, wind-whipped and floundering in deep snow. Dolores said she skied all day and dreamed about skiing all night. On Monday she showed up for her first week of college at the University of Denver with a badly sunburned face. But all she could think about was when she'd get to ski again.

Dolores had always been a good student, and she was a voracious reader and writer, but college felt unfulfilling. As a history major, she felt she was being fed stilted Eurocentric stories and half-truths. She finished her classes in 3 years, minoring in botany and teaching and graduating as a Phi Beta Kappa, with the goal of getting a job in a mountain town.

When Dolores graduated in the summer of 1947, she put in applications for teaching jobs in the mountains through DU's teacher placement agency. "The first one is Aspen," the agent said over the phone. Dolores accepted before hearing her other options. She knew Aspen had just installed the longest chairlift in the world.

Aspen's fancy new Lift 1 was indicative of how recreation, and skiing in particular, was changing. Before the chairlift, Aspen skiers were pulled up the mountain on toboggans driven by a truck engine, as well as by rope tows that were popular in other small ski areas. But in the wake of World War II, the return of veterans and gear, and the injection of quick capital into the economy, new technologies emerged. Aspen became—and still is—a mecca for celebrities, athletes, and socialites.

Aspen Mountain is steep, snowy, and complex, with leg-burning groomers and seemingly endless bowls. These days there's a gondola that brings you up from the heart of town, but to get there you walk through what is essentially an ultra-luxe shopping mall, past Prada and Gucci and Louis Vuitton. It's beautiful, but it's rarefied, and if you want to live there, you'll have to pay a premium. The average home price hovers around 3 million dollars, but most of the people who work there, particularly in the service sectors necessary to maintain a place like Aspen, don't live there. Much of the time I've spent there has been spent covering the ripple effects of that disparity.

Aspen is a clear example of how the outdoor experience became financially inaccessible to many when we started commodifying recreation in a serious manner, particularly in that flush postwar era. It's what Dolores—and Anne and Georgie—rightly worried would happen to the places they loved.

But Aspen in the '40s, when Dolores got there, was something very different. Like the Grand Canyon in the early days of boating, it was populated by a small, wild group squeezing the most out of the outdoors. Many were World War II veterans, trying to shake off the violence of their war experiences before settling down. They created a culture driven by hedonism and adventure, and that attitude would pervade Aspen for decades. But when Dolores came to town in the fall of 1947, the scene was only just emerging.

She lived with other teachers in employee housing and found a coupon for locals that let her take 10 ski lessons for cheap. She took those lessons and then kept going, skiing every day she could. She was the only schoolteacher who skied, so she became a de facto ski instructor, taking the younger students skiing every Wednesday, when the Aspen Ski School took the older kids. She became a part of the community.

Over her first winter, Dolores fell in with a group of fresh-powder obsessives. They'd climb up to the ridge of Bell Mountain, which now sits under the line of the Silver Queen Gondola, and ski down from there, lapping unlimited powder runs, no one else around. Dolores said the snow and the mountains felt endless.

Those new friends, including 10th Mountain veteran Lefty Cormier, taught Dolores a new way to ski. At the time, the prevailing method was the Arlberg technique, where the shoulders lead the body through a wide arcing turn. It was made for racing and groomed runs. Skiers doing it often felt like they were fighting against the pitch of the mountain.

Lefty taught her the single dipsy—the lilting, floating powder turn technique that Dick Durance, another 10th Mountain guy, had recently developed at Alta. He'd named it after the 1937 song "Dipsy Doodle" because it was bouncy and soft, more like dancing than fighting down the hill. "Few people could learn it because it violated all the skiing rules of the time," Dolores wrote.

With her new technique she could venture into untouched terrain, turning where other people were scared to, navigating narrow, steep chutes. She grew even more obsessive, practicing all the time. She'd soon be called the best woman powder skier in the world.

The technique was groundbreaking, but finding a group of like-minded, passionate people was foundational. The skiers shared work and food and bills. They didn't talk about feelings. If you couldn't keep up, you got dropped. That was the only drama. Dolores often wrote that her time in Aspen was one of the most idyllic periods of her life. "During my three years there, I had a brief taste of true community," she said.

Yet that was only part of the truth. She was also feeling unsettled. You can see those early seeking qualities in the paper trail of letters she was sending to her soon-to-be husband, Ed LaChapelle.

In the summer of 1949, she went to Seattle to check out the teaching program at the University of Washington. She wasn't impressed by the academics, but she liked the access to the Cascades. She climbed Mount Rainier with the famed Whittaker brothers, who would go on to found REI after becoming the first Americans to climb Mount Everest. From there she headed north with the Alpine Club of Canada to the Freshfield Glacier.

On the glacier she slipped and nearly fell into a crevasse. One of her hiking partners, a man her age named Ed LaChapelle, reacted fast, grabbed her arm, and saved her.

She went back to Aspen, and he went back to Washington where he was studying math and physics at the University of Puget Sound with the intent to be a snow scientist. They struck up a correspondence. In her letters to Ed, which he saved, she laments the lack of snow that winter and the changes coming to Aspen from the mountain's owners. They started sketching out a future together. She said she could live anywhere as long as there were mountains.

Dolores visited him in Washington over Christmas and returned home to a snowless drought that sent her into a funk. She sent him a series of heartbreaky, desperate letters about how the skimpy winter was driving her crazy. In the letters, she seems single-minded and unnecessarily bereft over a weak winter.

She was also frustrated by social constraints and insulted when Ed worried that she'd want to settle down into a domestic life. "You should rather worry about my lack of domesticity in a future wife," she wrote. "You need never worry about me wanting to quit climbing mountains because that time could never come."

In the spring, Ed proposed by mail after he found out he'd been accepted to what's now the Institute for Snow and Avalanche Research in Davos. After their wedding in June, they went back to Canada to climb for their honeymoon and then headed to Switzerland as a married couple.

In Davos, Ed was embedded in avalanche dynamics and snow science, a field that was rapidly changing in the wake of the war, as more people ventured onto bigger peaks, and artillery was used for avalanche control. Dolores was a tag-along wife on his program, thrust into the domestic sphere in a country she didn't know, where she couldn't speak any of the languages, and where she had to learn to run a household on Ed's skimpy research salary. She was isolated and frustrated. But she had skiing.

In Davos, she could ski every day. She began exploring the surrounding valleys, taking advantage of the interconnected ski areas and the train service between them. She'd take the lift up and then ski long, winding descents into the next town.

Almost immediately, skiers around Davos started noticing the new American woman with the strange technique, and within a few weeks she was teaching the Davos Ski School how to do the dipsy. She became known as a powder-snow specialist, particularly proficient and graceful, somehow able to float when other people fell. That reputation would follow her back to the States and become a fixed part of her identity.

She was also thinking about *why* skiing felt so important to her. Later she would turn to European philosophers like Heidegger and Jung, but at that point she was focused on her senses. She and Ed spent the summer hiking the high alpine peaks, and she started to notice that when summer storms, known as the foehn winds, would come through, she'd get splitting migraines. She grew interested in how places impacted her, not just how she impacted the place.

After Davos, they spent one winter in New York City, where Ed was working for the American Geographical Society. She became pregnant and went back to Denver to get ready for the baby while Ed took off on an expedition to the Arctic. Their son, Randall (who would change his name to

David), was born in October, and 2 weeks later they moved to Alta for Ed's job as a Forest Service Snow Ranger at the burgeoning center of snow research.

Alta sits at the head of Little Cottonwood Canyon, the granitic funnel that pulls moisture up and away from the Great Salt Lake, dumping snow against the wall of the Wasatch mountains. Alta is notorious for that good snow, deeper than Aspen, lighter than Davos. It's a proving ground for a certain kind of skier. I send myself there almost every year, like a pilgrimage, soaking in the sparkle of the crystallized air, listening for the compression of avalanche explosives in the morning.

Alta is special, but it's not straightforward. You'll miss most of the good skiing if you just ride the main lift. You have to work to find hidden chutes and sidestep up ridges to the powder pockets. It's full of skiing you have to work for.

During the 1860s, Alta was a busy mining town, but when the silver vein went dry in 1871, it became a ghost town, in part because the terrain was so treacherous. A chunk of the land was eventually deeded to the Forest Service. In 1935, the government brought in Norwegian ski-jumping champion Alf Engen, who had settled in Utah, to see if the area was usable for winter recreation. He decided Alta was the ideal location for a ski area. The Collins Lift started turning in January of 1939, making it the second chairlift in the western US.

Engen sited the ski area up at the top of the canyon where the mountains pitched up and caught storms. The area is great for skiing but is also incredibly avalanche-prone. Three quarters of Alta's ski terrain is known to slide. Football-field-sized patches of snow can come pummeling off the peaks above the canyon, covering the road, breaking trees, burying buildings.

Multiple factors cause avalanches, but the most significant one is slope angle. A slope anywhere from 25 to 60 degrees can slide, and the most common slope angle to slide is 37 degrees, basically the pitch of a perfect black diamond ski slope. To this day the canyon often closes, sometimes for days at a time, until the risk of avalanches has been mitigated. In the '40s, Alta was the perfect proving ground for avalanche control.

Ed's work was to manage those avalanches and make the canyons safe. He was hired by Monty Atwater, a 10th Mountain veteran and polymath who wrote children's books about avalanches and had an English degree from Harvard. They mapped out slide paths and monitored snow metrics, digging pits to see where the layers were. The techniques they came up with, which had roots in Ed's research at Davos, are still used today in everything from highway-hazard management to recreational backcountry skiing. Ed would go on to invent the first avalanche transceiver. And while Ed was the one with the government title, Dolores was immersed in the work.

Lodging for the Snow Rangers was a Forest Service cabin on the mountain only accessible by rope tow in the winter. Dolores—who was toting along 2-week-old David when they showed up—was thrilled that she could ski out her front door. It was the first place that they, as a married couple, would stay for more than a season.

As she had sworn to Ed in her early letters, she happily built a life that revolved around the mountains. Even when their kid was tiny, skiing was a priority. She took care of David, but Ed usually came home in the early afternoon and she could go out to ski, as long as she got back to breastfeed.

She claimed to have invented a back carrier so she could take the baby skiing with her as soon as he could hold his head up. She says she only fell once when he was on her back. It was so radical at the time that *The Salt Lake Tribune* reported on it. They interviewed her when she and Ed were down in the city Christmas shopping, toting David on their backs.

She also said she essentially invented the baby monitor. When David was napping, she would hook up the Alta radio in David's room and leave the mic keyed so she would know if he woke up. She didn't need it for long. David was skiing by the time he was 2 and picking up poles at 4. He had great balance, she said, and once he was big enough to ski on his own she became a ski instructor, back in the rotation of the mountain.

In the '50s, the ski industry was exploding. New resorts were cropping up across the country, metal skis made the sport easier, and more people had time and money to go skiing. Alta attracted some of the best skiers in the country, and Dolores was on the front edge. Her ski ability, which had shone in Davos and Aspen, stood out again at Alta, as she and her cadre of local skiers pushed into deeper, more technical terrain, perfecting their turns. She skied first descents through the range, including one down the famed Baldy Chute, the steep gully off the top of the 11,068-foot summit of Mount Baldy. She even skied for seminal filmmaker Warren Miller, but she didn't like it because she had to think about where to turn for the camera instead of listening to the mountain.

Dolores's friend Wilma Johnson, who worked at the Rustler Lodge and starred in early ski films, called her the Witch of the Wasatch for her ability to know when storms were going to clear, or where the wind would blow in. Her intense attention was different but adjacent to what Ed was doing: forecasting snow, learning patterns, observing the weather. It was a softer kind of science, a sort of intuition that came from connection to nature, one that she would continue to calibrate for the rest of her life.

When I'm at Alta, I try to channel some of that intuition. One morning, a few days out from a storm, in the gray haze of another one, I ride up the Collins Lift and cut across the High T, the traverse that takes you across the face of the mountain. It's rutted, sunbaked skiing, uneven and chossy, and I have to hold my speed to make it across. On the other side I'm on top of the steep lines of High Rustler, the valley glinting purple and gold in the distance.

I am following a friend who ski patrols here, and we drop off the edge of the ridge into Lone Pine, the chute that was reportedly a favorite of Dolores's. He makes one smooth turn and then disappears downhill. I try to follow, but I fumble, tangled in my skis. I have to stop, breathe, rebalance myself. I let him go, giving up the chase, and then let myself relax, feel the pitch, and finally point downhill again, trying to do what Dolores would have done. "Living and skiing at Alta all those years showed me that living on this earth is its own intrinsic reward when one decides to live in one place and cultivate a lasting relationship to the other beings of that place: soil, animals, plants, beings in the sky; clouds, rain, snow, thunder, and the gods of the place," she wrote in *Deep Powder Snow*.

She said that when she quit trying to force a path downhill and instead let the mountain turn her, she felt the boundary between herself and the world around her blurring.

That metaphysical connection might sound a little hokey, and it does to me sometimes, but what she's describing is a flow state, the melding of action and consciousness that feels like being in the zone. Psychologists say flow is one of our deepest intrinsic motivators: It feels good, and it often comes from our connection to nature. Dolores was decades ahead of the research that gave it a name.

In the late '80s, when he was in grad school, psychologist Mihaly Csikszentmihalyi became fascinated with the way artists became engrossed in their work. He noticed that when they were really engaged, the final product was less important than the way they felt when they got there. There was something about the combination of desire, skill, and an engaging activity that was intrinsically satisfying and pulled them into a deeper sense of consciousness.

In 1990, he published *Flow: The Psychology of Optimal Experience*, in which he said that to attain flow you had to be both highly skilled and highly challenged. If you were flailing as an artist, you couldn't get there, but if you were brainlessly painting by the number, you couldn't either. Flow is the edge between control and arousal that occurs when you're actively engaged with the environment around you.

Maybe you've experienced that kind of flow. I've felt it in the fleeting rush that some people call *runner's high*, my feet finding the ground of a well-worn trail. I've felt it on a river, when I'm in the literal flow, feeling where the water wants to move me. And I've felt it on a mountain.

"Powder snow cannot merely be considered a metaphor for living, but rather, skiing powder shows us how to live." This is one of Dolores's most famous aphorisms. The spine of my hand-me-down copy of *Deep Powder Snow* is broken open to the page that includes it. People usually stop the quote there, but it goes further: "If we insist on proceeding arrogantly in the narrowly human-centered world of modern culture we will continue to not only destroy the earth's species but the very water and air on which we depend to live."

Skiing taught Dolores to live in concert with the world, but she was also thinking about that destruction. Flow had been a driving force for her since she was a kid under the cottonwoods, and as an adult she found it in every season. She, Ed, and David began to spend summers on the Blue Glacier of Washington's Olympic Peninsula, where Ed would do research and she would run the field camp. She took David berry picking and climbed with him through pristine meadows. She observed the meteorological definition of *glory*, which is when your own shadow is surrounded by a circle of rainbows due to moisture in the air. She said she could start to sense encroaching thunderstorms from the electricity in the air, just like she could with snowstorms. Her friend Jody Cardamone, a deep ecologist who was the first director of the Aspen Center for Environmental Studies, told me that Dolores's ideas about philosophy really started to crystallize there on the glacier.

She read Martin Heidegger's philosophy on the state of being. She picked up Greek and Roman myths, Chinese history, traditional Indigenous religious texts, and tried to figure out where they all touched. But she was still very much on Ed's program. They moved and worked based on his schedule.

Dolores told Ed in early letters that she didn't want a typical domestic life, but she was pregnant with David less than 2 years after they were married. More than Georgie, who had lost her daughter by the time she went to the canyon, and more than Anne, who never had children, Dolores had to face the constraints of traditional gender roles. At Alta, she taught school for him and the other young children, like Kim Morton, the daughter of the couple who owned and managed the Alta Lodge, even though she was distracted by the mountains. Later David would say that she prioritized skiing over being a mother, which left him feeling wounded. But she also showed him how to build his own relationship with the outdoors by teaching him ritualistic ways of welcoming in the seasons: meditating over candles in the winter, finding wild plants in the spring.

She was progressive in ways that might seem normal now—making a backpack to take her baby skiing, making time for exercise, skiing with a crew of guys, pushing her body—but she had to carve out that space and cut away other people's expectations to do so. And some of those expectations are still limiting women in the mountains. When female athletes, mountaineers, and guides have kids, they're frequently judged harshly for continuing to prioritize physicality and adventure. I often think about ski mountaineer Hilaree Nelson, who achieved first descents on the world's biggest peaks. She had 2 kids in her early thirties and climbed Mount Everest when they were 3 and 4, intentionally trying to show them a parent with passion, someone who had dreams. She was a hero for many women coming up behind her, for her mentorship, and for how she modeled balance. She said that thinking about her kids helped her make good decisions in high-stakes mountain settings.

In 2022, when she died at 49 in an avalanche on Manaslu, one of the high peaks of Nepal, the mountaineering community suffered a huge loss. There was grief and reflection and celebration of all she had accomplished. And then there was blowback about the selfishness of being a mother in the mountains and about what it meant for a woman to put herself in a risky position. Every article about her mentioned that she had left her children. Every comment section had at least one nasty reaction. That doesn't happen in the same way when men die in the mountains.

For her, or Dolores, or so many of us who feel most at home outside, you're damned if you do, damned if you don't when it comes to parenting. Even though research has shown that it's good for children to have independent, fulfilled parents. Even though plenty of famous fathers have lost their lives exploring. That double standard existed in the '50s when Dolores was parenting, and it still exists now. Hilaree was already walking a tightrope, balancing so many expectations and working at the most elite levels, and being a parent added another heavy thing to balance. Not because of the parenting, but because of the social pressure.

Dolores was bucking against those expectations in her relationship with Ed and with motherhood. She spent her twenties and thirties in Alta, skiing and building her philosophy, but she didn't start writing about it until David had left home. Her role as a mother was hard to divorce from her role as a wife. And as time went on she struggled to fit into that role as a dutiful wife, and as Ed's wife in particular.

Part of the tension was that, although superficially they seemed well matched, Dolores and Ed didn't prioritize the same things. Ed was specific and tactile; Dolores was chasing ideas. Dolores's friend Steve Meyers, who knew them both, said Ed would belittle her. Steve said that even at her funeral Ed made disparaging remarks about her thinking. "She was trying to tease out of all these profound traditions about what is a good life for a human, and Ed finds it silly, even after she's dead," Steve told me. Dolores was disparaging and judgmental, too.

She said Ed wasn't deep or serious. They both looked past the other's good qualities and nitpicked the bad ones. I think Dolores might have been that way with everyone. She was hard on herself and hard on the world.

As their time at Alta went on, she began to wrestle with her feelings about marriage, parenthood, and spirituality. She went to church every Sunday, and part of why she stayed with Ed was because of Catholic guilt. But she now had a growing awareness that the rigid framework and the belief in a singular Western God no longer squared with her ideas. She became interested in Eastern religion and began to coalesce a philosophy about the sacred nature of mountains, making her argument like a magpie, picking the pieces of different traditions and putting them together. In her second book, *Earth Wisdom*, she said all major religions began when someone had an epiphany on a mountain. Dolores was trying to align what was happening in her body with a bigger sense of meaning. She wanted logic, structure, ceremony, and faith.

I'm not religious, so wrangling with spirituality is often the hardest part of Dolores's ideas for me. Sometimes I think her approach feels pushed together and forced, like she's trying to fill a gap for herself. But I also know that I've had experiences in the outdoors that I can't quite explain, that feel much bigger than myself.

The year after the avalanche, when she was 38, she told David that she was going to try to become a writer. He was sitting at the table, chomping toast when she told him, and he got the feeling that she was prepping him to be more independent. Their life was changing, albeit slowly.

In 1973, Ed took a job with the Institute of Arctic and Alpine Research at the University of Colorado Boulder. His post was based in Silverton, 7 hours away from the bustle of Boulder. He was contracted to study the impacts of cloud seeding in a project funded by the Bureau of Reclamation. It was ostensibly an avalanche-research project, but it was tied up in water systems, human dynamics, and the way we try to control the weather.

When you drive into Silverton from the south, like I usually do, you sweep around the curves of Coal Bank and Molas Passes, flashing past views of the Needles and Twilight Peak, before dropping down toward the town. The highway is a skinny two-lane, without guardrails, and it can feel like the mountain is eroding under the road. Kendall Mountain cradles the town to the southeast, shading the grid, making winter nights come fast. Everything about Silverton is harsh and compressed.

Today the area is known for its backcountry skiing, and for Silverton Mountain, the hardcore ski area. But Silverton wasn't a ski town when Dolores showed up. It was still a backwoods, end-of-the-road, sputtering mining town, an hour and two passes away from the nearest grocery store. There was a one-chair ski area run by the local hotel, but other than that, all skiing was human-powered, and there were only a few other people in town who skied.

Silverton didn't have the softness or the snow of Alta. And compared to Silverton, Alta was cosmopolitan. But Silverton did have a ring of spiny, snow-blasted mountains with pointed summits. It had crystalline ice-blue lakes, dense aspen networks, and solitude. It was harsh, and it had been mined and hacked up, but it was still wild and lonely. There was no one to fight for the powder turns.

Dolores initially told locals she was a children's book author because she was worried about what they might think about her if they knew that she was exploring radical environmental philosophy, and the community slowly welcomed the LaChapelles in. Everyone in town would come to winter potlucks, regardless of relationship strife or political acrimony, because nights were long and cold in their leaky mining shacks. Dolores didn't want to go to Silverton, but once she did, it unlocked something. She would stay there for the rest of her life.

There, Dolores cobbled together a community of people who felt similar sparks in the mountains. And now, 15 years after her death, many of those people have gathered for the equinox celebration where I hear Katrina talk.

One evening, before the light fades, a crew of us tromp up a hill above town to a shrine built for Dolores. The path weaves through skinny aspen trees and winds up to a meadow where there's a stone kiva overlooking the valley. There are some pictures of Dolores hidden inside the rocks, if you know where to look. We make a circle around it: Art Goodtimes, poet and environmental activist, who has carried Dolores's deep ecology torch; Steve Meyers, the philosophy professor who was one of her closest ski partners; and Jen Brill, who started Silverton Mountain ski area, and who loved Dolores before she came to town. They trade stories about her until it gets dark. We will find our way back down the hill by headlamp, but as the sun drops, mellowing out the gold in the aspens, Katrina and Art lead us in a chant. It makes me a little uncomfortable, but it's the kind of thing Dolores liked to do, and I am following the threads, back here in the place where she found them.

ROOTS OF DEEP ECOLOGY

After the summit, I am itchy to move my legs. I drive up Mineral Creek Road and start hiking into the Ice Lakes Basin, a cluster of startlingly blue alpine lakes set into a cirque at nearly 12,000 feet. Jen told me it was another one of Dolores's favorite places. Hiking up I can feel the way different aspects of the mountain receive different light and heat. Up above the road, the aspen have already dropped their leaves, and the willow and brush have turned ruddy. Once I'm up in the alpine I'm surrounded by waving golden grasses and the deadheads of wildflowers.

The trail is nearly empty today, which is unusual. The lakes are often so overrun with hikers that it can be impossible to find solitude. The climb becomes a conga line, and volunteers are staged at the trailhead, politely reminding people to stay on the trails, to pick up after their dogs, to avoid shredding the foliage or cutting down trees. It's a necessary precaution because that traffic has led to damage. Visitors have burned fires in the alpine tundra—sometimes using wood from historic mining structures to do so—and left feces and trash strewed around the lakeshore.

There are also signs of the diffuse human impact of climate change. This stretch of the state is known for its glowing, sweeping aspen groves, and at this time of year they look lit from within, shimmering and golden. But now, across the range, they're struggling. Cytospora cankers are creeping into the trees, aspen borer beetles are carving into their trunks, and the persistent drought thins their roots, making it hard for them to be resilient. Some of the stands are faded, their bark turning parchment-colored, their leaves drooping or gone. I feel the fragility.

I come up here for solace, but it's also where I can sense things changing. Like these women, my love for being outside has also made it hard to be outside. The more I see the more I can't unsee.

In 1973, when she moved to Silverton, Dolores was coalescing her ideas about environmental harms at the same time Georgie was fighting with federal permitting in the Grand Canyon and Anne was working on her first draft of *Woodswoman.*

The Endangered Species Act passed that year, as part of a wave of federal policy including the National Environmental Policy Act, the Clean Air Act, and the Clean Water Act, which were all directed at addressing the accrual of point source pollution, habitat destruction, and overuse of resources. The fossil-fuel-induced warming that we're currently feeling was just coming into public consciousness, but it was clear, from the shrinking rivers and disappearing forests, that the developed world had overleveraged its use of the planet. In trying to grasp those changes, Dolores fell into the burgeoning field of environmental philosophy.

You can trace the ideas that undergird environmental philosophy as far back as you'd like, to Aristotle's thoughts on psyche and Plato's ideas of flourishing, or to Thomas Hobbes's musings on the divides between society and wilderness in *Leviathan*. But the field as we know it started in the early 1970s, as a response to the environmental thought and action of the previous decade.

Environmental philosophy developed concurrently in the US, Australia, and Norway, all places with a history of white, Western Judeo-Christian morality that had long been operating on a philosophy of liberalism and individual freedom and the broken idea that nature was there for the taking. As new fields like conservation biology and environmental science coalesced, environmental philosophy emerged from the burgeoning awareness that the environment wasn't just going to take care of itself forever. "It was the intellectual response to what was happening on the ground," environmental philosopher and skier Alex Lee told me.

The new environmental philosophers, starting with Richard Sylvan, whose 1973 essay "Is There a Need for a New Environmental Ethic?," began to codify the field. He took ideas that had been percolating for a long time about intrinsic value, moral extensionism, and ethics as a tool for environmental problem-solving and applied them to the questions about resource use, animal ethics, land management, pollution, and more.

Early environmental philosophers were trying to figure out the moral relationship between humans and the environment and to break down the dualism between nature and people. They were teasing out thorny questions we're still wrestling with today: What does nature mean, and what is its best use? Are humans a more important or a more moral species than any other? At what rate should we deplete finite resources, and who gets to decide?

Dolores, who was trying to mesh what she was feeling in the mountain with what she was reading, hooked into a particular strain of environmental philosophy called *deep ecology.* It echoed her thinking about connectivity, and it came from the high mountains.

Norwegian philosophy professor and environmentalist Arne Næss is considered the father of deep ecology. He was a precocious thinker who became the University of Oslo's youngest professor at 27, but before he was thinking about empiricism or logic, he was thinking about climbing mountains. He'd summited all of Norway's highest peaks by the time he was 17, he led expeditions to the high peaks across the globe, including the Himalayas, and he formed some of his ideas about morality and interconnection in the mountains. He said that the reverential ways he saw Nepalese Sherpas treat the high peaks helped shape his ethics.

Næss was also involved in early conservation biology work. In his first paper explaining the roots of deep ecology—published the same year Dolores moved to Silverton—he said that the philosophy drew from international ecological work, science, and social science. He was trying to conceive an ethical framework for the connections he saw between people and places and every living thing.

The core tenet of deep ecology, which was radical at the time, is that humans are just one part of a wild, interconnected system, and that any separation between humanity and the world around us is a false dualism. Næss said that we should strive for an ethical relationship between all pieces of an ecosystem, and that separating out natural resources creates an unnatural rift. He thought nature had inherent value and that to truly, ethically exist with nature we couldn't just try to cut back pollution or conserve beautiful places, we had to rethink how people fit into the picture and stop seeing ourselves as the most important piece of it.

He argued that most modern environmental thinking, which he called *shallow ecology*, was anthropocentric—too focused on conservation and land management for human benefit. It addressed the symptoms of environmental degradation instead of the source. He wanted to go deeper, hence the name.

Though Næss was a professor, he developed his philosophy outside of the academic vacuum. Næss and the followers he quickly accrued were worried that an increasingly industrialized, capitalistic society posed a threat to nature and humans' connection to it. They disparaged any kind of thinking that put financial advantage above collective or ecological good. They worried about nuclear bombs and the purported population bomb—the idea made popular in 1968 by Stanford biologist Paul Ehrlich that the growing global population would deplete all food resources. They leaned into bioregionalism, degrowth, the importance of local ecosystems, and into ecopsychology, the idea that the health of our planet is directly linked to our mental health. They were trying to live within the carrying capacity of the planet and trying to quantify what that limit was.

Deep ecology was most controversial when it came to population dynamics. Some deep ecologists believed that the human population needed to decrease to make living on Earth sustainable. Næss came up with eight principles of deep ecology, the fourth of which was "The flourishing of human life and cultures is compatible with a substantial decrease of the human population. The flourishing of nonhuman life requires such a decrease." That antinatalist idea alienated a lot of people, including other philosophers. "To shallow ecologists, deep ecologists are fascists because they would assume they're better than us, and we can all die," Dolores's friend Steve Meyers, who hung out with the deep ecologists, told me.

Like Dolores, they were unpacking Judeo-Christian ideas about morality. They challenged the concept that people were created in God's image, and that the garden was theirs for the taking—an idea that had been dominant in Western culture and Western expansion since biblical times, and which is still seeded in so many of our political and environmental decisions. They were also paying attention to traditional Indigenous knowledge and touching on topics that were radical at the time. Should rivers have rights? Who is responsible for curbing warming? If you have multiple children, are you harming the planet? How do we unravel the harms of our history?

They codified the idea that everything is connected. You think you're on one mountain peak and then you see it's attached to the whole range. You get up high and it all spills out in front of you. Creeks run into the river, bisecting the valleys that go on and on. We exist tangled up with nature; there are no bright lines between us and it. Everything we eat, the silicone and copper in our computer chips, it all comes from the earth.

Like Næss and other environmental thinkers, Dolores saw the negative impacts of tourism on the environment. Alta was increasingly crowded. Aspen had already broken her heart. The mountain clubs she came up through, and the easy outdoor access she took for granted, felt like they were all being subsumed by the rush of consumerism and overuse. She felt like the integrity of her life in the mountains was at risk because of growth.

As her relationship to Catholicism slackened, she wanted a new moral framework. Steve says she was the most compulsive person he knew, and she researched ideas about morality and environmentalism obsessively.

The Silverton library is a boxy redbrick building, built with funding from Andrew Carnegie in 1905. It's cozy, with dark wood, rugs, and a relatively modest book collection. Dolores started pestering the librarian, calling in obscure books on subjects ranging from medicine to mapping to microwave technology from specific, hard-to-reach libraries, like the Air Force Academy in Colorado Springs. The house she shared with Ed started filling up with files and clippings and books. She had her own reference system. All of her personal books had indexes written into the back, in spidery pencil handwriting: *Ritual, p.14, 112, 234* the notes would say. She liked Jung's ideas that we had gotten too far away from nature, and that by doing so we were denying parts of ourselves. She also loved Heidegger's idea of *Gelassenheit*, often translated to *releasement* or *yielding*, which he described as the process of attunement and letting things unfold. To her, it perfectly encompassed the way a skier had to be in tune with the mountain, letting the snow turn them. She learned Heidegger, too, had been a skier, which made his ideas more resonant.

Dolores felt that Western religion separated people from nature and set up a patriarchal sense of conquering and domineering. She wrote that cathedrals rose after forests were flattened. She dived into Eastern religion and art. "For some years I had been aware that only Chinese and Japanese paintings depicted nature as I saw it in the mountains; therefore, I felt that they knew something we in the West didn't know," she wrote in her book *Sacred Land, Sacred Sex.*

She became fascinated with Indigenous cultures because, as she wrote, "most native societies around the world had three common characteristics: they had an intimate, conscious relationship with their place; they were stable, 'sustainable' cultures, often lasting for thousands of years; and they had a rich ceremonial and ritual life." Those characteristics felt core to the philosophy she was building about how to be in tune with the earth.

That philosophy clicked into place when she found deep ecology. In 1980, she gave a talk at a University of Denver conference on environmental ethics. There she met George Sessions, a philosophy professor at Sierra College. They bonded over the burgeoning ideas of deep ecology, and he inspired her to connect with other environmental philosophers, like Paul Shepard and Bill Devall. She began to call in articles from academic journals. In 1976, she published *Earth Festivals*, a book of ways to celebrate and reflect on living seasonally. She was part of a building zeitgeist. *Earth Festivals* was published right around the time that Arne Næss's papers were becoming widespread.

Earth Festivals feels a bit like an instruction manual for how to incorporate environmental awareness into your life. It's light, and some of it feels painfully dated and lacking awareness. Dolores co-opts and smashes together Indigenous (which she broadly refers to as *Indian*) traditions like medicine wheels. She slices out pieces of Tibetan Buddhism and pulls in whatever suits her ideas of ritual from seasonal songs to creation stories. But 2 years later, she published *Earth Wisdom*, which was wider in scope and more ambitious. She begins with the idea that morality is linked to being outside and being in balance with the world. The book includes everything from the history of cave paintings to the physiology of breathing. It's dizzying in its breadth and occasionally moves too fast to connect the dots, but sometimes her insights about the importance of ecosystem connectivity or the health impacts of environmental change feel shockingly modern. Thanks to her connections with people like Sessions, the book traveled out into the world of environmental thinkers and found an audience.

Michael Zimmerman, a Tulane professor who was one of the early proponents of deep ecology, said he hadn't heard of Dolores until she invited him to Silverton and sent him a copy of *Earth Wisdom*. When he asked around, he learned that she was a highly regarded skier and a mountaineer. In reading the book, he was impressed by the way Dolores wove together the threads of modern science, traditional knowledge, and philosophy. This random woman in the San Juans was pulling together insights that he wasn't reading in the academy or elsewhere. "When Dolores was researching a book, the little Silverton library led the state in the number of interlibrary loan requests!" he wrote.

She was able to access books and receive material at her outpost in the mountains, but it was harder to penetrate academic circles. She reached out to people like Zimmerman, inserting herself in the conversation, trying to show them she was relevant.

In 1976, after *Earth Festivals* was published, she was invited to a conference in Claremont, California, by Joe Meeker, a professor at UC Santa Cruz, and Paul Shepard, who taught at Pitzer. They'd invited Arne Næss, and Dolores struck up a conversation with him about Mount Baldy, which was 20 minutes outside Los Angeles. The next morning, after Næss gave his talk, he blew out of the room and grabbed Dolores, ready to head for Baldy. She could barely keep up with him on the trail, but their time in the mountains bonded them. They spent the rest of the conference talking about climbing and environmental work, and he pulled her into the deep ecology circle. The next year she sent him Edward Abbey's *Monkey Wrench Gang*, and from there they kept in touch by mail for decades.

Her ideas about sustainability, rights of nature, ecosystem connectivity, and respect for Indigenous wisdom are still bearing out today. But in her time and in her field, Dolores struggled to be taken seriously. Like Anne, she was operating in a nontraditional way, from an off-the-map place. Steve said she had a slight chip on her shoulder about not measuring up to what she called *the big guys*. "I think that if you have a male writer who is where Dolores is, they're an Aldo Leopold, but if you have a female writer doing the same thing, people will say she didn't quite nail it down," he told me. He said that he knew she had other marks against her, like her lack of academic affiliation, but he thought that when it came down to it, sexism was the thing that most stood in her way.

There were a few other women involved in the emerging environmental-philosophy world, like Val Plumwood, who was one of the first people to espouse ecofeminism—an idea Dolores didn't like—Donna Harraway, and Flo Krall, Shepard's eventual wife, an education professor at the University of Utah who would strive to include Dolores in her work. But both philosophy and science skewed male. Dolores connected with people like Krall, but she also shied away from being bundled in with other women. She wanted to be judged on her work, not her gender, and she often got some perverse joy from being the only woman among the men.

Her insecurity about not being a part of traditional philosophy kept growing. She didn't want to leave Silverton, but she didn't want to be excluded, so she decided to bring some of the deep ecologists to her. In 1981, she invited Zimmerman, along with Bill Devall, George Sessions, and Steve Meyers, for what she called the Heidegger in the Mountains symposium. The deep ecologists came to Silverton to sort through some of the pressing philosophical tensions in their converging work. Zimmerman wrote that he and Sessions argued about anthropocentrism—a concept that was only just emerging—and about the value of human existence in a broad ecosystem.

Dolores wanted their conversations to be grounded in nature, so she took the men hiking to Engineer Mountain, a prominent, solitary peak south of Silverton where wildflowers studded the meadows after a wet summer. She wanted to show them the peak she considered the middle of the mandala of the San Juan Mountains, and she also wanted to test them out for her next phase of the meeting.

Engineer is easily accessible. The summit is just a few steep miles from Coal Bank Pass, where Highway 550 cuts through a skinny gap. The next day they hiked into the Weminuche Wilderness, geared up for an overnight backpacking trip. They were headed for Eldorado Lake, a clear teal body of water nestled in an alpine cirque above 12,000 feet. They hiked in slowly, taking in the broad views across the continental divide, dropping into the meadow that cupped the lake. As they did, a thunderstorm split the sky, driving them into their tents, where they spent the rest of the night trapped by the weather. Although Dolores had wanted to showcase the beauty of the San Juans, she knew there was something powerful about being at the mercy of the unforgiving weather and terrain. In those mountains, Dolores was able to prove her mettle as a climber and a thinker. On her home turf she could stand up to the philosophers who were embedded in academia. "Among deep ecologists people would come to be with her, and they would be in awe of her," Zimmerman wrote after she died.

That meeting in the mountains went on to shape deep ecology. In 1983, Zimmerman published a paper based on what they discussed, "Towards a Heideggerian Ethos for Radical Environmentalism." Sessions would edit the first major book about deep ecology, 1995's *Deep Ecology for the Twenty-First Century*, which included chapters from Dolores and Arne Næss.

The conference in Silverton became the backbone of deep ecology's origin story in America. And while Dolores was responsible for it, she still struggled to gain institutional credibility. Many of the thinkers she respected admired her back—I found a note from Gary Snyder that said *Though we've never met, I feel I know you*—but in her archive there are also folders full of rejection letters from traditional publishers. She felt snubbed and sidelined, and she was sure that at least some of it was due to her gender.

Like the other deep ecologists, she was trying to make a moral and emotional argument for saving nature, instead of the kind of economic or resource-based rationale that had driven environmental thinking in the past. Steve says that although she was rigorous in her research, she could be loose in her arguments, relying on a pastiche of established ideas and techniques. She thought you needed "direct experiences where you know you are part of nature with no questions asked." She was looking for traditions and practices that could lead people back to nature in a physical way, from chanting and tai chi, which she'd do on mountaintops, to skiing and to wilderness retreats where she'd take people into the backcountry. "Rituals affirming the interconnectedness of the human and nonhuman worlds exist in every primitive culture. They also point to directions where we can search to recover the lost connection," she wrote in *Earth Wisdom*.

Around the same time as the Heidegger conference, a group of disenchanted environmental advocates were starting a new activist environmental group called Earth First! "The central idea of Earth First! is that humans have no divine right to subdue the Earth, that we are merely one of several million forms of life on this planet," they wrote in their first newsletter.

Dave Foreman, one of the founders, had defected from the Wilderness Society, where he led policy work in the Southwest. Like Næss and the deep ecologists, he thought they needed to go deeper, to shake up the system more. His group was inspired by writers like Ed Abbey, who espoused civil disobedience on behalf of the ecosystem. Their slogan was No Compromise in Defense of Mother Earth, and their first major act of public subterfuge was "cracking" the Glen Canyon Dam, which, like Georgie, they saw as the most hated structure in the West. In the middle of the night, they unrolled a 300-foot-long strip of plastic that looked like a crack down the face of the dam, creating an image that underscored the dam's fragility. From there they staged protests at large-scale logging sites—including sit-ins and tree spiking—wrote policy to preserve wilderness, and protested nuclear waste dumping. The group was loose, verging on anarchic. You became a member of Earth First! simply by participating.

They were among the most prominent of the new radical environmental groups. And in the early days of their coalescence, when they were looking for a way to explain their wild frustration around environmental degradation, they stumbled into deep ecology, which aligned with their ideas about bioregionalism, biodiversity, and balance.

Dave Foreman liked Dolores's spiritual bent, her uncompromising desire for embodiment, and her way of rejecting the yuppie consumerism of the early '80s. He started introducing her books to the group.

In a lot of ways, her ideas are old ideas; many of them, like the idea that mountains are sacred, draw on Indigenous wisdom that tracks back to time immemorial. Some of them are as simple as the social and physical value of being outside: the same concept that drove veterans out camping after the Civil War, and spurred the Civilian Conservation Corps. Dolores's philosophy was similar to the Romantics, who were looking for transcendence. It was similar to the back-to-the-land movement that predated and encompassed Anne, rooted in simplicity and bioregionalism.

And at the time, Dolores's words were a balm for the activists' worries. She was putting what they were feeling in context. Ed Abbey name-checks her in *Hayduke Lives!* By the late '80s, she was writing for Earth First!'s *Wild Earth* journal and showing up at their gatherings.

I'm curious about how Dolores's words galvanized the movement, and I know just who to seek out for answers. From Silverton I drive over Red Mountain Pass to Ouray, where I roll up the windows to cut the buzz of ORVs and try not to hit any visitors shopping for T-shirts. Then I roll out through the pastoral fantasy of megaranches around Ridgway. Some of them are historic homesteads, others owned by out-of-state celebrities like Ralph Lauren. I skip the turnoff to Telluride and keep heading west, to Norwood, the tiny town on the top of Wright's Mesa, where the real people live.

I pull into the ramshackle yard of Art Goodtimes, and he leads me into a home piled with books and clippings and baskets and boxes. There are copious bottles of mushroom tincture and a note from Gary Snyder tacked up on his wall. Art, in addition to being a Dolores disciple, is a bardic poet, political activist, and elected official. A small man with a big beard, his hands are often busy basket-weaving or thrashing animatedly as he talks. He sits me down at his massive desk, right in the middle of his kitchen, and starts making me a hot drink. I sip my mushroom hot chocolate, taking in his stories as he brews and steeps his own.

Art came to the mountain from San Francisco, where he grew up immersed in the labor movement and beat poetry. He studied to be a Roman Catholic priest, but he pulled himself out of the seminary to teach on a tribal reservation and work on antinuclear campaigns, which led him to Earth First! He became the poetry editor of the *Earth First!* journal in 1981, and in 1989 he helped organize the group's annual gathering, the Round River Rendezvous on Uncompahgre Plateau. When Dolores showed up, he was immediately infatuated. "I was like a little cub reporter taking notes," he says. "I found Dolores, and I found the intellectual philosophical base of my environmental inclinations."

She taught him about ritual and community building and the ways poetry and music can be tools to address climatic disagreements—ones he still uses in legislating.

In 1975, Dolores started her own publishing company and learning center, which she called Way of the Mountain. In addition to publishing books, she also held retreats like Anne did. People would travel from all over to see her. Even after her body slowed down and she couldn't hike or ski in the same way, people would come over the mountains just to hear her talk.

Art is an elder now, like Dolores was when he met her. He says that she became like a grandparent to him. Her ideas helped him find balance. I ask him how, because I'm still trying to figure that out for myself.

Art leans in closer to me. More emotional now. He draws a circle with his finger in the mess on the table to try to explain an idea to me. "This is the beauty way, the line between dark and light," he says, pointing to the edge of the circle. "And we're always trying to figure out how to walk that line."

He says that even though Dolores often felt hopeless about the future of the planet, she didn't act hopelessly. She gave people ways to act, by creating rituals that interwove ancient practices and psychological attunement to place. The rituals gave people a stake and a way to understand the system.

Art says that eventually Earth First! became too violent for him. The group had always been diffuse, but by the '90s some sects had turned toward more extreme acts of monkeywrenching. The founders fell off as the actions became more radical.

We hear a knock on Art's door. It's a neighbor and his young kid, delivering cookies, coming over to chat. Art has embodied that community-building part of Dolores's work. I decide it's a good time for me to be on my way. I head back east, into Telluride to see a friend, still wrestling with the notion that we've spent the past 50 years chewing on the same ideas without much change, and that maybe things could have been different if people like Dolores had been taken more seriously.

The problem with looking for heroes is that when you go digging, you find dirt. I know that if I want to rethink history by way of these women's stories, I have to consider what their work and lives really mean, and how they could have steered us wrong as well.

Dolores was a lot of things—intense, smart, talented—but even the people who loved her the most say she was tricky and harsh. Set in her ways, and sometimes unable to hear the other side of an argument. "One of her favorite phrases was *You wouldn't understand*," Steve told me. Art said she was dismissive of things she didn't believe in. She was spiky and judgmental, and she was particularly hard on other women. Jen Brill says you had to earn her respect, and she could make snap judgments about whether she thought someone was worthy of her time.

Much of her bad behavior seemed to come from insecurity. She was quick to burn a bridge and perpetually paranoid that other people were stealing her ideas. Steve said she felt like those ideas were her only currency, so she gripped them tight, even if she had assembled them from pieces of history or other thinkers.

Being in Silverton let Dolores dive into her research without distraction, but it also meant that she was intellectually isolated. Starting with *Earth Wisdom*, she largely self-published her books, except for her 1996 book, *D. H. Lawrence: Future Primitive.* Without an editor or peers to review her work in its early stages, her ideas, even in their final published form, could be poorly rationalized or sloppily co-opted.

She fetishized Indigenous cultures and oversimplified ideas about hunter-gatherer societies, which led to flawed arguments about overpopulation and resource use. "She was deeply disturbed by fascism, but she said she would die today if she could take 2 billion people with her. That's where we diverged philosophically," Art told me. And at her most egregious she was co-opting Native culture in an inappropriate, extractive way.

She grabbed and smashed, sticking Taoism next to ideas that originated in North America, conflating culturally significant rituals and trying to pull on common strings, even if they weren't there historically. She wanted history to show her a way forward, but sometimes it felt like she was forcing it.

The end of *Sacred Land, Sacred Sex* is a rundown of what she calls "Seven ways toward human/earth bonding: Boundary crossing between wilderness and civilization," and of the seven, from talking-stick councils to tai chi, most of them have been lifted from other cultures and presented out of context.

In doing that, Dolores reflected a larger practice among white-led environmental groups in the '70s and '80s, wherein First Peoples' ideas became synonymous with better, older practices of land stewardship and environmental ethics. At the same time, the US government, states, and private business were taking advantage of Native lands and people, mining and leaving pollution and slag, using tribally designated water, redrawing boundaries where it was convenient, and cutting off tribes from resources that they'd been promised through federal treaties. They were continuing the history of bait and switch that went back to the beginning of European settlement in America. People like Dolores failed to acknowledge this darker side of history, but took the symbols and practices that seemed appealing: dream catchers and smudge sticks and sweat lodges and songs. That act of lifting and revisioning is where Dolores makes me the most uncomfortable.

I don't think Dolores was intentionally trying to cause harm, but the fact is she adopted certain ideas out of proper and necessary context. She was operating in an intellectual vacuum, and elements of the material she generated are insensitive as a result.

At Ice Lakes, the purple-blue cloud shadow ripples across the water, and I twist my neck to see where the weather is coming from. It changes fast up here, and I still don't know the patterns. But I am starting to know the skinny river valleys and the names of massive peaks: Twilight and Sultan and Turk. I'm learning the avalanche paths named for mining claims named for women: Bonita and Maggie and Cora Belle.

Dolores said that the point of deep ecology was to restore what she called *topocosm*. It is a term that was Frankensteined by biblical scholar Theodor Gaster from Greek—*topos* for place and *cosmos* for world order—and it means the specific ecology of a place. "The topocosm is the entire complex of any given locality conceived as a living organism—not just the human community but the total community—the plants, animals, and soils of the place," Dolores wrote in an article for the Art and Ceremony in Sustainable Culture issue of *In Context* journal.

Topocosm provides an environmental ethic, a road map for engagement with nature. For Dolores it also gave her faith in something bigger. How did we get into this mess, and how do we get out of it? Those were the questions Dolores was wrangling with. And in doing so, she was trying to show that we can garner clues from the past about how to sustain our ecosystem. More recent thinkers like Robin Wall Kimmerer have underscored the idea that people can have, and historically have had, positive impacts: propagating native species, setting healthy fires, fighting erosion. There can be symbiosis, but it takes concerted effort.

Ethical action is at the heart of everything I've been thinking about, from Georgie's first hikes to Anne's boardroom fights. And when I'm feeling particularly overwhelmed, I can remind myself that action is the opposite of apathy.

I hike down from Ice Lakes, out of the alpine back down into the trees, still worried about environmental erosion, about new energy development in the area, about whether or not the mines would be usable again and what would happen if they were. And then, before the trailhead, I stop and lie down in the rocky, uneven grass under a stand of aspen trees and watch the light flicker through them, letting things settle for a second, letting myself remember why it's all important in the first place.

HOW DID WE GET INTO THIS MESS?

Baker's Park is a geologic anomaly. It's a swath of level valley floor carved out where the Continental Divide switchbacks west for a bit. Everything around it is spiky and steep, carved out by high-elevation winds and cold, harsh winters. Three streams, Cement and Mineral Creeks and the Animas River, coalesce and flow south toward the San Juan River, the Colorado, the sea. The flat stretch of land is home to the town of Silverton, and it's named after Charles Baker, one of the first white men who came here looking for minerals in 1860, after a gold rush kicked off in Colorado the previous year. His party climbed into the cold, spiny peaks searching for veins of silver and gold.

People still tend to come to Silverton like that, on a mission, hunting for something they're not quite sure they'll find, fighting the ruggedness and the weather and the isolation for a chance to prove themselves. A century after Baker broke over Molas Pass, Ed and Dolores showed up. Ed was trying to see if scientists could make it snow; Dolores was looking to understand how connection to place could lead to environmental action.

After Baker, the Civil War slowed the push of prospecting, but postwar it came back in force. The predatory Brunot Agreement, which was ratified as an agreement (not a treaty, because the US had stopped recognizing tribes and sovereign nations in 1871) in 1874, took 3.7 million acres from the Ute Reservation and made it available for mining and prospecting to nontribal members. The Utes believed the acreage would be much smaller and that they'd still have their historic hunting and fishing rights. Instead the land was opened to exploration and exploitation.

Silverton officially became a town that same year, and like a lot of the other cold, remote rocky towns—Leadville, Golden, Gypsum—prospecting, and then mining, became the backbone of the economy and the culture.

Prospector life in the mountains was harsh. Miners frequently died in avalanches, and anything they mined had to travel over the treacherous passes to Ouray or Animas City by mule. There were shootings and standoffs on Greene Street, the main drag, and there was an active prostitution trade on Blair Street. But there was money to be made, and the enclave of mining shacks swiftly morphed into a proper town of ornate Victorian buildings. In 1880, railroad speculators from the Denver and Rio Grande Western Railroad formed the town of Durango, 60 miles south in the Animas River Valley, as a hub for transporting minerals. Two years later, they brought the railroad to Silverton, cutting through what is now the Weminuche Wilderness, eager to get a pathway to the mines.

Silverton boomed in the 1880s because of the train. The population shot up enough to support 13 newspapers and 29 saloons. When the gold mines slowed down, the industry turned to silver, and it kept growing until the national silver crash of

1893. The town would never be as big or profitable as it was in the late 1880s, but it limped along on the boom-and-bust of mining for the next century. It boomed again when World War II kicked up desire for domestic minerals, and when the Cold War created a uranium boom, which reopened the shuttered smelter in Durango.

By the '70s, when the LaChapelles came to town, only two mines, the Sunnyside and the Idarado, were still operating. New techniques helped miners drill deep under the mountains, stacking the deck for future environmental disasters. Mining was still a major part of the town's identity and history, but as the ore veins tapped out, the town turned to tourism to try to create another economic source.

In the 1950s, Hollywood producers found the historic train and started using it in movies. The wild, windy canyon was a perfect background for Wild West tales and heist films. Visitors started coming to ride the train up the canyon from Durango. They'd get a few hours in Silverton to eat lunch and buy tchotchkes before taking the train back. By the time the last remaining mine, the Sunnyside, shut down in 1991, those tourists, along with some summertime hikers, backpackers, and off-road drivers, kept the economy propped up. The town was quiet, especially in the winter.

Even though the mines were slow when the LaChapelles arrived, Silverton was still an industry town, and most of the people who lived there were from mining families generations deep. It was hard to break in. But there were a few other people in town who skied, including Dick and Betsy Armstrong, who worked with Ed at the Institute of Arctic and Alpine Research. Together the four would ski the bowl of McMillan, the gullies of Sam's Trees, and the skinny finger of snow called

Cemetery, which is accessed by a committing cliff-riddled entrance. In October after they moved, she wrote that she'd spent the first fall in Colorado since her Aspen days. "Did tai chi on a rock in Lime Creek facing Engineer and realized I felt perfectly good and fulfilled all by myself with it and nature," she wrote. Holed up in a leaky former mining shack in Silverton, she started writing in earnest.

The amount of space an animal uses on a regular basis is called its *home range*, and Dolores was expanding hers. She went east, into the Weminuche, and west to Wilson Peak. She climbed the high peaks close to Silverton, like Sultan and Snowdon, and found river valleys where the aspens turned perfectly gold in the fall.

As she learned the details of the range, her ambivalence about Silverton gave way to a kind of knowing. She was inspired by thinkers like Peter Berg. "Find the place you love enough to fight all the battles necessary to protect all the natural beings and just stay there and do it," he wrote, and in Silverton she could inhabit that idea. She could stay.

Both Heidegger, the scholar of phenomenology, and Hal Rothman, the tourism historian, said that all places have a particular unnameable essence. In Silverton, the thin air makes everything feel harsh and clear, even when you can feel the dirt of the past. Dolores said she loved the light. She found the same kind of connection to the landscape that Georgie found in the Grand Canyon and Anne felt in the Adirondacks. Psychologists call that sense of connection *place attachment*, and there is quantitative and qualitative proof that it exists and that it leads to care, well-being, and a greater sense of self. I'd been searching for that feeling for most of my adult life, hyperaware of how I felt in any particular place, trying to find the right one. I know that feeling of having your heart split by place and always feeling like something small but sharp is missing when you're not in the right place. I thought about the pull of desert rivers, and I felt the hooks of the Northeast, where I'm from, where the seasons and the topography have always seemed correct to me. But my mind and then eventually my body kept coming back to the peaks of the Colorado Plateau. It felt right in ways nowhere else had. I wanted that deepness. So I moved to Durango, just south of Silverton in the San Juan Mountains, with the intention of digging in.

I chose Durango because I loved the way the mountains opened up into the desert, wide-shouldered and red, spilling down to New Mexico. I liked how quickly the landscape could change, how dense and wild it seemed, furrowed and faulted and endlessly deep.

I thought I'd acclimate quickly, but a year passed and I felt more disoriented by what was around me. I was trying to take it in too fast. Trying to conquer it in my mind. To actually understand the range I had to slow down. I had to stop looking at the map and start looking at the mountains.

My second winter there was a violent one where the snow never seemed to settle. I went backcountry skiing into the same safe places over and over again and watched how the sun changed the snow's surface, turning it crusty and then soft. I learned the skinny bits of terrain that held powder even when the wind howled across the ridge. I learned which way the prevailing wind blew. On my skis, my body finally started to learn when the turn was coming and where the mountain would push me. Like Dolores, I adjusted to my new home range slowly, putting things together piece by piece.

•

Unlike Anne, Dolores didn't think being in nature necessitated living in a cabin alone. She thought people should keep their footprints small and live in community, on the edges of wild places. In Silverton, she had that small-scale access, but she struggled to find the community that had come so easily at Alta, and in Aspen.

In the past, she'd always bonded with people through the ritual of being outside. Steve Meyers said that the first time he saw her, she was skiing. He was in the process of moving to Silverton, and he'd come to visit over Christmas, to find a house. He and his wife were at the base of Kendall Mountain, trying to cross-country ski for the first time, when they saw two people slicing perfect turns down the slope above. It was Dolores and Ed. They invited the Meyerses over for dinner that night. It led to a lifelong friendship between Dolores and Steve. The next winter she taught him to ski so they could go into the mountains together. "If you followed her, you felt like you were flying," he said. Dolores was in her head in town and in her body on skis. Steve, who had a background in philosophy and art, could meet her on both levels.

Steve said that over the next decade she started teaching tai chi and formed drumming and chanting circles to try to find some connection. Still, her life in Silverton was isolated. She was consumed with her deep ecology work. "When we weren't skiing, she was working," he said.

Her work started to take precedent over other aspects of life, including her marriage. She and Ed had been on a seasonal cycle, rotating between Ed's mountain post, Silverton or Alta, and the Blue Glacier in Washington, where he did summer glaciology research. She felt unsettled, exhausted, and disenchanted.

By the winter of 1978, Ed went back to Washington, and Dolores stayed in Silverton, despite her initial ambivalence about the town. She told Steve that even though she missed Alta, she'd fallen for the high alpine light in Silverton.

Dolores and Ed's marriage had been collapsing for years because of infidelity, miscommunication, and the way that Dolores wanted to be more than a mother and a partner. Back in Washington, Ed wrote heartsick letters, part yelling, part begging her to come home. At the same time, he asked for recipes and housekeeping details, proof their lives had long been intertwined. But she was done; she was in love with something else.

On Christmas Day 1983, as "Jerusalem" played on the record player, she typed out a note to herself that she titled *About Me Staying Here.*

"Now we need learning from nature itself—we cannot isolate ourselves like Proust in a cork-lined room. I don't come and go from nature to civilization and back. I'm within it and I see its sufferings day by day."

She filed the scrap of writing under a tab titled *Deep Ecology* in her compendium, her overflowing book of notes about subjects that interested her, and stayed in the uninsulated, foundationless house she and Ed had bought when they first came to Silverton. She stayed because the front window faced Sultan Mountain and because she could feel all the seasons there, even if her pipes froze every winter, even if she was lonely and untethered. For more than 20 years she'd followed her husband and conformed her life to his work, subsuming her own ideas. Shortly after the divorce, she wrote a note to herself listing out her goals: "Be in nature as much as possible, live in one place and watch the seasons go by, reclaim the land."

Silverton isn't exactly a ski town. Unlike Alta, there are no real ski resorts, but the peaks that ring the town hold all kinds of ski terrain if you're clever and careful and willing to work for your turns. From the front door of Dolores's house in Silverton she could walk to the base of Kendall Mountain and be on her skis within minutes. She would go outside almost every day, in every season.

Dolores called powder skiing the *loss of ego boundary*. "When that happens, the entire landscape comes alive with relationships and relationships within relationships," she wrote in an issue of the *Earth First!* journal. She wasn't chasing adrenaline; she was chasing that feeling of being at home in nature, the one she'd first felt under the cottonwoods as a kid, the one she thought was the core of deep ecology. When she was in a state of flow, she felt blissful, relaxed, and tuned in.

Writer Brooke Williams, who wrote the intro to *Deep Powder Snow*, said Dolores threaded a needle between adrenaline and ethics. "My sense of what she represented was pretty unique. She would always talk about how she would become a part of the earth's force, and powder skiing was one of the ways she discovered the powerful blending of her own body being a part of this force of nature." The feeling helped other environmentalists explain their ethics, too: the deep ecologists and the Earth First!ers and the growing number of conservationists.

"Environmentalists like myself are most aware of nature when we backpack, climb, and ski. Then we are acutely aware of our bodies. The labor of our bodies tells us the texture of snow and rock and dirt. We feel the grade of the incline. We know and care about weather," Richard Wright wrote in his essay in *Uncommon Ground*.

Now when I go skiing around Silverton, I often start at the old Gladstone mine site, where the EPA is still treating water and removing heavy metals. I ski past the tailing ponds and wreckage, a reminder that the damage doesn't go away even when it's mitigated. As I climb, I've learned to dig into the snowpack and see the story of a season left in layers by the storms. Up high I get an understanding of how the mountains spill out into each other, a learned map of landscape connectivity that changes every time I notice something new.

It's why Georgie was so heartbroken about the Glen Canyon dam, even if she wouldn't call herself an environmentalist. It's what Anne was trying to tell her guiding clients. The idea that context leads to care goes back to the Transcendentalists. "If a man would be alone, let him look at the stars. The rays that come from those heavenly worlds, will separate between him and vulgar things," Emerson wrote in "Nature."

In the early '70s, when the LaChapelles came to Silverton, the wave of ski-resort construction was cresting. Telluride opened in 1972, just across the ridge from Silverton, and by the end of the decade the resort was synonymous with wealth and celebrity. Ski areas were turning into ski resorts, focused on real estate and family vacations. Snowbird, which opened next to Alta in 1971 just as the LaChapelles were leaving, became a hub for a new style of skiing called *freeskiing* or *extreme skiing*, where skiers would prove themselves on the steepest terrain, constantly pushing the envelope. Those skiers were lauded for their risks. They were sometimes given gear sponsorships, and movie parts, and a modicum of fame. They became role models for average skiers.

And it wasn't just skiing that was changing. In the '80s and '90s, many individual outdoor sports—climbing, biking, kayaking, the nascent sport of snowboarding—grew more extreme, influenced in part by the growth of surf and skate culture, which valorized risk and progress.

That obsession with progression hasn't stopped since. These days in Silverton, where the backcountry skiing has put the hard-to-reach town on the map, it feels like everyone is pushing harder, farther. There's a local homeschooled teenager who is often the first person to ski big lines after a storm. On weekends the parking lots are full, and I often find myself looking at tracks on steep committing faces, even when the snowpack seems shallow and weak. We're still glorifying high-consequence free solo climbs, or hairball best-trick competitions, or the few remaining mountains that haven't been documented as climbed. That desire to push and compare is made even more prominent and immediate by Strava and social media. I am guilty. I have taken and retaken pictures to ensure that I look cool.

Dolores was worried about the commodification and commercialization of skiing. She had been since she left Aspen in the '40s. She was concerned about the ways that upholding a tourism economy might hollow out the culture of the places that people visited. "What do we who love the mountains do to live in the mountains?" she asked in a story in *Mountainfreak* magazine in 1998. "Industrial tourism. We bring capitalism here. For instance, here in Silverton people jump off the train and run into the stupid knick-knack stores."

Dolores thought that extreme skiers, in their quest to push harder, were missing the flow. But she had also explicitly and inadvertently led to the growth of the sport. From opening up ski terrain at Alta to pushing the edge of what was considered skiable in Silverton to the lessons she imparted in *Deep Powder Snow*, which was published in 1993, as extreme sports were coming into focus. She spent her winters chasing snow in big mountains and her summers scrambling into the same high peaks, going as hard as she could. Like Georgie, she was trying to have it both ways—she wanted to stretch her own physical experience, but she didn't want the world to change.

The cover copy of *Deep Powder Snow* sounds like the teaser for a ski movie. Dolores talks about outrunning avalanches and skiing every day. It's easy to skip over the philosophy and focus on the glory of feeling your body in motion. And that's largely how her book was interpreted. With her words she inadvertently gave a generation of skiers permission to devote themselves to obsessive powder chasing, and many of them missed her message of connection and care.

In 1975, two sociologists from Washington State University, Riley Dunlap and Robert Bruce Heffernan, studied the relationship between recreation and conservation. They sent out a broad survey to Washington residents asking about their recreation habits, their environmental concerns, and their opinions about government expenditures on things like pollution control and forest preservation. They divided outdoor recreation into two categories: appreciative activities, like hiking or skiing, and consumptive ones, like hunting or fishing.

The researchers found that a responder's emotional attachment to the environment drove advocacy more than any single activity. Dunlap and Heffernan attempted to quantify those feelings, and over the next few decades, as outdoor recreation and environmental attitudes changed, more studies corroborated their findings. There was a minor positive correlation between recreation and environmental ethics. In the end, people were still more concerned about local issues, like noise pollution in their nearby pond, than they were about diffuse issues, like drought or climate change. Similar to when Anne was trying to educate people about acid rain, the scope of care was small and personal.

Dolores was trying to show how recreation could dissolve your ego boundary and make you part of a whole. But the philosophy and the connection aren't completely clear. Experience *can* lead to stewardship, but it's murky. Like Dave Foreman said, recreation can often lead to preservation of landscapes for anthropocentric reasons, for human use, which has historically failed to consider ecosystem connectivity and the consequences of our actions. If you just think about landscapes as a canvas for recreation, and think about protecting them just for that, then you're still stuck in a colonial, anthropocentric, extractive mindset, barely better than the miners chopping slag out of the hills.

By the early '90s, Silverton was getting by on tourism. It was just enough to support a few burger and pizza joints, a coffee shop, and some T-shirt and jewelry shops, open seasonally. Over the next decade, the town's population shrank by nearly half, and unemployment was 4 times the state average. Families moved out, and their houses became mostly vacant second homes for visitors, or they crumbled on their foundations.

But things started to change in the early 2000s, when a

couple from Montana came to town, sniffing around about opening a ski resort.

In the late '90s, a snowboarder named Aaron Brill started traveling to undeveloped parts of the mountain west. He was looking to open a ski hill, inspired by the low-key, single-lift ski areas he'd seen in New Zealand. He'd initially written off Colorado as too built-up, but he stopped through the southwest corner of the state, just to look.

He thought about Lake City, on the north side of the Weminuche Wilderness, but decided it wouldn't get enough snow, and then he noticed Storm Peak, just up Cement Creek from Silverton, which seemed to have the right alchemy of steepness and snow, and which was largely on Bureau of Land Management land, which meant that it might be possible to develop.

He rented a place in town and started looking at maps and land-use codes. Then he came back with his girlfriend, Jen, who helped make the ski area a reality.

The Brills were part of a change in the skiing world. Better backcountry gear, big powder skis, and that push toward extreme sports led to a sect of skiers who wanted high-adrenaline ski experiences. The Brills saw an opportunity to create that experience in Silverton. Their plan was to build the first new ski area in the state in decades, across a beautiful swath of private and public lands. They wanted the infrastructure to be simple: one lift with access to prime skiing.

A lot of locals didn't like the idea, especially because the Brills' operation would close off wide swaths of popular backcountry skiing in the winter. To this day there are locals who don't like the Brills because they think they stormed in and changed the culture of the town.

But eventually the town government, and many residents,

ultimately came down in favor of the new ski area, called Silverton Mountain. "The winter economy is less than 10 percent that of the summer economy, and the community has experienced, and continues to experience, the highest winter unemployment rates and highest average annual unemployment rates in the entire state of Colorado since 1992," the mayor wrote to the Bureau of Land Management in a letter supporting Brill's proposal.

Because Silverton was so economically depressed, the Brills qualified for state business-development loans. "The state of Colorado loaned us money when nobody else would," Aaron told *Snowboard* magazine. "It wasn't enough money to complete the project, but it was enough to get started."

Even Dolores told *High Country News* that she thought the Brills' ski operation could "make Silverton a real mountain community again."

This was high praise for Jen Brill, who had encountered Dolores's writing through her Pitzer College professor, deep ecologist Paul Shepard. "Aaron convinced me to come [to Silverton] by saying 'Dolores LaChapelle lives in this town,'" Jen said.

Jen heard that Dolores was known to be standoffish, especially to young women, but she was determined to befriend her, so she joined Dolores's tai chi class. She found her to be a tough, judgmental instructor, but over time Dolores opened up to her.

"We met one or two times at first, where she questioned me a lot: 'Who are you, ski area developer lady? I've met your husband. This isn't going to work!'" Jen said. "She wanted to make sure the ski area I built was reflective of what she was trying to do in ski culture."

Jen said they were trying to make Silverton Mountain both an economic boost and a pure experience, a nearly impossible combination. To their credit, it was a different kind of ski mountain than the ones that had come to clog the nearby valleys like Telluride. Now, 20 years later, there's still just one lift, the base lodge is a canvas-wall tent, rental gear comes out of a converted school bus, and the only bathroom is a porta potty. There is no lodging, no restaurant, no other activities. It's just about the skiing. But even the Brills' low-key approach changed the town's image.

The economic boom wasn't as big as they might have thought, but it was part of the wave of new recreation. Silverton Mountain championed soul skiing, but it also sliced a chunk of land away from the public. They brought jobs, but for a specific group of people, and they brought attention, which led to more winter visitors, for good and bad. "We're recovering," former miner Willie Tookey told the *Westword* magazine as the ski area was opening. "But it's a different community."

Recreational development comes with a series of complications, from crowded streets to skewed housing prices. Lindsey Halvorson, a Town of Silverton board member, says that the town is trying to walk the unsteady line of growth without trying to damage the natural beauty that brings people there to begin with. They don't want to price out locals or ruin the culture, but they want to build a sustainable economy, at a scale that supports the town. Right now, it doesn't quite work. For instance there's not enough housing—especially affordable housing for seasonal workers like ski guides—and because of the small local tax base, the town is dependent on grants and outside money. Halvorson says Silverton needs more people, more economic opportunities, and more third places for community building, especially when so many of the services and business are directed toward visitors. It's not quite big enough to support itself, but the town's government is also worried about getting too big.

In 2023, the Brills sold Silverton Mountain to a group of young venture capitalists from Aspen who largely invest in heli-skiing operations. It's unclear how they'll change it, but they're already helicoptering in clients from the fancy towns.

Before she came to Colorado, Jen was one of the only women in the early days of snowboarding contests. When she and Aaron came to Silverton from Montana to open the ski area, she was leading construction projects and building the business, heading up a crew of men. Then, when the mountain opened, she was one of the only mountain guides. She liked being a leader. She liked working with a pack of guys and doing hard physical work, but she also said she was caught feeling like she had to be the toughest, strongest person on the mountain. Like Georgie, she felt like she had to be superwoman, both better than all the men and singular. "That's how we were raised: There was room for one girl in this space, and you had to protect your spot," she told me. "That's where Dolores was coming from, too, as a mountaineer and a writer. She had to be better than the men to be the same."

Jen says she worries that she perpetuated the trend of exclusion. She knows that she has been shitty to other women because she was defensive of her singular status, but she says that it was so hard to hold on that she couldn't see any other way to exist and feel respected. There was no model, and she felt like she was under the microscope from the staff and the skiers and the Silverton locals. She sounds a little wistful when she talks about seeing younger women in Silverton connecting with each other instead of competing. She thinks they are carving out more space through their collective presence. "They're bringing each other up. It's not 1970 or even 2002 anymore," she says.

It's not 2002 anymore, and there are often groups of women bootpacking the ridge at Silverton Mountain—there are more women backcountry skiing than ever before—but the boys are still largely in power. For instance, the staff and guides at Silverton are still largely male, and that's true in nearly every facet of the ski world. There might be more women at the bottom of the pyramid, but the top is still predominantly male. I've often been the only woman skiing in a pack of men. And just as often I've made myself breathless trying to keep up, because I felt like I'd let my whole gender down or never be invited again if I didn't. Some of that feeling was in my head, but some of it was real, made so by snide comments. And I felt a leering kind of satisfaction when I *was* the only woman who could hang.

Dolores saved bundles of Ed's letters, from the early ones he sent when they were first dating to the acrimonious ones in the depths of their divorce. I found them in a crowded box in her archive, which has been moldering in the spare room of Ananda Foley, the LaChapelles' son David's partner, since Dolores's death. They're crammed in with other correspondence, newsletters, and book invoices. Through Ed's words I learned the pain of their conflicts over money and sex, and their deeper battles over priorities and power. I could feel Dolores pushing against the constraints of gender and the structure of marriage. She was, as she said, "a fierce Catholic virgin" when they got married, and once she realized how much she felt trapped by the morals she grew up with, she was constantly trying to break free from them, academically, emotionally, and philosophically.

In their exchanges, I could see their stubbornness and the ways they talked past each other, but Ed surprised me on the page. I'd pegged him as an icy scientist, but his words were romantic and charged with emotion, especially as they worked through their split. He said love was an action, and he wanted to work on their life together, even if their problems were complex. He forgave Dolores's infidelities and empathized with her struggles, but he also wanted her to drop back into the life they had been living.

Dolores, on the other hand, wanted progress. She concluded their marriage couldn't be repaired. Once she was on her own, Dolores had what she jokingly referred to as *seasonal boyfriends*, who would come and stay for a winter or spring. She said she liked that rotation, having time alone and time in partnership, but Jen says she might have struggled to find someone who could align with her life. "I really loved that concept that she loved the mountains first, although I think she wanted a partner, but the kind of mountain men she was into didn't fit into Silverton," Jen said.

The same seemed true in motherhood. She couldn't quite find the mold. She said that watching David grow up in the mountains helped inform her work, and she often wrote about how important it was to introduce children to nature. She wrote in her compendium that 1953, the year after David was born, was a "happy year, new baby, beautiful place." But according to David's partner, Ananda, he was hurt by Dolores's lack of interest and engagement, and the way she prioritized skiing above him. And he wasn't wrong. "I knew Dolores for

19 years before I knew she had a child," a neighbor said at the Silverton gathering. Others agreed that when they thought about Dolores, they didn't think about her as a mother or a wife. That was partly by design. Dolores wanted to exist outside of gendered expectations while leaning into the appealing parts of feminine wisdom. Her ambivalence and contradictions showed up most clearly in her engagement with ecofeminism.

The term *ecofeminism* was coined by French writer Françoise d'Eaubonne in 1974. It was born out of environmental-philosophy conversations about how patriarchal ideas of dominance and unchecked growth, going back to biblical times and earlier, harmed both women and nature. It became its own strand of advocacy.

According to *Britannica*, the early ecofeminists "noted that women and nature were often depicted as chaotic, irrational, and in need of control, while men were frequently characterized as rational, ordered, and thus capable of directing the use and development of women and nature." The first ecofeminists were teasing out the cultural history of how women and nature have been treated like disposable property. They argued that we couldn't truly understand how we were abusing the planet if we didn't understand how women were being abused, undervalued, and discounted. Like deep ecology, ecofeminism is a way of looking at the planet as an interconnected system.

But while Anne called herself a "fierce eco-feminist" and saw a clear connection between her ecology research and her work to get women outside, Dolores was against the philosophy. In a March 1989 *Earth First!* journal essay titled "No, I'm Not an Eco-feminist: A Few Words in Defense of Men," she laced into feminism and ecofeminism in particular. To her, ecofeminists were missing the true work of ecological unity by dividing men and women. She could not see the value in highlighting the ways women had been harmed. Instead, Dolores saw herself as a Taoist who needed male and female energy. She said feminists were "so trapped into outdoing men that they are now just as enslaved as men by the Industrial Growth Society."

At the same time, she believed in the fundamental differences between men and women, which she cited as showing up everywhere in nature. She said that, as a woman, she worried about other people's emotions differently than men did. But she also felt those differences should be secondary to her accomplishments. She was giving in to an old, destructive trope, one that has always been a dark shadow of women's liberation: blaming women for the ways they've been confined. It's the same thing that sets up the trap of the superwoman syndrome, and the loneliness of being the only woman on a peak in a group of men. "I have never considered being a female as the deciding factor in what to do with my life. I did not consider myself a woman and then a mountain climber," she wrote.

"It's like you," Steve told me. "You don't want to be a woman writer, you just want to be a fucking writer."

But the playing field has never been level, and you can't break down the binary if you don't acknowledge the context. Ecofeminists were trying to acknowledge past harms that made that playing field uneven and point to a way forward.

Part of why I have been pathologically interested in Dolores and Georgie and Anne is because their stories outline a common struggle to make space in arenas that are both implicitly and explicitly male dominated. Ecofeminism helped me make sense of the connections and contradictions that underpin their narratives.

How did we get into this mess? is one of Dolores's core questions. She was perpetually peeling back layers to try to understand the depth of our relationship with the earth, and to put modern behaviors into historical and social context. I can see the work she did to try to connect the dots across decades and centuries, digging into old belief systems. So it feels particularly frustrating that this complicated intersection with gender is where she falters.

In some of their later letters, Ed wrote about his empathy for the way Dolores felt trapped by the ideas she grew up in. He was writing about Catholicism, but he could have just as easily been writing about problematic individualism and the bootstrapping American myth of conquest and personal liberty. Those ideas go back as far as the idea of wilderness does, and Dolores was still wrangling with them, trying to find her own place, and lashing out at anything that made her feel minimalized.

Dolores's myth of exceptionalism negates community—ironically the very thing she most craved. When she rejected ecofeminism, she was failing to see the very web she claimed was crucial.

After I found her *Earth First!* column about ecofeminism, I had to walk away from Dolores for a while. The dissonance made me mad. She should have known better. She should have seen the structural reasons why women's opportunities were limited. Other people did.

I was mad at her, and mad at myself. Had I just spent all this time and energy digging into a trio of problematic women?

Ones who upheld the same broken patriarchal standards that we're still dealing with because they couldn't get out of their own ways? Had I picked the wrong heroes?

These worries first emerged when researcher Denise Mitten asked me why I was looking at these particular women. They weren't good feminists, she told me. They were self-centered and dismissive of other women, and they weren't carefully making a path for the rest of us to follow.

But after being away from their work for a while, I softened. I could see that claiming a label isn't the whole picture. And I didn't come to these particular women in hopes of discovering their feminist politics, or even because I wanted to directly emulate the way they presented themselves in the outdoor world. I came because of what I'd seen them do outside.

When I focus on the good side of Dolores's ethics and ideas, I can see what she was trying to explain and create: more freedom in her marriage and parenthood, more space in the sport, more ecological awareness. She was prying open the bars of environmentalism and recreation to make spaces for the kind of connection and flow that lead to sustainability. She was trying to form a life for herself, based on her gut-level sense of what was important and true.

In the end, I love how Dolores, Georgie, and Anne followed their own intense interests and curiosities. I wanted to see myself in a lineage of competent women, to see my desires reflected. In them I could see parts of my own obsessive brain. They all chased that feeling of clarity, even if they compromised or failed, or showed their ugly sides along the way. That kind of intellectual and physical independence is a big part of what I see as feminism. It's what I'm looking for in heroes. I just wish they'd seen it, too.

THE SACRED IN THE EVERYDAY

"I'm overwhelmed," Ananda Foley tells me. "It just feels like so much to deal with, and I think I've been building it up. Hopefully you can help me move through it."

She leads me into her home office. The tiny room is stacked with boxes and file folders; there is barely a path to the closet in the back. We stare at Dolores's personal archive, which has been hiding there for years.

When Dolores died in 2007, her reams of papers—her correspondences and her books, and her compendiums full of notes—went to David. And then, 2 years later, when he died of throat cancer at 56, they went to his partner, Ananda, along with David's belongings and some of Ed's files. All of it—the painting David did of Dolores near her death, Ed's immaculate travel journals from their time together, scads of paperwork from their book sales—has been stacked up in Ananda's office for the past 16 years.

It has stayed there because she's struggled to find the best place for Dolores's work. Ananda was connected to David, not Dolores, and relationships between the LaChapelles had been complicated for decades, but Ananda remains a diligent and thoughtful custodian. This week she's finally decided to give the collection to the San Juan County Historical Society in Silverton, which has expressed interest since Dolores died.

I met Ananda at the equinox celebration for Dolores, the same one where I started to understand her complexity and how everyone there saw her differently: the ski hero, the philosopher, the sage. Everyone knew a different texture of Dolores, which is one of the reasons that Ananda has struggled to decide where her archive should land.

Ananda knew I was interested in Dolores's legacy, and we live in the same Durango neighborhood, so when she decided to organize and donate Dolores's archive, she asked if I might help.

I head over on an evening full of heavy, electric summer heat. In the kitchen, I sit in front of the fan as Ananda snips chives from the garden onto a homemade curry and tells me she knows the archive is doing no good in her spare room, but she's unsure how best to honor Dolores's complicated legacy.

We pull the boxes out one at a time, separating Dolores's papers from David's paintings and Ed's careful logs of his life. There are boxes of slides from her time in Europe with Ed. Folders of drafts for her *Earth First!* column, with notes from her editor, John Davis. Programs from ski events where she was lauded, letters from publishing companies rejecting her manuscripts. Notes about art and culture she liked: Melissa Zink's art, a movie review clipping about *The Gods Must Be Crazy.* I find plans for a remodel of their Silverton house, painstakingly drawn by Ed before he moved away. I find a photo of Dolores standing with Michael Zimmerman and Bill Devall at the Heidegger in the Mountains event, their names scrawled in pencil on the back in her spiderweb handwriting.

There's a box of her books with handmade indexes penciled into the backs, cross-referencing concepts she thought were important, outlining her web of connected ideas. Ananda says that Dolores created her own library system. I open up the boxes of compendiums, and the rest of the evening disappears as I read through the recorded history of her philosophy, the one she made for herself. I can see her striving and her obsessiveness, her self-flagellation and her hard work, how she tried to prove out her ideas.

My back cramps from sitting cross-legged on the living room floor, feeling Dolores's life take shape in front of me. I open diaries that kept track of what she ate, the weather, her heart, and how she dealt with age and her crumbling body.

As Ananda and I sort, we try to put things in order, from her Phi Beta Kappa card and pictures of her Aspen classroom to images of her with a long white braid leading a circle of young people through tai chi. In archiving, we have to decide how to tell the story: What's important? What's connected? What will carry through?

I think about the way Leslie spent years wading through Anne's pack-rat stash of slides and papers under her porch. And how the exhibit of her cabin at the back of Adirondack Experience Museum felt like a polished approximation, one that didn't quite convey the whole truth.

It's the same with the dusty, two-line plaque about Georgie in the back of the River History Museum. Or the way Dolores has been flattened into a single-minded ski guru. It all feels too small to encompass their baggy stories, but how do you do it right?

When I talked to Brooke Williams about his time with Dolores, he said something, out of nowhere, that surprised me. "The dead are out there all around us, and there are kind of holes in the membrane, whenever it is," he said, after he asked me why I was interested in Dolores's story. "I'd be asking *Why you, why now?* And why is there such a gap in the time between when we last thought about her? You kind of got picked. I think that's really interesting."

Ananda and I work into the night, moving boxes out of the office and into the living room, holding slide film to the light. We do it until our eyes fuzz, and then I walk home through the dark neighborhood, thinking about what it meant to be chosen.

When I come back the next morning, two of Ananda's friends are helping sort, and there are photos spread out across the living room floor. I find a little bit of bare ground by the box of compendiums and keep sorting through. Midmorning, Katrina Blair comes in with her dog Jasper in tow.

She brought us fermented burdock root and sprouts to snack on. Katrina's farm, Turtle Lake Refuge, is exploding with fruits and vegetables this time of year, but she also runs programs that regenerate parks and restore ecosystems with native plants. She's devoted to the health of those plants, something Dolores pushed her to do.

The food perks us up, and then Katrina sits down in the middle of the pile of pictures and papers and she starts to tell us stories. Katrina names people and fills in gaps. With her plant medicine, and the ways she works to heal the patchwork of landscapes around us, she is living out Dolores's legacy.

The circle of people who loved Dolores are still trying to uphold her ideas. Art hosts talking gourd circles to keep Dolores's ideas about sharing stories alive. Steve is still teaching writing and philosophy, even though he could have retired long ago, because engaging with a new generation of students keeps him jazzed. Jen Brill is up in the big mountains, still living out Dolores's ideals. "Dolores was carving out the path that we could all follow," Katrina told me. "She had to do the work to make the connections that now feel obvious." But despite those connections, Dolores's work is still difficult to find. I had to hunt for any information beyond the superficial ski stories, just like I did with the other two women.

Steve said that beyond the people she knew and influenced personally, Dolores was trying to make her ideas widespread. Dolores had been a teacher of some sort since she moved to Aspen, and over time, she leaned into it more as skiing began to hurt, especially in the joints and bones she'd crunched in the avalanche. "When she couldn't ski, she threw herself into writing and the role of teacher," Steve told me.

As her reputation grew, she began to get some of the recognition she desired. "*Deep Powder Snow* was a pretty reliable North Star for a lot of us in the late '90s and early 2000s," Jen Brill told me. Fans showed up in Silverton, looking for her, bringing gifts. Sometimes she would put them up for a few days. "She was not patient," Art said. "She preferred her own company to idiots. But if you could go along for the ride with her, you could learn a lot."

Dolores told Steve that the problem with women was that they didn't know what they wanted. When I asked him if she knew what *she* wanted, he laughed. He said she was stuck in the swirl herself, fighting through a dense web of ideas about the best way to live. In her notes, I can see her struggle. She could never relax into nuance and uncertainty.

Steve told me Dolores had a fear of being obscure. And that became more true as she established her strand of deep ecology. I think that's why she disparaged ecofeminism. She was scared there wouldn't be a place for her intellectual legacy, especially if she was pigeonholed as a woman. Like Anne and Georgie, she wanted to be revered in a way that we typically code as masculine.

Ritual was one of the most common themes in Dolores's work. "Ritual is essential because it is truly the pattern that connects," she wrote in *Deep Ecology for the Twenty-First Century.* "Ritual provides us with a tool for learning to think logically, analogically, and ecologically as we move toward a sustainable culture. Most important of all, perhaps, during rituals we have the experience, unique in our culture, of neither opposing nature or trying to be in communion with nature, but of finding ourselves within nature."

For a long time, skiing was Dolores's steadiest ritual, starting with the pattern of afternoon runs at Alta. "I did not 'get into' ritual. What happened was that ritual engulfed me before I had a word for it or knew anything about such a process," she wrote in *Deep Powder Snow.*

In Silverton, she started chanting groups, she led large-scale retreats, and she started seasonal festivals. She had her own smaller seasonal rituals, too. Jen said that she'd call you up and force you to come over when a certain flower was blooming in her yard or when the sun was setting at a particularly perfect angle. As she had learned through her research on Indigenous cultures and on the history of religion, practices disappear if we don't pass them down.

Part of it might have been the repressed Catholic deep inside her, which loved the purposefulness and routine of religious rites, but as her focus widened and she started connecting the dots of environmental history, philosophy, and anthropology, ritual became a core way for her to live out those tenets of deep ecology.

I think ritual can be big things like religious rites and weddings, but also secular, specific celebrations like Georgie's river rat initiations, or the celebratory slug of booze below Lava Rapid. Stopping to mark the equinox. Noticing the freeze-up on the lake every year. To me it feels like a way to make meaning, closing the gap between body and brain.

Dimitris Xygalatas, the author of *Ritual: How Seemingly Senseless Acts Make Life Worth Living*, says one of the paradoxes around rituals is that we can't really explain or think through them. "People often swear by the importance of rituals without being able to articulate why they're so important," he writes.

I struggle to articulate why it feels important for me to be outside. The closest thing I've found to explain it is *hierophany*, a word sociologist and religious historian Mircea Eliade coined to explain the way the sacred expresses itself in the real world. I feel that when I'm particularly tuned in, noticing the sunsplatter of shaking aspen leaves or feeling the glitter of snow underfoot.

Dolores said we wouldn't notice the sacred in the everyday or see how much we were enfolded in it if we didn't have rituals, even ones we might not think of as such. We notice changes in the world around us when we come back to the same practices and find them changed. When our summers along the Adirondack lakes are too smoky, or when we come back to the river to find a beloved beach washed away. Ritual is the fragile, fading freeze-up at Twitchell Lake, or the way Georgie couldn't feel the spring swell of the river after the dam went in.

This last winter, ritual clarified an alarming truth, like Dolores said it could. Storms dissolved to the west before they even reached us. Snow quickly melted, frying to lace in the sun. I stuck to shallow slopes almost all season; I never felt the momentum build, and my body never found the rhythm.

In the summer, it stayed strange, wet and hot and wild. Instead of the usual monsoon, which tends to show up in the afternoon when pressure builds over the La Plata Mountains to the west, storms flashed through the night. I came back from a rainy weekend of backpacking in the Weminuche to find that a chunk of the mountain behind my house had slid across the highway, the mud mangling the road.

Other places had it worse. My local river, the Animas, runs from Silverton down to Durango, flushes into Lake Powell, and joins up with the Colorado before flowing through the Grand Canyon. This year, the whole river system seemed either too dry or too inundated. In August, exactly a year after I'd been in the canyon, Havasu Creek flooded, forcing hundreds of visitors to be evacuated by helicopter. One woman died, her body flushed all the way to the river where a group of rafters found her. It could have been us.

Right now, the planet is constantly breaking records for ecological unraveling: the hottest year on Earth, the warmest day on record, the most money spent in a single hurricane season, the peak of global energy use. There is severe flooding in the Adirondacks, and decadal drought in the Colorado River Basin. The reservoir above the Grand Canyon hovers just around deadpool, in part because the snow in the San Juans sublimates off in the spring.

I know climate and weather are different—one is point source, one is pattern—but I can feel one reflected in the other, often visible to me through my rituals of recreation. I started this inquiry with recreation, but I can't untangle it from conservation, and from what we're doing—or not doing—to sustain the places where we go out.

Dolores, and the thinkers that came after her, carved out three ways we can do that. First, to hold the line on destruction, to stop and slow down ecological damage, and to clearly communicate what's happening. Then, to change economies and ecosystems to operate at a smaller, more sustainable scale. This is the meat of what Dolores thought was important. She was trying to understand, as modern environmental thinker Joanna Macy wrote, "what interlocking causes enslave us to an insatiable economy that uses our Earth as supply house and sewer?" That necessitates taking the idea of bioregionalism and writing it large, through everything from housing and how we live, to transportation. Changes have to happen in recreation, too. To do that we need a value system at the heart of any kind of sustainable change. That's the third step. For deep ecologists, it's the idea of inherent interconnectedness, and the value of every living thing. Macy says this step is liberation work, too, because, like ecofeminism, it prioritizes marginalized communities and ecosystems and strives for some kind of level playing field.

In laying out those values, it's hard not to think about how things could have been different if we'd heeded these three women's warnings. If we'd heard Anne's calls about dead lakes and destruction, and how small impacts added up. If we'd held a line on preserving land. If we'd listened to Dolores's ideas about living in line with the season and the place. If we'd embraced more of Earth First!'s early ideas, like the ones about fighting deforestation and dam construction, that proved to be prescience. If the three of them hadn't been discounted as angry women, or weird crones, or illegitimate strivers.

But I also know hindsight isn't very helpful. It's one of my least favorite parts of Dolores's work. She spends so much time looking back, stuck in a kind of nostalgia that can feel like wishful denial. I'm not immune to that feeling—one piece of these women's appeal is the landscapes they were in at the time, which feel wilder and less damaged than mine. But I live now, when the canyons are often either flash flooding or dry, and no amount of nostalgia is going to change that.

This time of year, as summer slips into fall, I hike into the higher peaks, toward Silverton, and see strands of dead aspen among the golden ones. I walk over creeks stained orange from acid mine drainage and skirt the ponds impacted by the pollution dredged up decades ago.

I know that sustainability can't just come from awareness and ritual—it needs action, too—but it's still an important piece. Georgie showed me how you can feel the transcendence of tiny miracles in the canyon if you pay attention. Anne underscored the importance of independent thinking, and all the ways we need to fight and observe. Dolores did the research to back up those ephemeral feelings of connection and show how we need them to forge a path toward a more sustainable way of living.

Georgie is the *where*, and Anne is the *how*, but Dolores is the *why*. Why it's important to be outside and be immersed. Why we need to pay attention to the coalescence of all the ways we live within a broader system, for better or worse.

Dolores died at 80, after her heart, which had been stuttering along for years, finally gave out. Silverton isn't an easy place to get older. It is harsh and cold, and there is no local health care. And it's particularly hard if you've staked your worth on what your body can do.

In her final years, she grew increasingly dependent on neighbors and friends, like Steve Meyers's wife, Debby, who is a nurse. After her body slowed down, she relied on her brain and her quick wit to keep her connected to people. She was always cutting out articles for Katrina. But eventually she became less sharp. She felt like she always had to be producing something or pushing the limit or proving she was capable.

That was true of all three of them—Georgie didn't want anyone to see her at the end—and I think that's an unforeseen hazard of pegging your life to motion. Who are you when your body fades? How do you hold on to your sense of self-worth if you're not the river guide or the woodswoman or the best skier on the mountain?

Some of Dolores's friends told me that, for all her learning and striving, she didn't seem very happy. She had lots of ideas about what it meant to be enlightened and fulfilled, but she could never relax into what she learned. She was always moving the goalposts.

The same is true of the other women, too. They were so mission-driven that I worry they missed out on contentment. By the time Anne built Thoreau II, she wanted to hide from the world. Georgie was so worried about business that she rarely relaxed into the canyon.

I worry that my own sense of self-worth is too tied to my body's ability. I worry that when I'm somewhere beautiful I'm still often frantic, unable to really tune in. TA Loeffler told me, way back, that it's often easier to learn the hard skills—the ones coded as masculine, the knot tying and rowing and building houses—than it is to learn emotional resilience or compromise or attention. I can try to push myself in the mountains, or ski something big and scary, or hike deeper into the woods, but I can't force myself to be calm and release.

I do know that the good part of being outside—of going down a river or up a mountain—is that on some level you have to give in to the pace of your surroundings you can only rush so much. I know that the only time Dolores could shirk the pressure of her frantic brain was when she was skiing. In all her intellectual quests for enlightenment and connection, the place she absorbed the ideas was on the mountain, in motion.

On a Thursday, when the leaves are peaking, I drive up past the trailhead to Engineer Mountain where the Heidegger crew hiked and stop at the edge of Lime Creek where it spills past the highway. I start running downhill through the tunnel of aspen, past the tapestry of colors on the ridges, green pines stippled with gold, patches of umber and red. It was a wet summer, which apparently makes the colors brighter, and the mountains glow. I run farther than I have in a long time, eyes on the horizon, feet flinging out over the rocks and ruts. It is nearly 2 years to the day after I stood under the turning aspens with Dolores's disciples and started to understand the breadth of her curiosity.

There's a continuum from personal to systematic. That's what I'm learning over time, by tracking these women's stories. I might not have been able to see how I got to the river before learning Georgie's story, but now I know I'm part of the curve.

I now know that Georgie's radical sense of adventure led to expanded recreational land use, which opened up into Anne's independent venture into the woods, which led to her concrete understanding of our changing climate. From there, Dolores was able to build an ethic of ecological connectivity. And all of their lives, and the things they worked toward, had ripples that expanded far beyond their personal stories. Things that seemed radical in their time, like talking about industrial pollution, are now mainstream. That I can go to the woods alone without thinking too much and that I take those freedoms for granted mean things have changed, even just by a margin.

I am a similar age to Dolores when she came to Silverton. She was 38 when she decided, finally, to be a writer. I was 38 when I moved to these southwest mountains and decided to write this book—two decisions that didn't seem connected at the time, but which are now irrevocably tied. My curiosity, like hers, stemmed from the connection between my body, my desire to be outside, and the ache I felt about the environment degrading. I found context for my feelings the way Dolores did: by digging through the past to see myself in a system, to find proof that what I felt was real.

I run through that golden tunnel of leaves, pushing my lungs to the edge, and follow the creek as it dips and weaves, enfolded in a feeling of fierce delight.

CONCLUSION: HEROES

I go back to the desert like I do so often in the fall, when it is mellow and red gold, when the rocks still hold the heat of the summer. I drive into the canyons to the east of Bowknot Bend, above the river. Last time I came through here I was on a mission to find Georgie's name, desperate for some proof that she had been here. This time I'm not searching, I'm just out for myself.

Nights like this, alone in the echo of canyon country, were some of my first attempts at feeling independent outside. I'd camp outside my car, vigilant for weird noises in the night but elated by being alone. For a long time, it was a way to test myself, to prove that I could make it through the night and that I was bigger than my fears, both irrational, like ghosts, and less so, like other people.

Now a night out alone feels more like a retreat. Just me sloughed down to my simplest parts: water, food, a notebook, a sleeping bag, the sky. I rarely set up a tent because I am lazy and I like to see the stars. I feel like I'm coming back to myself.

I have sifted through so many stories of these three women that the details feel like they're sitting under my skin. I think about Georgie cackling through the big rapids, or cracking open a beer on the beach, ready to launch into one of her tall tales. I think about Anne scuba diving to see what was really going on under the surface of the lake. And Dolores, up early, skinning her way uphill. I feel like I'm part of that.

I feel like I have heroes now. I'm moved by their drive toward resonance and truth. They each carved out their lives around a mission. Even when they didn't have many people in their corners, even when their life choices were unpopular and unsupported, even when they were exhausted. In the end, they wedged open space for people like me, even though there is still so much more space to be claimed.

It's not that I necessarily want to go live at Thoreau II or be the one gambling with flood-stage rivers or unskied avalanche terrain. And I've seen how they could be brutal and biased and bullheaded. But I've learned that Dolores was a magpie, picking what she liked, pulling out the threads to shape her beliefs, and I think that I can magpie the parts that I like, too.

That, Maureen Murdock says, is the heroine's journey: continued curiosity, constant cycles of alignment, choosing the parts that work and moving forward, staring the ugliness in the face, acknowledging it in yourself, and still wanting more.

The last step of that journey Murdock outlined is breaking through constraining stories, taking stock of history, and using the parts that make sense to build up a new paradigm.

I thought it didn't matter much that they were women at first, because I was still stuck in old expectations. I didn't identify my bad attitude, or my superwoman striving, or my dismissal of gender restrictions for what it was until way too long after the fact. That's because I've been told things should be different by now. That we could be whatever we wanted without the necessary work to reframe a system that drastically confines what it means to be a woman. But that's not true, we're still wading through the sludge, and that's why it feels important to tell the stories of people who made things change. I'm not saying they were perfect, but I came in impressed by their feats and came out impressed by their backbones.

And I do think their feats matter. I have noticed when I tell other women about Georgie, Anne, and Dolores, they light up. And that is a reason enough to ensure their names don't just fade into pale scratches on remote rocks.

I might never get my own wild cabin. I will never be the first to explore an unseen river canyon, and I'm nobody's guru, but I can take what I've learned from them: a fierce love of place; a rejection of unnecessary social constraints; the feeling that things can change. The knowledge that everything else is hollow if the places we love aren't healthy and sustained. Being outside is tied to pleasure and independence. For me it's tied to my body. And being outside here is irrevocably connected to a particular kind of American story of land use and freedom, ugly and open and tricky and changed. Impossible to ignore, because we're still part of the story.

So I wake up early, just as the light breaks. I make coffee, walk to the edge of the soft sandstone canyon, watch the sun gild its edges. Later today I'll be back in the morass of cell service, probably frantic and staring at screens. But for now, I can sit and listen to the wrens and to the wind coming through the curve of the canyon like Georgie might have. I can dangle my feet off the edge and feel alive, like Anne on the dock, or Dolores on a ridgeline, hitched up to everything around me, home.

ACKNOWLEDGMENTS

The best part of this work is getting to hear other people's stories, and trying to pull together history from the vault would have been unimaginable without the people who are the keepers of memory and knowledge, and who shared some of that with me, including Renny Russell, Jody Cardamone, Steve Meyers, Art Goodtimes, Marty Hogan, Tom Martin, Roz Jirge, Ray Gorospe, John Shocklee and the whole crew at OARS, Teresa Matheson, Ann Friedman (thank you for all the walks and talks), Clare Menzel, Penny Harr, Alex Lee, Katrina Blair, Ananda Foley (thank you for reminding me to think about my teachers), Brooke Williams, Becca Lawton, Louise Teal, Leslie Suprenant, Lynn Hamilton, Caitlin Kelly, Jim Lassoie, Megan Mayhew Bergman, Jen Brill, Lindsey Halvorson, TA Loeffler, Denise Mitten, Sally McCracken, Lew Steiger, and the folks at the Cline Library.

Once you get the stories, you have to turn them into a book. I'm grateful for so many people who helped make that happen, including my thoughtful and kind editor at Hanover Square Press, John Glynn, who is excellent at knowing when and where to cut my rambling, and the agents who have been in my corner, Zoe Sandler (sorry, you're on my team for life) and Andrianna deLone.

I mean it when I say my friends are my heroes. Much of this book was hashed out on runs or skin tracks or over long car rides or long phone calls or longer text chains. My life is incalculably richer because of the women in it. I am constantly in awe of how brilliant and thoughtful and funny you are, and of how you put the pieces together and work to break down systems that aren't working. Thanks for checking in on me, for making me think big, and for getting me outside.

None of this would have been possible without my family. The big irony of this book about women is that it would have been impossible (or at least much harder) without one particular man. Biggest thanks to T, who constantly reminds me why it's important to tell stories and to dig for the truth, who holds me up when the work of writing wears me down, and who lives with a spiky, stubborn woman who likes to be gone a lot. Thank you for doing it all with me, what a gift.